THE HEADLESS STATE

The Headless State

ARISTOCRATIC ORDERS, KINSHIP SOCIETY, &
MISREPRESENTATIONS OF NOMADIC INNER ASIA

David Sneath

COLUMBIA UNIVERSITY PRESS   *New York*

COLUMBIA UNIVERSITY PRESS

Publishers Since 1893

New York   Chichester, West Sussex

Library of Congress Cataloging-in-Publication Data

Sneath, David .

  The Headless state : aristocratic orders, kinship society, and misrepresentations of
  nomadic inner Asia / David Sneath.

    p. cm.

  Includes bibliographical references and index.

    ISBN 978-0-231-14054-6 (cloth : alk. paper)—ISBN 978-0-231-51167-4 (e-book)

    1. Asia, Central—Politics and government—1991– 2. Tribal government—Asia,
Central. 3. Clans—Asia, Central. 4. Power (Social sciences)—Asia, Central. 5. Aristocracy
(Political science)—Asia, Central. I. Title.

DS329.4.S64 2007

958 .042—DC22

2007020899

References to Internet Web sites (URLs) were accurate at the time of writing. Neither the
author nor Columbia University Press is responsible for URLs that may have expired or
changed since the manuscript was prepared.

DESIGN BY VIN DANG

This book is dedicated to Lisa, Adam, and Emily—
as representatives of long-suffering families everywhere.

| Contents |

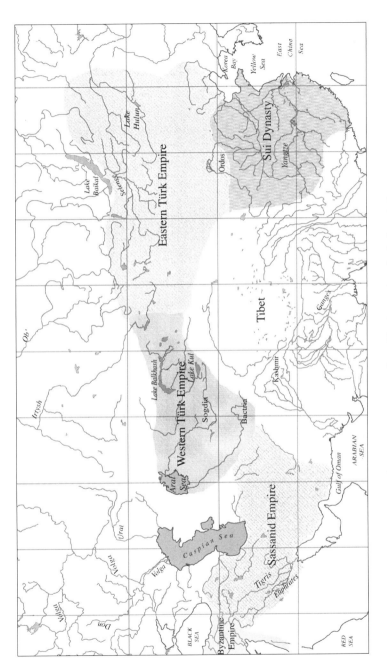

MAP I. The Eurasian Steppe and neighboring regions in the late sixth century.

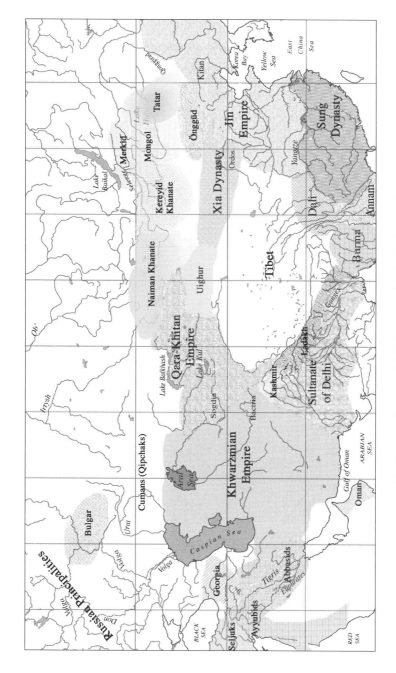

MAP 2. The Eurasian Steppe and neighboring regions in the late twelfth century.

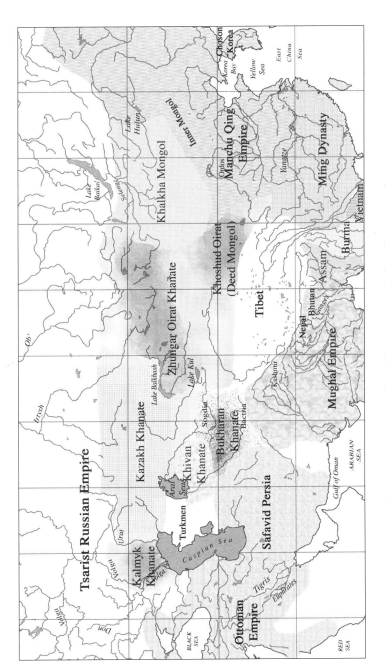

MAP 3. The Eurasian Steppe and neighboring regions in the mid-seventeenth century.

THE HEADLESS STATE

I

Introduction

This book has two aims: the first is to expose a misconception that became firmly rooted in twentieth-century social science, journalism, policymaking, and popular culture. Since the colonial era, representations of Inner Asia and its traditions and histories have been dominated by images of fierce and free nomads organized by the principles of prestate kinship society into *clans* and *tribes*. Anthropological fieldwork in Inner Mongolia and Mongolia in the 1980s and 1990s convinced me that nothing like the popular image of kinship society had existed recently in Mongolia, and the more I studied the history of Inner Asia, the more apparent it became that colonial-era notions of tribalism had powerfully distorted representations of steppe societies and their past. On closer inspection, it was not "kinship society" but aristocratic power and statelike processes of administration that emerged as the more significant features of the wider organization of life on the steppe.

This brings me to my second aim: to rethink the traditional dichotomy between state and nonstate society and to approach the state in a different way—in terms of the decentralized and distributed power found in aristocratic orders. Viewing the state as a form of social relation rather than a central structure avoids the evolutionist dichotomy between state and nonstate society, and it makes it possible for us to conceive of a "headless state," a configuration of statelike power formed by the horizontal relations between power holders, rather than as a result of their mutual subordination to a political center.

MISREPRESENTING INNER ASIA:
A SUMMARY OF THE ARGUMENT

The roots of the myths of tribal society lie in the evolutionist social theory of the nineteenth century, which saw kinship as the organizing principle for nonstate society. This was elaborated in the twentieth century, with the structural functionalist model of segmentary kinship proposed by Fortes and Evans-Pritchard in *African Political Systems*, and this Morganian tradition was also highly influential in Soviet ethnography of Inner Asia. As Kuper (1988, 239–240) notes: "The idea of primitive society served imperialists and nationalists, anarchists and Marxists." Twentieth-century social science, both Western and Soviet, represented political centralization as a key feature of "the state," and the notion of acephalous society represented its antithesis. Nonstate society was pictured in terms of kinship organization, made up of clans that united to form tribes and tribal confederations.

Models of tribal, nomadic, and kin-organized society were applied to the indigenous societies of Inner Asia, and this led to the consistent misinterpretation of historical and ethnographic materials to support the vision of tribal societies organized by principles of kinship. Where named groups of "nomadic" people appeared in the historical texts, they were generally assumed to be tribes or clans. The genealogies of noble houses were taken as evidence of the general organization of society on kinship lines. Within anthropology, kinship and descent theory have now been all but abandoned as a result of critiques by Schneider, Kuper, and others. But the use of derivative models of tribal society has continued largely unchallenged—particularly in historical studies of pastoral nomads. In describing Inner Asian pastoral nomadic society, for example, Barfield (1989, 1992) applies a model of clan society and tribal confederation originally proposed by Lewis Henry Morgan in 1851 to describe the Iroquois, a scheme itself derived from Grote's 1846 theory of ancient Greek society.

Rather than one of the "earliest acts of human intelligence," as Morgan supposed, the organization of people into named unilineal descent groups with political functions was an act of state administration in much of Inner Asia. Comprehensive kinship organization, where it appeared, seems to have been a product of the state, not a precursor to it. In the Mongolian case, the units later described as clans (*obog / obúg / ovog*) were largely imposed on common subjects by the Qing state as administrative devices, with limited success. In the tsarist Russian state, the *rod*, or administrative clan, was also used as a unit for the government of Inner Asian subjects. However, this should not be seen simply as a case of "secondary tribalism," in which the tribe becomes a product of the colonial state. These units never operated in the way that the theories of kinship society supposed, but they provided an idiom of administration that could be misread by later scholarship as evidence of autochthonous kin organization.

The discourse of tribe and clan also obscured the continuities between the state and decentralized aristocratic power in Inner Asia. The notion of a timeless, traditional, nomadic, tribal society organized by kinship made the emergence of steppe states a puzzle to be explained away in terms of contact with the urban and agricultural polities on their borders. But a critical reevaluation of the material shows that the dichotomies of tribe and state, tradition and modernity, kinship and class, have been projected onto material that cannot be usefully analyzed in these terms. The earliest Inner Asian steppe society for which we have historical records, the Xiongnu empire of the third century B.C.E., for example, was ruled by an aristocracy of three noble families who governed their subjects using a military-civil administrative system of decimal units. These characteristics—aristocracy and decimal military-civil administrative units—persistently appear in steppe societies until the twentieth century. But the exotic image of the nomadic pastoral lifestyle and the dominance of notions of kin-organized tribal society meant that scholars were inclined to contrast steppe polities with agricultural and urban-based states, rather than exploring their common features.

Classical social theory sought a clear distinction between territorialized, stratified state societies and nomadic, egalitarian nonstate societies. These narratives conditioned the understanding of Inner Asian mobile pastoral society, and images of nomadic life were fed back into them and used to support wider theories of state and society. Deleuze and Guattari, for example, represent an influential strand in Euro-American social sciences, which essentializes "the State" as a single timeless form, closely identified with its titular head. In Deleuze and Guattari's case, this is also character-ized by the dual nature of this head (magician-king and jurist-priest) and by state order being internalized. As we shall see, the trope of the free, egalitarian nomad provided an irresistible counterpoint to the notion of the interiorized, disciplinary state for these theorists.

But steppe society was stratified for much—probably all—of its history, and the study of these aristocratic orders demonstrates the implausibility of the dichotomized distinction between state and nonstate societies. In actual polities, power is evidently distributed between myriad sites, prac-tices, and persons. Given the aristocratic values apparent in the historical literature, the key distinction between noble and common status has as much reason to be thought of as interiorized as the governmentality pos-ited for state subjects. The political relations of aristocrats determined the size, scale, and degree of centralization of political power, and these var-ied in historical time. The history of the region shows no clear dichotomy between highly centralized, stratified "state" society and egalitarian, kin-based "tribal" society, but rather displays principles of descent deployed as technologies of power in a range of more or less centralized polities, rul-ing subjects engaged in various kinds of productive practices—pastoral, artisanal, and even agricultural.

Without the a priori separation of social forms into tribe or state by their presumed essences, we can see state and state-conditioned processes distributed throughout the lifeworlds of those subject to all manner of po-litical authorities. This appears to have been as true of pastoral aristocratic orders as it is of the industrial "governmental" state. Power relations were inescapably present; certain configurations—such as domestic and aristo-cratic orders—have been reproduced and have acted as the substrata of power in a series of historical polities that have resembled the centralized, bureaucratized "state" to a greater or lesser degree, depending on histori-cal contingency. The early Chinggisid and Qing empires, for example, had high levels of centralization, while the Oirat and Ming-era Borjigin poli-ties were relatively decentralized.

The broader picture that emerges is of power structures, more or less centralized, interacting in various modes of articulation, competition, and superimposition as part of contingent, path-dependent historical pro-cesses. An examination of the substrata of power that underpins these

processes reveals aristocratic orders that include many of the power technologies associated with states—stratification, forms of territorialization,
taxation, corvée, and military service. The local power relations that since
ancient times have made the Inner Asian state possible were reproduced
with or without an overarching ruler or central "head." Although more
and less centralized *polities* may be clearly recognized, the distinction between state-organized and stateless *societies* becomes meaningless here.

This political environment, in which almost all of the operations of state
power exist at the local level virtually independent of central bureaucratic
authority, I term the "headless state." Inspired by the work of Gramsci and
Foucault, recent scholarship has stressed the distributed, rhizomatic nature of power in liberal democracies, and there seems no good reason to
exclude this as a possibility when examining techniques of power in other
political environments. The aristocratic orders of Inner Asia were based
upon decentralized power and exhibited aspects of both governmentality
and sovereignty in the Foucauldian sense. It is not that these aristocratic
orders simply stand somewhere between the state and "nonstate" forms,
but rather that in Inner Asia many of the forms of power thought to be
characteristic of states actually existed independently of the degree of
overarching political centralization. The centralized "state," then, appears
as one variant of aristocracy.

THEORIES OF THE STATE AND ITS OTHER

Visions of society without the state have long served as elements of the
origin myths of the state in political thought. Hobbes's seventeenth-century vision of a stateless society was one condemned to the "calamity of a
war with every other man" (1996 [1651], 222). Such societies were bound to
be "fierce, short-lived, poor, nasty." Escape from anarchic misery required
a state or commonwealth whose members agreed to the absolute rule of
a single authority so as to maintain peace, law, and order. But for Locke,
concerned as he was with refuting justifications for monarchy, the basis
of political power must be the general consent to obey one's rulers on
condition that they exercise their power for the public good. Thus, society
without the state was one in which all men were equally free to choose
to form a political society on this basis. These conditions existed, Locke
thought, in the indigenous American societies of his day, where men "had
neither kings nor commonwealths, but lived in troops" (Locke 1978 [1690],

167), and the figure of the noble savage, free and uncorrupted by hierarchical civilization, also provided a starting point for Rousseau's philosophy of the social contract as the basis for legitimate state authority.

The social sciences that emerged in the age of the populist nation-state continued to conceptualize "primitive society" and its replacement term "tribal society" as a sort of inverted mirror image of life in the modern state (Sahlins 1968, 5). As Kuper (1988, 235), notes: "From Maine and Morgan to Engels and Childe, the basic assumptions were that kin-based communities gave way to territorially based associations, which developed into states." Although various social theorists offered very different characterizations of the state, they all reflected rather similar visions of nonstate society as organized by kinship. In the Marxist tradition, the state is the instrument of repression necessary for the maintenance of class relations of exploitation. It ensures that, through control of the means of production, some are able to consistently exploit the labor of others. The other key feature of the state is that it claims to represent the "illusory general interest" of society, simultaneously representing the interests of the dominant class and representing itself as the guarantor of general social justice. So for Engels (1959 [1886], 236), "the state presents itself to us as the first ideological power over man." Since in the Marxist scheme nonstate society must be composed of kin communities, the primary state was one that supported the Asiatic Mode of Production—kin communities, which still largely organized their own productive relations, dominated by a central power that extracted tribute. Clastres (1977, 167) follows in this tradition, distinguishing primitive society and state society in terms of the presence and absence of exploitation: "the difference between the Amazonian Savage and the Indian of the Inca empire is . . . the first produces in order to live, whereas the second works in addition so that others can live." For Clastres, the state came before class. "The political relation of power precedes and founds the economic relation of exploitation . . . the emergence of the State determines the advent of classes" (Clastres 1977, 167–168). In this formulation, the impersonal and exploitative relations of class stand in contrast to the apparently personal and affectionate bonds of kinship. This has been widely echoed by other Marxian treatments of state formation. For example, Patterson (1991, 5) declares "when a class structure is erected, a state is born."

The two central elements of this characterization of the state have remained highly influential. First, the notion of the state as an object of ideological reification was developed in the Gramscian tradition and is reflected in the work of those such as Abrams (1988) and Mitchell (1991).[1] Second, although the direct identification of the state with class interest was seen as a characteristically Marxist argument, the notion that the state permits classlike stratification was widely accepted by scholars of state-emotion (e.g., Fried 1967, 109; Service 1975, 285).

The Weberian tradition also linked the state to stratification and hierarchy, although the strata might be thought of as "status groups" rather than classes in the Marxist sense. A selective reading of Weberian thought was particularly influential in structural-functionalist approaches (Fortes and Evans-Pritchard 1940; Parsons 1951). Fortes and Evans-Pritchard took the Weberian characterization of the modern state as their starting point in the identification of state societies in Africa. Two aspects were selected in particular to capture its essential nature. The modern state was, Weber (1947, 156) wrote, "a compulsory association with a territorial basis. Furthermore, to-day, the use of force is regarded as legitimate only so far as it is either permitted by the state or prescribed by it." In this tradition, the monopoly of the legitimate use of force in a given territory became the litmus test for statehood.[2]

Alongside the old theme that states were territorialized, appeared the notion that they must be centralized. The state had, after all, long been seen as manifest in the authority of a ruler or centralized ruling authority, be it a monarch or senate. After all, the progressive centralization and bureaucratization of power had been one of the most striking features of the modern nation-state, which Weber (1947, 156) took to be the most fully developed form of the state idea. Fortes and Evans-Pritchard (1940, 5) thought of the state as a type of political organization with centralized authority, administrative machinery, and judicial institutions. In this tradition, Mann (1986, 26) defines the state, somewhat vaguely perhaps, as the "centralized, institutionalized, territorialized regulation of many aspects of social relations."

But this Weberian characterization of the modern state has increasingly been seen as a poor place to start when approaching state forms more generally. First, as Giddens (1985) points out, premodern states were often not really territorial, in that their rule extended over subordinate rulers and nobles, some of who could be relatively independent or even ambivalent in their loyalty. The borders of such dynastic realms were often ambiguous: the sixteenth- to seventeenth-century domains of the Habsburg Holy

Roman Emperors, for example, were scattered throughout central Europe and encompassed domains that paid homage to other monarchs, such as the king of France. And the Roman Catholic Church retained control of significant parts of even the more centralized European kingdoms until well into the eighteenth century. Until the "modern" bureaucratic state began to develop in northwestern Europe from the sixteenth century onward, monarchies, in effect, ruled sets of aristocrats, who in turn governed their local subjects and tended to exercise many of the powers of government for themselves, such as taxation and law enforcement (Mackenny 1993).

The difficulties of attempting to apply the model of the centralized territorial state to other polities quickly became apparent in the study of South East Asian states. As Nordholt (1996, 2) notes, such states frequently lacked a stable monopoly of power:

> The royal centre was unable to exert direct control over the whole realm. Instead the king controlled only a small domain, while the rest of the domain was divided between regional lords who managed to develop a considerable power basis of their own. At most, the king could exert some degree of influence in the territories of these lords, depending on the extent to which they were willing to recognise his authority. "Government" consisted in this context of a specific mixture of personal relationships between the king and his lords and a degree of bureaucratic administration, while no distinction was made between private and public interests.

As Gledhill (1994, 17) puts it:

> Imperial governments always claimed to be masters of all they surveyed, but lacked the administrative, communicative and military infrastructures to make that claim a reality. "Traditional" states had frontiers rather than borders. The administrative reach of the political centre was relatively low and its control was patchy on the periphery of its domains. The Weberian definition of the state as an institution that possesses a monopoly of the legitimate use of force within a territorial domain is therefore appropriate only to the modern European state.

In fact, Weber's work on the "premodern" state places much less emphasis on territorial control. In this case, the key step was the institutionalization of relations of dominance in the form of political office. For Weber, the "traditional state" emerged with the creation of patrimonial office, and in this early form, power is personalized and limited by nothing but the whim of the ruler. He called this "sultanism," reflecting the influence of notions of oriental despotism at the time (Weber 1949, 346; Vitkin 1981, 447).

However, in the postcolonial era anthropological interest shifted away from the premodern state and become more concerned with the modern nation-state. In this work, the Gramscian and Foucauldian approaches have remained influential. As Hansen and Stepputat (2001, 3) put it, Gramsci's understanding of state power was something that "emerged from the capacities, the will, and the resources of classes, or segments thereof." This "will to class power" led to projects of political and cultural hegemony that consolidated class domination. This has drawn attention to the distributed, noncentralized aspect of state power, and in this respect found a degree of common ground with Foucauldian treatments of the state that emphasize the "closely linked grid of disciplinary coercions whose purpose is in fact to assure the cohesion of this same social body" (Foucault 1986, 240). Power could not be seen as flowing down or out from the centralized state, which organized the society about it. Rather, in this view, "the modern state is not the source of power but the effect of a wider range of dispersed forms of disciplinary power" (Hansen and Stepputat 2001, 3).

Sovereignty proved to be a central concern in these debates, since for some, such as Deleuze and Guattari (1986, 15), "the State is sovereignty." Foucault treats sovereign power as the principle of monarchical government, which is embodied in the dominance of the sovereign over the subject and reflected in the legal codes and philosophies inherited by modern governments. However, the modern state was distinguished by the growing importance of an entirely different and ultimately incompatible form—disciplinary power—that Foucault saw as a key innovation of bourgeois society, based on the "biopolitical" normalizing practices of numerous institutions and disciplines. Agamben (1988), however, rejected the notion that sovereign power is an archaic type to be superseded by the disciplinary biopolitical forms. Following Schmitt, Agamben (1998, 2) defines as sovereign he who decides on the exception, that is, the ultimate authority, standing outside the law, who both guarantees the law and decides when it should be set aside. This form of sovereignty—ultimately, the power over "bare life"—Agamben argues, is as fundamental to the modern state as it was to its predecessors and, indeed, has expanded in scope with the increased power of the central authority over its population.

But do such treatises on the modern nation-state provide any insights that might sharpen our understandings of other types of states? I think they do. First, they further destabilize the notion that state power is necessarily about centralization, since this is not very clearly true of even the most centralized and bureaucratic nation-states. Second, they draw our attention to the distributed power of diverse practices and institutions that generate subjects and the political orders that define them. Third, the debates surrounding sovereignty emphasize that the key relationship of state is between the institutions of authority and its subjects, not territory.

This suggests we can regard the state as a form of social relation, rather than as the sort of distinct "extrasocial" structure that the state pictures itself to be. Chandhoke (1995, 49) makes a useful point on this: "Any definition of the state, therefore, needs to relate it to the wider society in which it is located; which it regulates; and whose political organisation it is. The state is simply a social relation, in as much as it is the codified power of the social formation." But this leaves open exactly what the nature of the social relation is, and here it makes sense to return, selectively, to the Weberian and Marxist traditions.

Is it possible to retain the central intuitions of these classical characterizations of the state and still make the concept more genuinely suitable for crosscultural application? Again, I think the answer is a cautious "yes." Weber's notion that the state requires the existence of political office seems a plausible basis for the sort of social relation I have in mind, and the constitution of this office could serve as the codified power required by Chandhoke. I could add to this the Marxist intuition that the state presents itself as the just arbiter in disputes between other social interests. Finally, the existence of rulers and ruled as distinct social strata, be they conceived in terms of Marxist notions of class or Weberian concepts of status groups, seems to be a persistent feature of descriptions of the state and accommodates the tradition of contrasting nonstate society with state hierarchy. In short, we might look for three features to identify the state as a social relation: political authorities, systems of rules or arbitration, and the distinction between governing and governed persons. This approach allows us to reconsider the old distinction between state and nonstate, to look for "state relations" in societies that do not seem to match the older models of the centralized, clearly bounded state. It also, I think, suggests we could usefully look again at societies that have been represented as nonstate "kinship" societies and rethink the nature of power relations within them.

ANTHROPOLOGY AND PROBLEMS WITH KINSHIP SOCIETY

At its outset, the anthropological specialization was concerned with presenting alternatives to the *ancien régime* of Europe, with its hierarchies, martial aristocracies, and monarchies that traced their origins to the Germanic invasions of the late Roman period. Morgan was passionately committed to showing that primitive "kinship" society was essentially democratic, and he was by no means alone. The impulse to find the nonhierarchical, ethnographic tribal "other" was deeply embedded in the emerging disciplines of sociology and social anthropology. As Thom (1990, 35) remarks:

> Within sociology itself, the special emphasis upon ethnology expressed a need, on the part of lay, republican intellectuals such as Durkheim and his pupils, to counter polemical celebrations of the martial and monarchical values of the ancient German tribes within France's national boundaries with the distant, purely human, universal values of tribes from without, from Australia, from Polynesia and so on.

The emerging discipline of anthropology made primitive society its primary object of investigation, and since the evolutionist thinking of the time identified primitive society with kinship society, anthropology made the study of kinship an early priority.

Schneider's (1984) critique of classical kinship theory forced a reevaluation of the Western social science tradition that represented kinship as a sort of human universal. His work on kinship in America and the Pacific island of Yap showed that relatedness need not be seen as necessarily about genealogical connection and reproduction. He questions kinship's "distinctiveness, its systematicity" (Schneider 1984, 194), and its privileged position in anthropological accounts. He illustrated his critique by showing how the assumptions of kinship theory had led him to misrepresent Yap society. The *tabinau*, for example, was the landholding, officeholding, political unit of Yap village life, analogous perhaps to a family farm or estate; the word also means house or dwelling (Schneider 1984, 21). Schneider explains that as a young anthropologist, keen to identify generic kinship structures, he had originally described the *tabinau* as a "patrilineage" in familiar anthropological terms, privileging kinship in his account. He then reexamined his work, starting with the recognition that the *tabinau* was a Yap institution in its own right. Rights to *tabinau* produce and membership derived from the *work* that a woman and her children did for the landholder, the *tabinau* head, and the respect they showed him, not kinship or genealogical connection per se. The "relationship is more one of *doing* than of *being,*" Schneider (1984, 75) notes, and if the junior members of the *tabinau* did not perform work or show respect properly they had no rights to the land or its produce. It made no more sense to think of the *tabinau* as a patrilineage than it would be to conceive of a family farm as one. Inheritance might usually follow the male line, but that was no reason to think of the institution as essentially about kinship when it was actually all about farming and land.

In this respect, Schneider's work echoed the point made by Godelier in his 1977 critique of the concept of "tribe," which was generally assumed to be a political unit formed on the basis of kinship. The empirical concept of tribe, he points out,

> reveals these social relations *only* as aspects of kinship and therefore prevents us from seeing social relations except as aspects of kinship. The very form under which social relations are described, some Anglo-Saxon anthropologists significantly call them "kinship societies," already contains a kind of unasked for answer to the implicit question about the real nature of these social relations. . . . Thus we can see how theoretical thought is engaged, consciously or unconsciously, in a direction already indicated by this "form" of the appearance of social relations.
>
> (GODELIER 1977, 94).

In general, the trend within anthropology has been to "denaturalize" kinship, and Schneider's work helped pave the way for studies that examined the particular "cultures of relatedness" of different societies. It also helped question the lingering association of automatic affection attached to Euro-American notions of kinship and the implication that "kin" relations are bound to be consensual and solidary. It strengthened the possibility, already well developed in feminist and Marxian anthropology, of regarding households as fields of power in which people were assigned various senior and junior positions by practices and discourses that ethnographers had conventionally described in the idiom of kinship but that might be usefully reexamined in terms of power. Furthermore, the old models of kinship society, based on assumptions regarding unilineal descent groups as the "building blocks" of nonstate social structures, were carefully reviewed by Kuper in his 1988 work *The Invention of Primitive Society* and shown to have been almost completely discredited.

Anthropologists have, I think, tended to search for signs of kinship society at the expense of examining aristocracy as a comparative theme. In part, this was because for a long time the discipline retained the distinction between "primitive" or "tribal" aristocracies and the more advanced sort found in Europe (e.g., Sahlins 1968, 20; Service 1975, 82). But another reason for this was that aristocracy could look, or be made to look, very much like the kinship society predicted by the nineteenth-century models of social evolution that anthropologists had studied.

For much of the twentieth century the intellectual apparatus that anthropologists took to the field with them predisposed them to identify kinship structures and attempt to discover their political roles. And since kinship stood opposed to class in their theories, it also directed anthropologists away from the terminology of class and aristocracy. Local officeholders tended to be regarded as leaders rather than rulers, representatives of the tribal or ethnic group under study, and this corresponded with colonial terminologies—elders, headmen, chiefs, and paramount chiefs—terms better adapted to ruling populations as a mass than reflecting the political ideologies of the subject societies.

The structural-functionalist school had developed a typology of political organization that reflected colonial administrative practice, as will be discussed below in chapter 2, and elaborated a particular model of the "kinship structure" of stateless societies that seemed to solve the perceived problem of maintaining social order they were deemed to face. The Marxist scheme of kin community predating class and state formation remained paradigmatic for many, such as Diamond (1974), Silverblatt (1987), Gailey (1987), and Patterson (1991). Works such as Gailey's *Kinship to Kingship*, for example, took for granted and reproduced the assumption that prestate kin communities could not be divided into real classes or have truly exploitative relations, however much it might seem that they had. In this tradition, class becomes—almost tautologically—the defining characterization of both exploitation and the state. Some of the difficulties with this approach can be seen from a brief examination of this aspect of Gailey's study.

THE KINSHIP MODEL AT WORK: THE CASE OF TONGA

Precontact Tonga was a stratified society divided between the *hau*, called "chiefly people" by Gailey, and the *tu'a* commoners. Land was controlled by chiefly families and "chiefly and nonchiefly people had differential access to basic resources" (Gailey 1987, 52). Hereditary titles and areas of territory were associated with the "chiefly" house (*ha'a* means, literally, "house"). The *ha'a* traced patrilineal descent and was therefore described by Gailey as a patrilineage, reflecting the traditional anthropological emphasis on kinship structures that Schneider noted. Commoners, in contrast, were matrilineal, although Gailey claims that ultimately both commoners and nobles traced descent from the same distant ancestors. She explains social stratification as the result of a "conical clan" system, by which social seniors traced descent from first-born ancestors and their social inferiors traced descent from more junior offspring. "Tongan people were ranked according to their closeness to a common ancestor, with preference given to patrilineal primogenitor" (Gailey 1987, 50).

Gailey begins from the assumption that this was a prestate, kinship society in which "there may be significant status differentials, but no real exploitation." She knows this must be the case, since "for exploitation to emerge, kin-based relations of work, distribution, and consumption i.e. the relations of production—must be subordinated to class relations." The commoner and "chiefly" strata might look like classes, but Gailey argues that class relations are only present when "a nonproducing group depends upon a producing one, *and can deny the producing group's continued subsistence*" (original emphasis). This is a hard test for any political order to pass, since it is questionable if any dominant group could practically starve its subjects to death, and it is difficult to see how one could know if they would be successful unless they had tried it. In any case, Gailey considers these strata to be "transitional" forms lying somewhere between kinship and class—and she calls them "estates." What happens in the next part of the argument seems very circular. Gailey (1987, 55) argues that "in those state societies where estates may persist, estates become jurally defined; in kinship societies estates may exist through customary descent and ranking principles." And only when estates became jurally defined could they become true classes. But since law is distinguished from custom by the notion that it is codified by a state (Service 1975, 86), class becomes impossible for a society deemed to be "prestate" in this formulation.

Gailey presents the "kinship structure" as the organizing principle of precontact Tonga, but it is possible to question the primacy of kinship itself in this regard. Urbanowicz (1979, 232; cited in Gailey 1987, 50) noted, for example, that the Tongan ruler, the Tu'i Tonga, "divided his lands between his kinsmen, his 'eiki [people of chiefly rank, whether titled or not]. The various 'eiki established and belonged to their own named groups of 'eiki or Ha'a, a corporate descent group." This suggests the noble houses, which Gailey describes as patrilineages, were created not by the internal logic of a kinship structure but by a ruler's division of lands, to which each was given title. Should we think of this as a "kinship structure," or was the "structure" that of political allocation reproduced by patrimonial inheritance? Similarly, although "chiefly" Tongans did not marry commoners, the children of chiefly men by commoner women were sometimes called disparagingly "half-chiefs" (*mu'a*) and, Gailey (1987, 57) notes, "were attached in service to their fathers and to their higher-ranking half-siblings. In this capacity, they were housed and fed as part of the chiefly retinue." In the wake of Schneider's critique, we might question the extent to which this should be seen as an element of a general system of "kinship" relations, or whether we should regard it as part of the practices of the noble house as a landholding corporation and field of power.

Gordon (1992, 603) found Gailey's distinction between kinship and state society to be unconvincing, and it seems to me that her model of kin community has distorted rather than sharpened her analysis. To my mind, the society that Gailey describes seems to more clearly bear the imprint of aristocratic power than of archetypal kin community. As Marcus (1980) notes, the *hau* aristocracy long predates the colonial-era Tupou dynasty that Gailey thinks of as originating the state, and whether we would wish to use the Marxist formulation of "class relations" to describe them or not, the powers that "chiefs" had over commoners seem comparable to those in many other aristocracies. Gifford (1929, 174) noted that "a chief . . . could dispossess his commoners at any time, or transfer them from one part of his land to another, even though they opposed the move." He also noted that, in some respects, commoners were treated in the same way as alien captives (Gifford 1929, 127). And more recent work based on archaeological evidence has challenged the notion that the conical clan was the organizational basis for precontact Polynesian societies (Sutton 1990).

I do not wish to try to replace "kinship society" with "aristocracy" as a general classificatory category or claim some sort of analytic primacy for hereditary political stratification as the defining feature of any given society. The point I am making is simply that the legacy of nineteenth-century evolutionist thought has been to foreground kinship as the natural organizational principle preceding the state and to place aristocratic power in the background. As Godelier (1977, 95) noted, the problems of the kinship/tribal society model have as much to do with its dichotomization with state society as with the content of the category. "Until [the concept of tribe] *loses its* object it will not lose its *place*, to exist as a shadow of a former mode of thought always open to spontaneous thinking, but which scientific thought will have learnt to suspect and do without" (Godelier 1977, 96). The concept of the tribal is generated by its relationship to the state. But aristocracy exists on both sides of the traditional dichotomy, and it seems to me that its exploration provides us with the opportunity to rethink the state as well as kinship society.

MOBILE PASTORALISM AS A POLITICAL ECONOMY

In an age of democratic populism, hierarchy seems to require explanation, whereas equality appears natural. Dominant models of pastoral nomadic society incorporated the assumption that without the political structures thought of as "settled," there could be no reason for stratification in a mobile society. The implicit question was: but *why* would nomads be stratified when they didn't need to be? But on reflection, this is an empty question. We might as well ask why agricultural or urban societies are stratified, since, as discussed below in chapter 5, there is nothing intrinsic to mobile pastoralism that limits political coercion, if the dominant are as mobile as the dominated. Elite theory may offer some insight into this process; Mosca's (1939, 53) original argument that "the dominion of an organized minority ... over the unorganized majority is inevitable" is plausible, if not entirely unanswerable. But there is a limit to the applicability of sociological elite theory, oriented as it largely is toward the analysis of political power in industrial society.[3] Mosca (1939, 51–56), for example, reproduced the standard evolutionist narrative of state development and saw the emergence of a ruling (or "political") class as a result of a society reaching a certain level of civilization.

Another strand of the tribal model was the environmentally determinist thinking that pictured mobile pastoralism as a simple subsistence economy unable to support great complexity or hierarchy. For example,

Barfield (1989, 6) locates the causes of nomadic states outside their own "simple" societies, and looks for them in their relations with sedentary societies, since, he writes, "historically known nomadic states were organized at a level of complexity far beyond the needs of simple nomadic pastoralism." Historians have begun to reject this view on empirical grounds (e.g., Di Cosmo 2002, 169), and one might, of course, question an implicit theory of the state that supposes it exists to serve the putative needs of society rather than reflect the interests of those who rule. But in any case, we need not accept the assumption that a nomadic economy is bound to be simple. Mobile pastoralism is framed and transformed by political power just as sedentary agriculture is, and, while clearly different, it allows just as many possibilities for the accumulation of wealth and the construction of large-scale systems as agricultural techniques do. In both cases, the economic possibilities depend upon the nature of the property regimes that exist for resources and products and the wider political systems that frame them.

A property regime in which one may own animals without looking after them oneself, for example, allows owners to "lease out" herds. This institution was called *emanet* among the Turkmen, *saun* among the Kazakh, and *süreg tavikh* (*sürüg talbikhu*—to "place herds" [4]) in Mongolia. It was one of the most fundamental relations of historical pastoralism, and it allowed those who owned livestock to have them herded by others while retaining ownership and receiving a large part of their produce. The herding family retained a proportion of the animal produce and sometimes some of the offspring.[5] In principle, there is no limit to the amount of livestock wealth that can be accumulated using these property relations, provided they are enforced. Indeed, owing to economies of scale, the benefits of specialization, and the reduction of the risk of herd losses, large concentrations of herd wealth seem to have been more secure and productive than small holdings (Shahrani 1979; Sneath 1999, 2000).

Mobile pastoralism can form part of large-scale complex systems regulated by local authorities. In the Mongol case, we have detailed accounts of such systems. The *khoshuu* (*khoshigu*) "banners" were administrative units ruled by hereditary lords or Buddhist monasteries and operated as small political economies in their own right. Pastoral families generally moved to different seasonal pastures with their livestock in an annual cycle, and land use was regulated by banner officials. In most *khoshuu*, large numbers of animals were owned by the nobles or monasteries and were herded for them by their subjects.[6] Most common subjects also had their own livestock, and the wealthier families sometimes had so many that they also "placed herds" with other households. But the poorest pastoralists had few animals or none at all and had to work for wealthier families to make a living. Households generally herded several different species of livestock, but there were also specialists who would look after large herds of a particular species (such as horses) for their noble or monastic masters.

In this system, the broad status of common subject was divided into four categories: personal servants of nobles and officials (*khamjilga*), the imperial subjects owing legal obligations to their lord (*sumun-u arad* or *albatu*), monastic servants and subjects (*shabinar*—described by Bawden [1968, 106] as "church serfs"), and slaves who could be owned by nobles or commoners (*bo'ol*).[7] The *sumun-u arad* were in a position analogous to serfs in a feudal society. They were tied to their banner and its lord and were liable for taxation and corvée duties, such as serving the officials as messengers, clerks, or laborers. In the seventeenth century, the Manchu formalized the number of *khamjilga* personal servants that the different grades of aristocracy were permitted, ranging from four to twelve families for the humblest nobles without *khoshuus*, and up to sixty families for senior nobles (Bold 2001, 120). Treated as part of a noble's retinue, these families were theoretically exempt from tax and corvée duties.[8] These "personal serfs" could be punished by their masters but not killed out of hand.[9] Commoners could occasionally be elevated—not to the nobility, but to the status of *darkhan*, comparable to the medieval European "freemen"—becoming nominally free of the obligation of corvée service.[10]

Overall patterns of land use were managed by the noble or ecclesiastical district authorities. The operations organized by the wealthy herd owners could be highly sophisticated and involve specialist herders moving large, single-species herds to selected pastures so as to make best use of the local ecological resources at given times of the year.[11] The property regime for land was complex and consisted of various prerogatives held by legal persons at different levels in the sociopolitical order. In the Qing period, authority over the use of land was ultimately vested in the Ejen Khan—the Manchu emperor.[12] The actual unit for pastoral land management was the *khoshuu*, and rights to land use were described in terms of entitlements to move herds or stay with them in a given locality.[13] This allowed flexible but managed access to large areas of grazing land and was a central element of the mobile pastoral techniques employed during this period.

A good description of this sort of pastoral management is given by the Russian Mongolist A. D. Simukov (1936, 49–55), who made a detailed study of Bayanzürh Uulyn *khoshuu*, in what is now Bayanhongor province (*aimag*). He described the pastoral operations managed by the Lamyn Gegeen monastery, which had administered the district until a few years before Simukov's visit. The monastery's subjects had been divided into groups that were responsible for herding different species of livestock for the monastery, moving the herds over different sets of pastures as part of their annual migratory cycle. These duties and movements were overseen by officials appointed by the monastery, who also saw that well-established quotas of animal produce from their herds were delivered to the monastery. Simukov estimated that before 1924, 70 percent of the population of the *khoshuu* herded livestock for the monastery.[14]

The political economy of the *khoshuu* required the social coordination of labor made possible by the framework of duty obligations (*alba*) owed by subjects to their masters. Crop agriculture, for example, was commonly carried out by families assigned to this work as an *alba* duty: thus the *khoshuu* economy was not bound to remain an exclusively pastoral one.[15] Some nobles, such as the prince Togtohtör (or To-Wang), made efforts to diversify their *khoshuu* economies by establishing productive activities to which *albatu* subjects were assigned, including textile workshops, tile and brick works, mines, and water mills. These two sets of power relations—the citizenship regime, whereby members of local political economies owed obligations to district authorities, and the property regime of local authority management of joint district land—remained important for the organization of pastoralism in the both the prerevolutionary and, in a new form, the state socialist period (Sneath 1999, 230).

I do not argue that pastoral societies of the Eurasian steppes are bound to have particular political forms, and I certainly do not seek to replace one brand of environmental or economic determinism with another by arguing that steppe societies were bound to have been aristocracies. Our understanding of the forms that social life took on the Eurasian steppe must be led by historical and ethnographic description, not a priori reasoning on the presumed limitations of "nomadic pastoralism." But having said this, it is, I think, possible to offer descriptions of the political economy of given steppe societies that, like good studies of littoral polities, pay close attention to the relationship between productive relations and wider political forms.

Shaped as it was by political relations, then, mobile pastoralism was as capable of generating concentrations of wealth and power as agricultural techniques were. After all, a sedentary lord ruling over wide agricultural lands cannot, strictly speaking, "centralize" these either. Some of the less perishable agricultural produce might be laboriously carted to granaries, but the real wealth—land—remains locked down in a form that the lord himself cannot possibly monopolize. While a pastoral noble might casually gather a herd of a thousand horses, as Jebe did when he jokingly gave a herd of identically colored horses to Chinggis Khan (Thackston 1998, 110), it is difficult to imagine how an equivalent amount of agricultural produce could be so easily concentrated in one place. What is really centralized with any concentration of wealth are the rights of ownership, and these are socially rather than environmentally determined. And when one turns from the means of production to consider the means of coercion, it is clear that mobile pastoralism allows for much more efficient concentrations of military power than most agricultural systems, since it can readily produce large numbers of horsemen and mobile food supplies in the form of livestock. Until the relatively recent dominance of firearms over cavalry, pastoralism had allowed the development of military power to a much higher degree than "pure" agricultural societies, and steppe systems were far more productive in this respect than farming ones. Had the history of Eurasian centralized polities been written from a pastoral perspective, pure agriculturalists might have been represented as an evolutionary dead end, stubbornly living in their immobile villages as they had done for thousands of years and generally unable to create the concentrated military power needed to construct genuine state structures, except when conquered by, or in contact with, the more developed steppe societies. Indeed, something a little like this appears in the thought of Ibn Khaldûn (1967, 276–288), in which real state-forming power is located in the pastoral "desert," not the agricultural center.

But one effect of the tribal kinship society model was to preclude the possibility of complex political processes. Social control had to be "bottom up," since the "higher authority" of the state was not thought to be present. But by regarding the state as a social relation, "vertical" power relations are seen to exist wherever there are governing elites. In this case, entirely distributed forms of power relations such as ownership are not dependent on the kind of centralized bureaucratic state, the "external" state—of classical social theory; they only require enforcement by local hereditary elites or some other means.

Much of this book is devoted to developing a critique of the kin-tribe model of Eurasian pastoral society, but it also attempts to provide a basis for an alternative analytical frame—a set of descriptive terms that may be used where the primary evidence allows. If, heuristically, these were to be assembled into a countermodel, they would describe a society with a largely aristocratic order, rather than a tribal one, in which descent and relatedness resembled those of the Lévi-Straussian notion of "house society" discussed below in chapter 4, rather than the Morganian model of segmentary lineage theory of the "pastoral-nomadic" ideal type reviewed in chapter 5. Here, mobility, rather than being the defining characteristic of a social type, appears as a flexible feature of the wider *political* economy that frames pastoralism in any given historical context. But none of these features require or imply the others, and for this reason I think of them as simply a set of alternative characterizations, rather than another social ideal type. They are also all entirely compatible with various forms of state organization, so that rather than filling the conceptual space occupied by the notion of "tribe" in the state/tribe dichotomy, these descriptions permit a disengagement from the old distinction and a discussion of more and less centralized political formations that does not invoke nineteenth-century evolutionist social theory. As I attempt to show in the rest of this book, for those engaged in filling in the gaps and ambiguities left in the historical accounts of steppe polities, the concepts of aristocratic order, house society, and mobile pastoralism within a political economy are likely to provide a better set of starting points than tribalism, segmentary kinship society, and pastoral nomadic society as an ideal type.

INNER ASIAN POLITIES: A BRIEF HISTORICAL OVERVIEW

Much of the classical literature on steppe society has treated it as a single, timeless, traditional complex, frequently ranging across different regions and epochs to construct general models of Eurasian pastoral nomadic society. The reexamination of these models involves reviewing understandings of a number of very different historical societies, selected largely because of the centrality of the tribal model in influential ethnographic or historical treatments.[16] For the orientation of readers unfamiliar with some or all of these societies, I try here to provide a very brief introduction to some of the more prominent polities found in the history of the Eurasian steppelands.[17] All of the steppe polities outlined here have been described as tribal in historical literature. When steppe rulers come to govern sedentary societies, they are generally described in terms of dynasties and royal houses. However, as discussed in chapter 5, the dominance of a certain model of pastoral nomadic political organization has meant that while they principally govern pastoralists, such rulers are usually described as chiefs of tribes or rulers of tribal empires or confederations. In this account, I have tried not to reproduce the tribe-clan model, for reasons set out in the following chapters, but I have used the same terminology for sedentary and steppe political forms.

The first steppe polity for which we have substantial historical materials is that of the Scythians, known to the Greeks as *skythai* and the Persians as *saka*, based in the southern Russian steppes. Archaeological sites and artifacts associated with the Scythians appear to date back to the ninth century B.C.E. and are found across the Eurasian steppe as far east as Tuva. They had come to dominate the region in the eighth century B.C.E., having defeated and replaced an earlier polity, the Cimmerians, about which less is known.[18] The Scythians were an important power in the ancient Hellenistic world, and for the Greeks they were distinctive because of their use of mobile pastoralism and housing. Herodotus, our major source for Scythian society, describes them with considerable admiration, noting that this lifestyle made them all but invincible in war. But the polity also included agricultural and urban elements. Herodotus mentions "Scythian tillers of the land" (Godley 2000, 218–219) and other agricultural subjects—such as the Budini, who live in houses and are said to have had a great city built of wood but who are also described as nomads. Herodotus describes a hierarchical society in which slavery was common. It was ruled as an empire, divided into pastoral districts (*nomoi*), each administered by a governor (*nomarch*). Scythian kings were buried with all the wealth and splendor of the rulers of mighty sedentary realms of the time, and rich tomb finds have revealed hordes of finely crafted objects, much of it showing the striking "animal style" art for which their culture became famous. In the third century B.C.E., the Scythians began to be eclipsed by a steppe power from further to the east, the Sarmatians, who were based north of the Aral Sea and who remained a significant power until coming under the rule of the Huns in the fourth century.

At the eastern end of the Eurasian steppe corridor, the polity for which we have the earliest detailed historical records is the Xiongnu. They appear in the Chinese records in the late fourth century B.C.E., located on the northern borders of China. In 209 B.C.E., a vigorous new Xiongnu emperor named Modun seized the throne from his father and embarked on a series of conquests. The enlarged empire included the Mongolian steppes, Ordos in modern-day Inner Mongolia, and the Tarim basin. Detailed descriptions of the Xiongnu appear in the classic Han text the *Shiji* (*Records of the Historian*) by Suma Qian (145–90 B.C.E.). The empire that he described was arranged like a vast army at rest, facing south and divided into left (eastern) and right (western) wings. Under the *chanyu* (emperor) were the *tuqi* (wise kings) of the Right and Left, who served as viceroys of the two halves of the empire, and a series of other high officials. The administrative system consisted of a series of decimal units that could raise a nominal number of horsemen in times of war (Di Cosmo 2002, 177). There were twenty-four hereditary myriarchs, "lords of ten thousand," who nominally ruled ten thousand households but could rule as few as four thousand in reality (Atwood 2004, 595). Beneath these were lords of one thousand subjects, who in turn appointed governors of one hundred, who commanded the heads of groups of ten. Like the Scythians and almost all premodern steppe empires, their military power was based on highly mobile cavalry, particularly mounted archers. Also like the Scythians, the Xiongnu made considerable use of slaves (Golden 2001a, 35).

The Xiongnu emperors were enormously wealthy and powerful rulers. They have been described as "confederate chieftains" (Kessler 1993, 52), but they were recognized as equals by the Han dynasty and at times received tribute from them. Archaeologists have found the remains of a series of Xiongnu forts and settlements, some as far north as Siberia, and huge tombs with rich grave goods revealing a distinctive artistic style reminiscent of the "Scythian" animal style. Rivalry with the Han dynasty led to periodic wars with losses and gains on both sides, and regions such as the Tarim basin passed from Xiongnu to Han control and back again more than once. The Xiongnu empire split in the first century B.C.E., and, although it was briefly reunited, in the end the Han won the allegiance of the southern Xiongnu and waged increasingly successful wars against the northern Xiongnu state, which was finally defeated toward the end of the first century. The northern *chanyu*'s forces fled west, and many of his former subjects were resettled in northern China. In the early fourth century, the descendants of the old Xiongnu imperial house defeated the Jin dynasty and founded the Xia and Liang dynasties, ruling parts of what is now western Inner Mongolia and northern China, before being eliminated by the Wei dynasty in the early fifth century.

Control of much of the Mongolian steppe passed from the Xiongnu to the Xianbei starting in the first century. The Xianbei were based in the area of what is now Manchuria and eastern Inner Mongolia and grew in strength as Xiongnu power waned. In the second century, the conquests of the Xianbei ruler Tanshihuai stretched as far west as Ili, in what is now Xinjiang. But Xianbei power did not stay unified for long, and there was no real successor to Tanshihuai as overlord. In the fourth century, Xianbei nobles established a series of dynastic states in northern China, such as the Northern Wei (386–528), in southern Inner Mongolia and the Shanxi region; the Later Qin (385–431), in Shaanxi; and the Yan dynasties (337–410), in the Beijing-Shandong region. The Northern Wei went on to unify northern China in the fifth century.

The similarity between the name of the Huns and the word Xiongnu and its variants have led some scholars to consider them to have been the same people (Grousset 1970, 19; Sinor 1990a, 177–179). Whatever the truth of this, the Hunnic empire emerged on the southern Russian steppes around the Sea of Azov, and by the late fourth century had defeated the powerful Ostrogoth state of southern Russia and caused the neighboring Visigoths to seek resettlement within the borders of the Roman Empire. Under Attila (406–453), the Hunnic empire reached its zenith. Attila forced the eastern Roman emperor Theodosius II to pay him tribute and was for a while allied with the western Roman emperor Valentinian III against Gothic power. The empire fragmented after Attila's death, his sons ruling some elements and others reverting to local rulers.

Back in the east, in the late fourth century the Rouran (Juan-juan) Khanate emerged as a major rival to the Northern Wei, ruling the steppes from Korea to the Tarim basin. But early in the sixth century, the Rouran *qagan* (emperor) Ch'ou-nu (508–520) was assassinated, leading to splits in the court and rival rulers seeking refuge with the Wei (Sinor 1990b, 294). In 545, one of the former vassals of the Rouran, the powerful Ashina family, who ruled territory near the Altai mountains, made a strategic alliance with the Yuwen family, rulers of the western part of the Wei state.[19] The next year, the Ashina ruler Bumin defeated a rebellion against the Rouran, and asked to be allowed to marry a Rouran princess in return. But the request was refused, and so in 552 Bumin rebelled and overthrew the Rouran ruling house (Atwood 2004, 478). The new Ashina rulers established the Türk empire, encompassing all the territories of the Rouran domains and extending them. Bumin's brother Ishtemi led armies to the west to attack the Haital dynasty. The Haital or Hephthalite empire had formed in the mid-fifth century in Turkestan, expanding to include Sogdiana, Bactria, and, in the sixth century, Kashmir and Punjab.[20] Ishtemi defeated the Haital and came to rule much of Central Asia, forming diplomatic relations with both the Sassanids in Persia and the Byzantine empire. The Türk rulers developed a unique runic script to write their own language, and a number of inscriptions survive on stone monuments such as those found in the Orkhon Valley, Mongolia.

The vast Türk realm split into the eastern empire ruled by Bumin's descendants, based in western Mongolia, and the western empire based in eastern Turkestan and including most of Central Asia at its height. But in the seventh century, rivalry between the eastern and western empires weakened both, and they were unable to resist the growing power of Tang China. In 630, the Eastern Turkish emperor (*qagan*) was captured by the Chinese, and Tang armies marched as far west as Persia, defeating the western Türks in 657. The breakup of the western part of the Türk empire led to a number of polities forming in its wake, such as the Pechenegs and Oghuz. The most powerful turned out to be the Khazar khanate, which emerged in the seventh century and was ruled by Ashina aristocrats; it came to play an important part in the rivalry between Arab, Byzantine, and Russian rulers. The Khazar rulers became famous for apparently converting to Judaism around the turn of the ninth century, perhaps to try to remain "nonaligned" in the face of Islamic-Christian rivalry. By the mid-ninth century, the khanate ruled a huge area of southern Russia—from the Volga to the Caucasus—with a diverse population including both settled and mobile pastoral subjects. The Khazar court wintered in its cities and moved out to encampments on the steppe in summer (Golden 1990, 266). In the late ninth century, they fell victim to the growing power of the Russian princes of Kiev and Novgorod, who formed an alliance with another steppe power, the Oghuz lords. The Oghuz had once been allies of the Khazar *qagans*, but now turned against them to help the Russian forces dismember their realm. In the tenth century, one of the Oghuz noble houses, the Seljuk, established a power base in Persia, and by the eleventh century had expanded it to rule much of the Middle East. Other Oghuz subjects of the Seljuk, known as the (Turkmen) Turkomen, established a series of vassal principalities in Asia Minor, largely at the expense of the Byzantine empire.

The eastern Russian and western Siberian steppe was ruled by the Kimek khanate, which seems to have appeared in the eighth century. Not much is known about this polity except that a tenth-century source remarked that its ruler held the title of *qagan* and commanded eleven lords who ruled hereditary fiefs (Golden 2006, 29). The Cuman or Qipchak polity emerged from the Kimek polity in the eleventh century, expanding to control the southern Russian steppes and invading parts of Moldavia, Wallachia, and Transylvania. Interestingly, the Cuman do not appear to have had a central qagan or overlord: eyewitness accounts from the twelfth century record that the Cumans "have no king, only princes and noble families" (Golden 1990, 280). Militarily powerful, the various Cuman princes became deeply involved in Russian, Georgian, and Byzantine politics.

Türk power had revived in the east toward the end of the seventh century, with the "Second Türk Empire" centered on Mongolia, but in 741 the Türk *qagan* was assassinated and usurped by one of his officers, who proclaimed himself Ozmish Qagan (Groussett 1970, 113). Former vassals of the Ashina rose in revolt, led by the Uighurs under Qullig Boyla. The Uighurs were former rulers of northern Mongolia; once defeated by the Ashina, they had become their subjects. But in 744, the Uighur Qullig Boyla toppled the Ashina rulers, locating his new capital, Ordu-Baliq, in the Orkhon Valley in Mongolia, just as had the Türk *qagans* and the Xiongnu *chanyus* before them.

The Uighur khanate expanded to include Mongolia, southern Siberia, and parts of western Central Asia. Its rulers retained good relations with the Tang dynasty—sending an army to put down the An Lushan rebellion against Tang rule (755–762), for example, and making diplomatic marriages with the Chinese dynasty. The Uighur emperors also favored the Sogdian merchants of Bukhara and Samarkand, adopted their Manicheist religion, and developed a modified form of the Sogdian script to use alongside the old Türk runic one. But in the early ninth century, the dynasty collapsed as a result of court intrigue, rebellion, and a harsh winter that wiped out many of their livestock (Mackerras 1990, 319). Again the dynasty was overthrown by former vassals—the Kyrgyz. A rebel Uighur general led an army from the neighboring Kyrgyz khanate to sack Ordu-Baliq and scatter or slay the Uighur aristocracy. Some Uighurs found refuge in the east; others relocated to the Turfan and Gansu regions, where they continued to rule until the thirteenth century.

To the east of the Uighur empire was the allied state of the Kitans. Chinese histories suggest that the Kitans originated from the Yuwen family, rulers of the western part of the Xianbei Wei state and sixth-century allies of the Ashina (Franke 1990, 402). Based in what is now southeastern Inner Mongolia, they had been vassals of first the Türk *qagans* and then the Tang dynasty in the seventh century. With the collapse of the Uighur dynasty in the ninth century, the Kitans found many Uighur nobles fleeing to join them, and by the early tenth century, they had formed a powerful state. The Kitan *qagan* was elected by the eight most senior lords and had a three-year period of office, but after the veteran general Yelü Abaoji became *qagan* in 907 he abolished these elections and crushed his political opponents, taking the Chinese title of *huangdi* (emperor) in 916 and building a new capital on the Inner Mongolian steppe (Atwood 2004, 315). Abaoji took control of most of Mongolia and conquered the neighboring state of Bohai (Parhae) in Manchuria and northern Korea (Wittfogel and Feng 1949, 571–576). His son Yelü Deguang extended Kitan control over much of northern China, at first supporting a rebel warlord to establish a client state (the later Jin) and then annexing it. Yelü Deguang changed the dynastic name to the Great Liao. The dynasty ruled northern China and, despite a number of rebellions, much of Mongolia until its overthrow in 1125.

The Liao used a dual administrative system for its "northern" steppe subjects ruled by Kitan nobility under Kitan law, and its "southern" Chinese and Bohai subjects were governed by Chinese landlords as well as Kitan nobles, using the well-established country-prefecture administrative system and Tang law. Senior positions were held by members of the royal Yelü family and the "consort lineage" of Xiao that supplied marriage partners for the royal house (Wittfogel and Feng 1949, 191). The Kitans remained "nomadic" in that pastoralism seems to have been thought of as their key economy, and the court remained mobile, moving between the five provincial capitals and seasonal camps on the steppe. Abaoji had two new scripts developed to write Kitan, and the dynasty sponsored monastic Buddhism, artisanal and agricultural production in the steppes, and established two hundred or more cities in what is now Inner Mongolia. The more important Kitan cities were built to a distinctive plan with northern and southern sectors for the different categories of imperial subject (Kessler 1993, 93).

The Kitans enjoyed military superiority over their southern neighbors, the Song dynasty, and in 1005 had forced them to agree to a huge annual tribute of silk and silver. The Song did their best to destabilize their rivals, and in 1114 one of the Liao vassals, Aguda, lord of the Jurchen in what is now Manchuria, rebelled, with Song encouragement. After defeating a Liao army, Aguda declared himself emperor of the Jin ("Golden") dynasty. The Song used the opportunity to recapture territory they had lost to the Liao, but Aguda laid claim to both the lands of the former dynasty and its annual tribute from the Song, and the result was a war that the Jin won, causing what was left of the Song government to flee south of the Huai River and establish a new capital at Lin'anfu. By 1128, the Jin empire stretched over most of northern China, and by the late twelfth century the dynasty ruled some forty million subjects. The Jin retained the Kitan dual administration for their Chinese subjects and the northerners associated with the core Jurchen domains. For these they used a decimal civil-military administrative system, very similar to that described for the Xiongnu, with a unit of a nominal thousand households (*minggan*) composed of smaller units (*mouke*) charged with raising one hundred troops each. But these were administrative rather than ethnic units and were expanded to include Bohai, Chinese, and others—a total of six million people, including over a million slaves attached to Jurchen households (Franke 1990, 421).

To the west of the Jin lay the Xia (Xixia) dynasty, based in the Ordus and Gansu regions. The Xia realm was established by Tangut rulers from the Sichuan-Tibetan region, who claimed descent from the Xianbei (Kessler 1993, 122). In the Tang era, the Tangut took control of the Ordos, and in the mid-ninth century the Tangut ruler Tuoba Sigong was awarded the title of duke of Xia and the Tang imperial surname Li in return for his aid in putting down a rebellion. In the early eleventh century, the Tangut ruler Li Yuanhao expanded his realm by conquest and in 1038 declared himself emperor of the Xia dynasty. As in so many other cases, Xia subjects included both "nomadic" pastoralists and sedentary agricultural and urban populations.

To the west of the Xia lay the Qara-Khitan empire. This conquest state had been founded in 1131 by the Kitan prince Yelü Dashi (1087–1143), who had fled with several thousand troops when the Liao dynasty had been overthrown by the Jurchen and rallied some Kitan loyalist forces in western Mongolia to carve out a huge new empire centered on the Kyrgyzstan region, where he had established his capital. This new empire rested on the ruins of older ones. The region had once been home to the Qarluq khanate, a polity that had emerged in the eighth century and was probably ruled by members of the Türk royal house, the Ashina (Golden 2006, 29). The Qarakhanid empire was established in the tenth century and eclipsed and incorporated the Qarluq. The second Qarakhanid ruler, Musa, had converted to Islam, and this gave rise to a set of Islamic royal families ruling domains in the Ferghana Valley and surrounding regions, including Kashgar. It was these states that Yelü Dashi subjugated one by one in the twelfth century, but he left much of the old aristocracy in place to rule as his vassals.

The new empire was called Qara-Kitai (black/vassal Kitai), to distinguish it from the Kitan original, and in Chinese it was called the Western Liao, for the same reason. It included most of Central Asia, stretching from the Oxus to the Altai mountains, and its ruler was titled both an emperor in the Chinese tradition (*huangdi*) and *gürkhan* (universal khan) in the Turkic one. The Kitan core of the polity, numbering perhaps some forty thousand households (Atwood 2004, 445), seems to have been organized into decimal military-civil units, each ruled by Kitan nobles of the Yelü or Xiao lineages (Biran 2006, 69).

The westernmost vassal of the Qara-Kitan emperor was the shah of Khwarazm, a powerful state centered on the city of Urganch by the Aral Sea, ruling both Turkic pastoralists and Iranian-speaking farmers. The Khwarazm shahs had been forced to swear fealty to the Qara-Kitans after their Seljuk overlords had been defeated by them in the mid-twelfth century. But the Seljuk empire had fragmented and collapsed soon afterward, and the Khwarazm shahs extended their rule over much of Persia before formally rebelling against the weakening power of the Qara-Kitan emperors in 1209. Faced with rebellion and the turmoil created by the expanding power of the Mongols in the east, the Qara-Kitan empire collapsed around 1213.

At the turn of the thirteenth century, the steppe of what became Mongolia was divided between a number of powers. In the east, in the Hulun Buir region, were the Tatar lords, ruling some seventy thousand households or more (Thackston 1998, 43). The Tatar had been an independent power in the tenth century but had been subjugated by the expanding Kitans in 942 and were later enrolled as border auxiliaries (*jüyin*) by the Jin dynasty (Atwood 2004, 529). To their west were the Mongols, who had once been vassals of the Kitans but had formed a khanate after the collapse of the Liao. The Mongols had attacked the Jin and had captured a number of frontier towns, until agreeing a peace in 1147 in return for generous subsidies. But in 1164, Qutula, the Mongol khan, was killed by Tatars loyal to the Jin. The khanate fragmented and the Mongols forced to pay tribute to the Jin. To the west of the Mongols lay the Kereyid khanate. This had, once again, been part of the Kitan empire but become independent after its overthrow by the Jin. We know that, like the Kitans, the Kereyid administered their subjects in units of a nominal thousand (Atwood 2004, 139). Under Qurjaqus-Buyruq Khan the Kereyid became a powerful polity, centered on the Tuul River region, but upon his death the khanate faced disunity, divided as it was into the appanages of Qurjaqus-Buyruq Khan's very numerous sons (Atwood 2004, 296), and it was only by force that the eldest son, Togril, managed to retain a tenuous overlordship. To the north of the Kereyid lay the lands of the Merkit, some of whom had joined Yelü Dashi in his establishment of the Qara-Kitan empire. To the west of the Kereyid was the yet more powerful khanate of the Naiman, which stretched from western Mongolia across the Altai mountains, to the Irtysh River. The khanate dated from the eleventh century and seems to have reached its zenith in the mid-twelfth century under Inancha Bilge Khan, who divided his realm between his two sons, although one of them, Tayang, subsequently reunited the two halves. The Naiman came under the rule of Qara-Kitai for a time, but were independent of them from about 1175 (Biran 2006, 68).

This was, very crudely, the political landscape of the Eurasian steppes on the eve of the Mongol conquests that were to sweep away almost all the existing polities of the region. The process began when Temujin (1162–1227), the son of the Mongol ally of Togril Khan of the Kereyid, defeated Tatar and Merkid rivals and, with Kereyid support, finally reunited most of the old Mongol khanate before turning on his ally and conquering Togril's Kereyid khanate. Temujin then subjugated the Naiman and in 1206 established the Great Mongol Empire, taking the reign name Chinggis Qan (khan). Chinggis organized his steppe empire along familiar decimal lines, with ninety-five nominal units of a thousand (*minggan*) ruled by a noble, each made up of units of a hundred households (*ja'un*) divided into groups of ten (*arban*). Each unit had a head and was required to raise the appropriate number of troops if so instructed. Some of the *minggans* were organized into yet larger myriarchy units of a nominal ten thousand (*tümen*), under senior officials of Chinggis Khan's court. A ten-thousand-strong imperial guard, the *keshig*, was created. This was an expansion of an existing institution; the Kereyid khanate had a royal guard of at least one thousand (Atwood 2004, 297), and it formed a core for Chinggis Khan's army, staffed by officers he appointed and supplied by recruits from the *minggans* ruled by the other nobles.

Chinggis lost little time in using his new army. He invaded the neighboring Tangut state of Xia, forcing it to pay him tribute, and in 1211 the Uighur and Qarluq rulers swore fealty to him. The Khan's armies then attacked the Jin in the east and were again victorious. In 1215, the Mongols captured the Jin capital of Zhongdu (now Beijing), and over the next nineteen years conquered most of northern China. In 1218, Chinggis Khan's dominions expanded further to the west, as his generals took Kashgar and gained control of much of the Qara-Kdhitan empire. This brought him into contact with the expanding empire of Sultan Muhammad of Khwarazm, whose dominions now included most of Persia, Afghanistan, and Central Asia. Chinggis attempted to establish peaceful relations with the Khwarazm-shah, but his overtures were rejected and his envoys killed (Ratchnevsky 1991, 119–23). Mongol armies swept into Khwarazmian territory and met with brilliant success. By 1221, the Sultan Muhammad was dead and his armies scattered.

The four sons of Börte, Chinggis Khan's principal wife, were each given large appanages within the empire. The eldest, Jochi, was given areas to the west of the river Irtysch as part of his *ulus* (domain, patrimony, appanage). Chagadai was to rule much of Turkestan and Transoxiana, and this domain later became known as the Chagadai khanate. Ögödei was given lands on the river Ili (to the east of Lake Balkhash). Tolui, the youngest son, inherited large holdings in Mongolia. Chinggis chose Ögödei to succeed him as emperor of all the Mongol dominions, and during his reign (1229–1241) the empire continued to expand rapidly. The remnants of the Jin empire were conquered, Korea was invaded, and by 1240 Georgia and Armenia were also under Mongol rule. Jochi's domains were divided between his eldest and youngest sons, Hordu and Batu. Hordu received the lands from the river Irtysh to the Aral Sea, a realm that became known as the White or Blue Horde, but Batu was assigned the area west of the Volga—a domain that had yet to be conquered. In 1235, Ögödei agreed to assemble a powerful army for Batu, and the next year it rode west, defeating the Cumans and subjugating all but a minority who fled west. In the winter of 1237, Mongol forces occupied Russia, and in 1241 they invaded

Poland and captured Hungary, destroying the European armies they encountered at Leignitz and Mohi. Batu's realm was based in the southern Russian steppes; it included Russia and extended as far as Bulgaria in the west and the Caucasus in the south. His khanate became known as the Golden Horde (the word "horde" derives from the Mongolian *ordo* [*ordu*, *ord*], which means "palace" and came to mean "principality"), and Batu's successors ruled for the next century and a half before their power was broken by the warlord Timur Lenk (Tamerlane).

Ögödei's death halted the Mongol advance and, after much political maneuvering, his son Güyüg was finally enthroned as emperor in 1246 but died two years later. His widow, Oghul-Qaimish, ruled as regent for three years until Tolui's son, Möngke, became emperor. Möngke sent his younger brother Hülegü southwest with an army, in order to extend the empire in the Middle East. In 1258, Hülegü sacked the great Islamic metropolis of Baghdad and executed the caliph. The following year, his forces invaded Syria and in 1260 occupied Damascus. Hülegü became the first of the Il-khans, the Mongol dynasty that ruled Persia and adjacent regions until the last of the line died heirless in 1335.[21] In 1299, even before the end of the Il-khante line, one of their (former Seljuk) Turkic vassals in Anatolia, Osman I, had declared his independence—and his principality (*beylik*) expanded in the fourteenth and fifteenth centuries to become the mighty Ottoman empire.

Möngke died in 1259, and this time the struggle for succession became an armed conflict between two of his other younger brothers: Ariq-böke, based in the Mongolian homeland, and Qubilai (Khubilai), who commanded the Mongol forces in northern China. Qubilai emerged victorious but did not inherit a unified empire. He was, in effect, the senior member and nominal overlord of a royal family that ruled relatively independent khanates in Russia, Persia, Turkestan, and northern China. War had already broken out between Hülegü and Berke Khan, who had succeeded his brother Batu as khan of the Golden Horde. Qubilai pursued the war against the Sung dynasty, and in 1276 he took their capital, reunifying China for the first time since the fall of the Tang. Mongol armies pushed as far south as Java, but in 1281 the huge armada that the Khan sent to conquer Japan was destroyed by a violent summer typhoon (later called the "divine wind" *kamikaze* by the Japanese); the Mongols never attempted to invade the island again. Qubilai enhanced his legitimacy by forming an alliance with the Tibetan Phagspa Lama, who identified Qubilai with figures in the Buddhist pantheon in return for the emperor's support for the religion (Rossabi 1988, 144).

Qubilai died in 1294, but the Yuan dynasty that he founded continued to rule China until a series of rebellions in the middle of the next century led to their overthrow by the Ming in 1368. Toghan Temür, the last Yuan emperor of China, retreated to Mongolia, and the dynasty continued to rule parts of Mongolia under the name of the Northern Yuan. The Chagadai khanate was beset by internal power struggles in the fourteenth century. In 1370, power was seized by a military leader named Timur Lenk (Tamerlane). Timur conquered an empire that stretched from Samarkand to Turkey, and although some of this was lost after his death in 1405, the Timurid dynasty ruled much of the Middle East until the sixteenth century before finally collapsing in the face of the waxing power of the native Persian Safavid dynasty in the east and the Ottomans in the west. Turkic groups that had been part of Timur's empire were incorporated into these new states and were often used as military forces, as in the case of the Qashqai, who seem to have been posted to the Fars region of southern Persia by the Safavids. In the late fourteenth century, two Turkmen dynasties emerged in the region of eastern Anatolia and Azerbaijan, the Aq Qoyunlu ("White Sheep") and Qara Qoyunlu ("Black Sheep"). The Aq Qoyunlu ruler Uzun Hasan defeated his Qara Qoyunlu rival in 1467, but he was defeated by the Ottomans in 1473, and by the early sixteenth century what was left of Aq Qoyunlu power was destroyed by the Safavids.

In Mongolia itself, disunity brought an end to the age of Chinggisid military supremacy, and the once mighty capital of Karakorum was sacked in 1388 by the armies of the Chinese Ming dynasty. In the fifteenth century, a new power emerged on the steppe: the Oirat Mongols, whose rulers had held senior office in the Mongol empire but were not themselves recognized descendants of Chinggis Khan. Ruling the region from the western part of Mongolia to the Irtysh, the Oirat lords threw off Chinggisid overlordship at the end of fourteenth century and became their major rivals. At that time, there were six *tümen* myriarchies ruled by Chinggisids and four ruled by the Oirat political alliance. In the fifteenth century, the Oirats extended their power eastward to control central Mongolia, including the old imperial capital of Karakorum (Grousset 1970, 507). Oirat rivalry with the Chinggisids continued, with losses and gains on both sides, but by the seventeenth century there were three Oirat polities: the Zünghar (Jungar) principality in the region of western Mongolia and northern Xinjiang, the

Deed Mongols of northern Tibet, and, far to the west, the Kalmyk khanate on the Volga.

The fortunes of the Chinggisid imperial house revived briefly after 1480, when Batmönh Dayan Khan assumed the throne of the Northern Yuan and managed to reunite most of the Chinggisid nobility under his leadership. However, this empire was, in effect, divided between Dayan's nine sons, who acted as overlords of its constituent elements. These quickly became practically independent principalities with their own names and whose rulers also began to adopt the title of khan. In the sixteenth century, one of these—Altan Khan of the Tümed Mongols (1507–1582)—revived something of the glory of the Chinggisid line, building a powerful realm based in Inner Mongolia. Altan renewed the alliance with Tibetan Buddhism that Qubilai Khan had pioneered; in 1578, Altan conferred the title Dalai Lama ("Oceanic Lama") on a leading Tibetan cleric, bSod-nams rGya-mtsho, first naming the office that was to become so important in Tibet. Other Mongol monarchs, such as Abatai Khan, who ruled much of central Mongolia, followed Altan Khan's example and converted to Buddhism (Elverskog 2006a, 109). The links between the Buddhist clergy and the Mongol nobility remained close. In 1639, one of Abatai's descendants was invested with the title of Jibzundamba Khutugtu, the "Living Buddha," whose subsequent seven reincarnations (most of whom were found in Tibet) headed the Buddhist church in Outer Mongolia until the twentieth century.

After the fall of the Yuan dynasty, the Jurchen of Manchuria had become vassals of the victorious Ming, but in the late sixteenth century they were unified by Nurhaci (1558–1626), who threw off Ming suzerainty in 1616 and proclaimed himself khan of the Later Jin dynasty. Nurhaci conquered parts of northern China and won the backing of Inner Mongolian nobles. This was partly due to the unpopularity of the Chinggisid overlord Ligdan Khan (1588–1634), the last emperor of the beleaguered Northern Yuan, who made vigorous and largely unsuccessful attempts to forcibly unite and control the other Chinggisid nobles. But Ligdan was defeated in battle in 1632 by Nurhaci's son and heir Hong Taiji. By 1636, when Hong Taiji proclaimed himself emperor and adopted the dynastic name Qing, his vassals included most of the rulers of what became Inner Mongolia, some of whom were related to him by his marriage to a Khorchin princess and two of Ligdan's former queens (Atwood 2004, 449). As part of his attempt to distinguish the new dynasty from the old Jin, Hong Taiji changed the name of his people from Jurchen to Manchu.

In 1644, under the pressure of Manchu attacks and internal rebellions, the Ming dynasty finally collapsed, and the Qing began to rapidly take control of China. To the northeast of the Gobi Desert, the three Khans of what had become known as Khalkha (later "Outer") Mongolia faced military defeat at the hands of the Oirat Galdan Khan. They turned to the Manchus for support, swearing fealty to the Qing emperor in 1691. Five years later, Galdan was defeated by the Manchus and their Mongolian allies. Over the next sixty years, the Qing armies destroyed the power of the western Mongols and returned the lands of Mongolia to nobles of Chinggis Khan's Borjigin lineage (referred to collectively by the plural term Borjigid). The Mongolian aristocracy enjoyed a high status under the Qing, particularly in the area of military appointments, and the Mongol and Manchu nobility had intermarried since the early days of the dynasty.

In the western steppes, the house of Jochi was deeply divided, and struggles for succession continually resurfaced. By the mid-fourteenth century, the most powerful Jochid ruler was Urus Khan, a descendant of Batu's brother Hordu, who ruled the eastern wing of the empire, the Blue or White Horde (Vernadsky 1953, 247). His nephew and successor Toqtamish came to rule the entire Golden Horde by about 1380, but his power was destroyed by Timur, and in the aftermath another branch of the house of Jochi emerged to dominate the eastern part of the former Golden Horde. The Shaybanids were descendants of Shayban, another brother of Batu, and the Blue Horde was forced to recognize their leader, Abul'l Khair, as overlord. Around 1450, two of Urus Khan's descendants, Janibeg and Qarai, rebelled against Abu'l Khair. They asked the khan of the neighboring Chagadai khanate for territory and were granted lands, which they expanded as they were joined by other nobles deserting Abu'l Khair. They became known by the term qazaq, meaning "exile," "rebel," or "freebooter," and formed the Kazakh khanate, divided into the Great, Middle, and Lesser hordes. The Shaybanids remained important in the Khwarizm region, founding smaller khanates in Khiva and Kokand. The rest of the Golden Horde continued to fragment in the fifteenth century, splitting into the Nogai Horde between the Volga and the Irtysh and into a number of independent khanates in the Crimea, Kazan, and Astrakhan. These divisions allowed the Russian princes to finally throw off Mongol suzerainty, and in the sixteenth century the growing power and firearm technology of Muscovite armies began to turn the military tide against the steppe powers. In the eighteenth century, the Kalmyks on the Volga

and the Buryats to the east of Lake Baikal had come under Russian suzerainty. By the nineteenth century, tsarist Russia had added most of Central Asia to its empire, although the independent Turkmen living east of the Caspian Sea were not finally subdued until 1881, and a technically independent khanate survived in Bukhara until 1920.

In Mongolia, the Qing helped the Chinggisids to finally eradicate their rivals, the Oirats, and Manchu-led armies crushed the power of the Zünghars in 1755. The Borjigid remained generally loyal to the Qing until the twentieth century; the few rebellions against their rule were usually limited and easily put down. Mongolia was divided administratively into two parts: Inner Mongolia was the term given to regions close enough to the seat of government to be administered directly by the *Li-fan-yuan*, the Court of Dependencies in Beijing, while the more distant Outer Mongolia was ruled indirectly, via the military governors of Urga, Uliasutai, and Khobdo (Khovd). With the continued support of the authorities, the Buddhist church expanded steadily, building temples and monasteries and amassing herds, lands, and subjects bequeathed by devout nobles. Over this period, Mongolia became increasingly integrated economically and politically with the rest of the Manchu empire. By the twentieth century, this had had a ruinous effect on Mongolian prosperity. Most of the population (both noble and commoner) was in debt to Chinese firms of merchants, taxes were heavy, and, in some regions, pastoral families were being turned off the pasturelands that the local lords were selling to Chinese settlers. As the Qing collapsed in 1911, Outer Mongolia declared its independence under the head of the church, the Jibzundamba Khutugtu, but the new state was too weak to resist either the Chinese warlord Xu Shuzheng, who captured the capital city of Urga in 1919, or the White Russian adventurer Baron Ungern Sternberg, who captured it from the Chinese in 1920. The USSR intervened to oust Sternberg, installing a Soviet-backed government. Inner Mongolia remained part of China, experiencing mass Han immigration during the republican and warlord periods, and, after the Communist victory, it gained a rather nominal form of recognition, with the formation of the Inner Mongolian Autonomous Region of the PRC.

Looking back over more than two millennia of history, it is clear that the steppes had been subject to a series of imperial projects based both within and beyond the Eurasian grasslands.[22] We see steppe rulers in continuous and complex sets of relations with one another and neighboring sedentary courts—peace, war, trade, and diplomatic marriage. Most of these polities were anything but isolated backwaters; they appear as active players in the wider political struggles of neighboring regions, and this generated intertwined aristocracies that ruled both sedentary and mobile subjects in China, Turkestan, and the Middle East, as well as in much of the steppe. As Di Cosmo (2002, 170) notes, we do not find sharp demarcations between "nomads" and sedentary peoples, "even though the core of the state may have been monopolized by the nomadic aristocracy . . . nomadic and non-nomadic traditions tended to merge and form original socio-political architectures."

Traditionally, this history has been interpreted in the light of the tribal model, and the succession of dynasties often written up in the style of the *Völkerwanderung* vision of Dark Age Europe discussed in chapter 6, so that whole tribal peoples seemed to emerge from the mysterious steppes and vanish again. The notion that nomads represented an earlier evolutionary stage remained influential throughout the twentieth century. For example, Deleuze and Guattari (1986, 73) remark, "It is true that the nomads have no history; they only have a geography." This almost zoological turn of phrase reflects the exoticization of "the nomad," which helped fuel the vision of traditional tribal society as essentially timeless and unchanging. It seemed entirely plausible that such societies must be completely different from our own: fluid, rootless, simple, and without fixed points. A state must be ephemeral in such circumstances, it seemed: a temporary structure resting on a tribal base. Free to move as they were, nomads would not support a stable hierarchy, and since they had not been fundamentally reordered by a state, the argument went, their basic organization must have remained a variety of kinship society.

2

The Myth of the Kinship Society

Evolutionism and the Anthropological Imagination

It was only with the sixteenth-century expansion of Europe into the Americas and Africa that the association of tribes with a more primitive order of mankind began, and only with the Enlightenment of the eighteenth century that this was formalised into that concept of progress which set tribal people outside the pale of civil society. It was then supposed that the natural course of human development was a progression to higher levels of social, economic and political organisation, which could be equated with civilisation; and that those people who remained grouped in tribes represented an earlier, lower form of life, left behind by the march of history and destined to be redeemed and refashioned by the intervention of superior forces. The epithet most commonly found in association with the word "tribe" was "savage."

| —M. YAPP, "TRIBES AND STATES IN THE KHYBER, 1838–42" |

The notion of the tribe as a descent group stretches back to the original thirteenth-century appearance of the Latin word *tribu* in English, when it was used for the thirteen divisions of the early Israelites.[1] By the fifteenth century it was being used in nonbiblical contexts in a way that overlapped with later notions of lineage and clan, and was, for example, applied to Irish groups having the same surname (*OED* 1933, 339). However, the association between the notion of the tribe and kinship society was given a particular form in the nineteenth-century evolutionist formulation of primitive society and sociocultural evolution. Morgan (1964 [1877]), following Grote's 1846 theory of ancient Greek state formation, saw the tribe as the political union formed by clans in the prestate period and described the confederated League of the Iroquois in these terms, providing an early model for anthropological accounts of "primitive" societies.

EXCAVATING THE NOTION OF KINSHIP SOCIETY

Nineteenth-century evolutionist social science saw descent groups as the elementary units into which humans organized themselves. Morgan, Maine, Marx, and McLennan all saw extended ties of kinship as forming the basis for prestate society. These kin relations later gave way to territory as the basis for social organization in civilizations. This theory of change, by which egalitarian kinship society preceded impersonal class society, became the frame in which the anthropological conceptions of tribe and clan developed.

Maine (1861, 106; cited in Kuper 1988, 80), who grounded his work on primitive society in studies of classical Greek and particularly Roman sources, wrote that "the history of political ideas begins, in fact, with the assumption that kinship in blood is the sole possible ground of community in political functions." This scholarship assumed a fundamental distinction between societies based on kinship (i.e., membership of clans—*gentes* in Latin) and those based on territory, a distinction Marx saw as between "blood" and "soil," and this opposition was mapped onto the dichotomies of primitive / civilized and prestate / state.

The most influential thinker in this regard, both for anthropology and Marxism, was Lewis Henry Morgan. For him, "all forms of government are reducible to two general plans. . . . The first, in the order of time, is founded upon persons, and upon relations purely personal, and may be distinguished as a society (*societas*). The gens [clan] is the unit of organisation. . . . The second is founded upon territory and upon property, and may be distinguished as a state (*civitas*)" (Morgan 1964 [1877], 13–14). Morgan's work, as well as articulating the evolutionism of the age, was also intensely ideological. His commitment to the articles of faith of populist democratic politics led him to conclude that the most ancient forms of society—kinship society organized into *gentes* (clans)—must embody the principles of liberty, equality, and fraternity. Morgan could not allow democracy to be an innovation of Athenian politics or the brainchild of Cleisthenes (as classicists did and continue to claim), but argued it must be an innate feature of the "gentile" (i.e., clan-based) kinship society that was thought to precede the city-state. One major problem for this scheme was that the earliest large Hellenistic social units, the *phylon* (translated as "tribe"), had a single ruler named a *basileus* or "king."

So Morgan (1964 [1877], 214) charges the classical historians with "monarchical bias"—even Grote, who is his principal source. He refutes the standard history with a general evolutionism, using evidence from Native American societies such as the Omaha to try to buttress his claim that a leader of an early kinship society could not have been a monarch: "under gentile conditions . . . rule of a king by hereditary right and without accountability in such a society was simply impossible" (Morgan 1964 [1877], 218). "Monarchy is incompatible with gentilism, for the reason that gentile institutions are essentially democratical [*sic*]" (Morgan 1964 [1877], 209). In Morgan's scheme, the *basileus* becomes a general military commander chosen for collective defense as part of a "military democracy" that might superficially look like monarchy but in reality embodied the spirit of liberty. To prove that this was possible, Morgan gives an example: "An Englishman, under his constitutional monarchy, is as free as an American under the republic" (Morgan 1964 [1877], 218). The same evolution must have occurred in all societies, and thus the Roman *reges* must also have been military commanders serving the will of their people, not kings, as generally thought. Where there was no evidence to support his model, Morgan simply assumes that it has been lost in the course of time. "The Latin language must have had a term equivalent to the Greek phylon or tribe, because they had the same organisation; but if so it has disappeared" (Morgan 1964 [1877], 266).

In fact, there is nothing to suggest Morgan's scheme was correct, even for ancient Greece. First, the "clan" does not seem to predate the state at all, but probably appeared after it, and like the later Roman *gens* ("clan"), it seems to be primarily an institution of the elite. Starr (1961, 134) remarks: "The genos (clan) only became important when aristocrats began to play a central role in Greek political life. They actually had no place in Attic law."[2] Second, the *phyle* (clan / tribe) does not seem to have been a kinship unit, but an administrative one, in which people were registered for the purposes of local civil and military government.[3]

But in the nineteenth century, Morgan's vision fitted well with both liberal and socialist philosophies concerned with such notions as the original natural liberty of man, or, in the Marxist variant, the idea of property as the basis for exploitation in the light of the universal sharing claimed for primitive communist society. The notion that without the state people organize themselves into descent groups and that these tend to be nonhierarchical became deeply ingrained in the Western social sciences.

Durkheim, the "father of sociology," conceived of clan-based society as a stage in the evolution of more complex systems, and he saw this as a special case of "segmental organization," that is, "societies based on repetitive parts which joined together simply through a sense of mutual resemblance" (Kuper 2004, 81). Evans-Pritchard's model of the Nuer segmentary lineage system seems to fit so perfectly with this thinking that one is tempted to feel in retrospect that if such a society had not existed it would have had to have been invented. Despite numerous subsequent critiques of the ethnographic basis of Evans-Pritchard's representation of the Nuer (e.g., Gough 1971; Beidelman 1971), the segmentary kinship model remained enormously influential in work on tribal and pastoral societies. The general frame into which it fitted remained so strong that Earnest Gellner (1994) continued to see segmentary society as the major predecessor and rival to "the state."

Well into the late twentieth century, the dominant view in both Western and Soviet anthropology was to regard tribes as "survivals" of earlier stages of political evolution, a view that continues to inform many state bureaucracies.[4] As such, the tribal continued to act as the primitive counterpoint to self-descriptions of Euro-American "civilization," narratives dominated by the discourse of class, kinship, territory, and function, where the Hobbesian brute contended with the Rousseauian noble savage. Sahlins (1968, 4–5, emphasis in original), for example, writes:

> Tribes occupy a position in cultural evolution. They took over from simpler hunters; they gave way to more advanced cultures we call civilizations . . . the contrast between tribe and civilization is between War and Peace. A civilization is a society specially constituted to maintain "law and order"; the social complexity and cultural richness of civilizations depend on institutional guarantees of Peace. Lacking these institutional means and guarantees, tribesmen live in a condition of War, and War limits the scale, complexity, and all-round richness of their culture. . . . Expressed another way, in the language of older philosophy, the U.S. is a state, the tribe a state of nature. Or, the U.S. is a *civilization*, the tribe a *primitive society*.

Kinship, egalitarianism, and, in Sahlin's account, endemic warfare had become naturalized as basic features of humans as a self-organizing species.

Despite some disquiet, the idea of tribal society as organized primarily by kinship rather than territory was retained, although it was acknowledged that there was rather little ethnographic evidence that clearly illustrated this.[5] The notion had been crystallized by descent theory into a model by which the units generated by kinship formed a nested series of descent groups. "The tribe presents itself as a pyramid of social groups, technically speaking as a 'segmentary hierarchy'. . . . The smallest units, such as households, are segments of more inclusive units such as lineages, the lineages in turn segments of larger groups, and so on" (Sahlins 1968, 15). This particular model of tribal structure could be disputed (e.g., Barnes 1962; Lévi-Strauss 1969), but the received idea of prestate, self-organized, kinship society remained.

So Khoury and Kostiner (1990, 4) conclude that "as ideal types, tribes represent large kin groups organized and regulated according to ties of blood or family lineage; states, by contrast, are structures that exercise the ultimate monopoly of power in a given territory." Noting that this distinction was generally far from clear in practice, they make use of another old anthropological concept to bridge the gap: the chiefdom. "Chiefdoms may be viewed as one type of intermediate political formation between tribes and states, incorporating some features and institutions of both" (Khoury and Kostiner 1990, 8).

TRIBES, CHIEFS, AND CHIEFDOMS

The era of European colonialism powerfully exported the term "tribe" as an administrative category and established it as a description of collective identity throughout much of the colonized world. Ranger (1983) takes John Iliffe's description of the creation of tribes in colonial Tanganyika (former German East Africa) as typical of the wider colonial process, and it is worth quoting at length:

> The notion of the tribe lay at the heart of indirect rule in Tanganyika. Refining the racial thinking common in German times, administrators believed that every African belonged to a tribe, just as every European belonged to a nation. The idea doubtless owed much to the Old Testament, to Tacitus and Caesar, to academic distinctions between tribal societies based on status and modern societies based on contract, and to the post-war anthropologists who preferred "tribal" to the more pejorative word "savage." Tribes

were seen as cultural units "possessing common language, a single social system, and an established common law." Their political and social systems rested on kinship. Tribal membership was hereditary. Different tribes were related genealogically. . . . As unusually well-informed officials knew, this stereotype bore little relation to Tanganyika's kaleidoscopic history, but it was the shifting sand on which Cameron and his disciples erected indirect rule by "taking the *tribal* unit." They had the power and they created the political geography.

(RANGER 1983, 250).

Anthropology also inherited the term "chief" from a colonial order in which civilizations were governed by monarchs and aristocrats and more primitive "tribal" societies were ruled by chiefs and paramount chiefs. The colonial authorities in Africa found it expedient to identify tribes and rulers to help maintain order, provide labor, extract surpluses, and so on, and they usually termed these rulers chiefs (Leys 1976; Hobsbawm and Ranger 1983; Ranger 1983; Chimhundu 1992). This was especially clear in the British system of Indirect Rule that developed in Nigeria and Tanganyika. In the early years of Indirect Rule, this meant creating chiefs or appointing some to be paramount over others and the creation of new tribal boundaries or ethnicities that had not existed or been prominent before (Iliffe 1979, Ranger 1989).[6] The most powerful African rulers were regarded as royalty, such as the monarchs of Dahomey, Benin, Ashante, and the Zulu, and as Cannadine (2002, 9) notes, the British imperial ideology contained a variety of "aristocratic internationalism" that recognized (and sometimes reinforced) aristocratic orders in its colonial dominions. But in general, local rulers were described using the less prestigious vocabulary of chief and paramount chief, rather than lord, king, or some other "civilized" noble title, and this became more widespread as time passed and colonial government became more secure. For all the salience of the capitalist economy of colonialism, aristocracy still commanded great prestige in Europe, and the use of titles had important political and diplomatic implications (Mair 1977, 134–139).

Ranger (1983, 239), for example, notes, "In the early days colonial administrators were happy to recognise African rulers as kings, and to present them . . . with the properties of stage monarchy. But as the colonial regimes established themselves and became less dependent on concessions extracted from African rulers, so there began a process of deflation." This variety of "divide and rule" undermined indigenous rulers by eroding their powers over subject nobles ("chiefs") and emphasizing the distance between all Africans and their colonial overlords. Thus, for example, King Lewanika of Barotseland was at first accorded full royal honors when the British gained control of the region at the turn of the twentieth century. But within a few years, the colonial administration declared that "Lewanika himself should no longer be referred to as 'King', since this elevated him above the other chiefs and drew what was considered to be an altogether inappropriate analogy with the imperial monarch" (Ranger 1983, 240). After all, colonial monarchs had to be very clearly placed above African / tribal ones. As late as 1947, when the Northern Rhodesian government issued printed instructions for the royal visit, they took care to emphasize this difference. The pamphlets explained: "King George is the biggest King in the world. He is not like an African chief" (Ranger 1983, 233).

The colonial usage was later rationalized by structural functionalist modeling of many African political systems as smaller in scale, less centralized, and territorially looser than "the state." But as the true grounds for the term had always been to distinguish civilized from barbaric societies, this terminology did not correspond to descriptions of any European forms of leadership since the Dark Ages. Each one of the hundred or so petty rulers of seventh-century Ireland was termed a king, for example, despite the fact that they governed a few thousand people at best. The hereditary ruler of the Bemba, however, governing some 140,000 aristocrats and commoners, was termed a "paramount chief" (Richards 1940). Elizabeth Colson (1986, 5–6) notes the double standards of this "tribalizing" discourse:

> In terms of territory, population, wealth, bureaucratic development, social stratification, and the centralization of power, the Hausa state of Kano far surpassed many of the kingdoms of Medieval Europe. Yet most of those who referred to the Hausa as a tribe were not being facetious in the fashion of Weatherford when he wrote of the tribes of Washington. . . . Too many social scientists, as well as the general public, use [tribe] to maintain a false distinction between us and them, those people who used to be called primitive because they did not originate within the European tradition. Tribe, then, signals something about political domination but says nothing about the social complexity or political organization, now or formerly, of those to whom it is applied who may or may not have formed a polity in the past or

present. In the seventeenth century when English-speaking explorers and settlers dealt with Native Americans as politically independent societies, they commonly referred to them as nations, placing them thus on a par with European nations. . . . As it became possible to ignore and inexpedient to recognize the full sovereignty of Native American rivals with whom the English settlements competed for land and political dominion, "nation" gave way to "tribe" which carried implications of lesser political status. Tribe thereafter became the term commonly used to distinguish among the populations being incorporated into colonial empires as these were created during the nineteenth century.

The chiefdom was fitted into the evolutionary scheme of development, and this was done most explicitly by anthropologists such as Sahlins and Service. "Tribes present a notable range of evolutionary developments . . . in its most developed expression, the chiefdom, tribal culture anticipates statehood in its complexities. Here are regional political regimes organised under powerful chiefs and primitive nobilities" (Sahlins 1968, 20). The distinguishing feature of "primitive nobilities" was, needless to say, the circular notion that they existed in chiefdoms or "primitive states." As an evolutionist concept, the chiefdom had to conform with the theory of change from egalitarian kinship society toward impersonal class society. It was said to be made up of descent groups that were simultaneously communities and therefore could not be *fully* stratified, as that was thought to be a characteristic of a later stage:

> A chiefdom is a ranked society. The descent and community groups of a segmentary tribe are equal in principle, but those of a chiefdom are hierarchically arranged, the uppermost officially superior in authority and entitled to a show of deference from the rest. A chiefdom is not a class society. Although a stage beyond primitive equalitarianism, it is not divided into a ruling stratum in command of the strategic means of production or political coercion and a disenfranchised underclass. . . . One particular type of chiefdom organisation, developed on exactly such distinctions of kinship grade, is so often called to anthropological mind it has come to epitomize the class. . . . The conical clan system. . .
>
> (SAHLINS 1968, 24)

As Kuper (1988, 205) notes, the conical clan model, originally proposed by the Engelian Paul Kirchhoff in 1955, was used to try to explain stratified social systems using the dominant model of kinship society. Sahlins (1968, 24) explains it thus:

> The conical clan is an extensive common descent group, ranked and seg-
> mented along genealogical lines and patrilineal in ideological bias. . . . Here
> clanship is made political. Distinctions are drawn between members of the
> group according to genealogical distance from the ancestor: the first-born
> son of first-born sons ranks highest and other people lower in the measure
> of their descent, down to the last born of last-born sons—everyone's com-
> moner . . . the chiefdom as a political unit is constructed on the clan as a
> ranked descent unit.

But the ethnographic basis for these ideal types began to dwindle on close inspection. Sahlins claimed the conical clan was widespread in Central Asia and parts of Africa, but he describes it as the "Polynesian type," considering it to be most common and perfectly manifested in that region. In fact, subsequent ethnography from Polynesia suggested that residential communities did not match descent groups and status need not depend on descent at all (Kuper 2004, 91).

As early as 1961, Leach had suggested that the supposed structure of unilineal descent groups might be a "total fiction" (Leach 1961, 302).[7] The ethnographic evidence for the segmentary kinship model had always been rather slight, and what there was faded away in the light of more critical later studies (Gough 1971; Verdon 1983; Southall 1988; McKinnon 2000). As Kuper (1988, 190–209) pointed out, the actual local categories used to designate groups of people did not resemble those of descent theory at all (Jackson 1989, 10–11; Gottlieb 1992, 46–71). There is no Nuer word for "clan" (Evans-Pritchard 1933–1935, 28); no Tallensi word for "lineage" or for the segments of a maximal lineage (Fortes 1949, 9–10); no Lugbara term for "lineage," "segment," or "section" (Middleton 1965, 36); and so on. As the dangers of foregrounding the analyst's categories at the expense of the indigenous ones became more apparent, these descriptions simply lost their plausibility. In retrospect, as Piot (1999, 11) notes, the structural functionalism that generated these theories appears deeply rooted in particular Euro-American academic debates.

As Kuper (2004, 93) writes, "in the end even the Nuer, Tiv, and Talis cannot be said to have 'true segmentary lineages.'" He concludes that "the lineage model, its predecessors and its analogs, have no value for anthropological analysis. . . . First, the model does not represent folk models which actors anywhere have of their own societies. Secondly, there do not appear to be any societies in which vital political or economic activities are organized by a repetitive series of descent groups."[8] Indeed, as

Goody (2000, 18) notes, it is doubtful if even the classical Roman agnatic descent group, the *gens*, was ever the dominant organizational form that Morgan supposed. It was certainly not the prestate social building block that the nineteenth-century social theory assumed. Cornell (1995, 85), for example, notes that the *gens* spread with the process of urbanization and administration. "This feature of the evidence runs counter to the well-entrenched nineteenth-century theory that the *gens* originated as a 'pre-political' organisation, which was weakened and ultimately eclipsed by the rise of the state. In fact the evidence implies the contrary." Rather than predating the state, then, the Roman descent group appears to have been produced by it.

Without its grounding in a distinctive form of kinship organization, the characteristics that are supposed to distinguish the chiefdom are reduced to the idea that societies termed tribal, ruled by chiefs, represent a "prestate" stage in political evolution.[9] But this parallel terminology by which the hereditary elites of tribes are termed chiefs and those of states are termed nobles is also problematic. The Weberian definition of the state—a political community possessing a monopoly of the use of the legitimate use of force within a given territory (Weber 1948, 78)—was actually devised to distinguish the "modern" state. But it was used by the structural-functionalist theoreticians to underpin the notion that the chiefdom was at least one evolutionary stage behind "the state." In retrospect, this approach seems limited historically and culturally and poorly suited for application beyond Weber's original subject. Applied to the medieval world, for example, this definition of state would rule out almost every kingdom in Europe, as the Roman church retained independent judicial jurisdiction over significant parts of most countries until well into the sixteenth century.

Fortes and Evans-Pritchard (1940) used the term "primitive state" for the evolutionary step after the chiefdom, a category into which they placed the majority of precolonial African polities. The working definition of this sort of state was a polity in which "a ruler who is recognised as supreme makes his authority effective through territorial agents chosen by himself. . . . The collection of tribute . . . is characteristic of all states" (Mair 1972, 124). This test of statehood is a hard one to pass for most early modern European states, in which the powerful aristocracies that controlled much of the territory can hardly be said to have been chosen by the ruler. But in the colonized world, only the most centralized and autocratic precolonial polities were considered primitive states; everything else was, by default, tribal. That we recoil from the idea that England or Portugal should be regarded as tribal chiefdoms until, say, the Elizabethan or imperial periods, reveals the residual ethnocentric evolutionism of the term. Europe had "passed that stage"—it had entered "historical time"—whereas polities in much of the rest of the world could be seen as examples of earlier stages, particularly in areas without systematic written histories to contradict the models projected onto them by the theorist.

Service (1975, 82) provides a typical justification for keeping Europe out of the evolutionary scheme imposed on "the rest." "European feudalism, then, was historically of a very complex, and perhaps unique sort. For this reason it cannot be considered a stage in evolution, or even a usual case of devolution." It was clear, however, that superficially, chiefdoms seemed very much like European aristocracies and monarchies:

> When [vassalage] systems become institutionalized as the power bureaucracies of hereditary chiefdoms, they resemble in certain important respects the hereditary aristocracies of late or postfeudal times in Europe. But none of these chiefdoms combine those features with the complicated land tenure systems and devolution in political unity of European feudalism closely enough to be classified with it.
>
> (SERVICE 1975, 82–83)

Without the mass of complicating historical detail available for Europe, then, more exotic societies could be cast as representing evolutionary stages. Although an earlier generation of scholars of Africa such as Rattray and Nadel had described precolonial African states in terms of feudalism, this terminology lost ground to the structural-functionalist scheme, which presented itself as a more general and objective classification of political society (Service 1975, 137). Similarly, Vladimirtsov's 1934 study of Mongolian society had described it as "nomadic feudalism," but this approach gave way before the advance of the tribal discourse of Radloff, Barthold, Fletcher, Khazanov, and Krader. The effect was to reproduce the old conceptual apartheid by which the colonized were subject to the primitivist language of tribe and chief while the colonizers only used such terms for the most distant eras of their own histories.

The attention of political anthropologists has drifted away from such classificatory wranglings to join sociologists and others in remarking on the distinctiveness of the "modern" state, the Weberian, Marxist, and Foucauldian characterization of which seemed more promising academic subjects (Gledhill 1994; Scott 1998; Mitchell 1991; Rabinow 1989). But this left the remnants of the language of an older political anthropology in widespread use—utilized by journalists, politicians, historians, and regional specialists, as well as by anthropologists themselves. Tapper (1990, 48) remarks, for example, that

> historians have sometimes employed anthropological theories or concepts that are outmoded, inappropriate, or controversial. Not least among these are the concepts of "tribe" and "tribalism." These terms refer to a category of society whose study was once regarded as the prerogative of anthropology, yet anthropologists themselves have notoriously been unable to agree on how to define them.

Khoury and Kostiner (1990, 5) characterize the tribe, following Tapper (1983, 6), as "a localised group in which kinship is the dominant idiom of organisation, and whose members consider themselves culturally distinct," and they contrast it with the state. The difficulty is, however, that it becomes clear that kinship is not the basis for social solidarity in many of the societies described. Hourani (1990, 304), for example, argues that "few people in illiterate societies know their ancestors more than three or four generations back or can extend their relationships beyond those whom they know personally or see frequently." Hourani observes that "tribes" do not share genealogical kinship, but he tries to keep the model alive by suggesting that tribes share "a myth of common ancestry." The notion of "fictive kinship" has been a common reaction to critiques of the concept of kinship society (e.g., Geiss 2003, 65)—it is not that people actually share descent, but they have an ideology that means that they think they do.

This idea does not stand up to any serious scrutiny. Quite apart from the ambiguities of what common ancestry might mean when three major Eurasian religions claim universal human descent from Adam, Khoury and Kostiner (1990, 5) follow Tapper in noting that some "tribes" never subscribed to an ideology of common descent. Indeed, as will be explored in chapters 4 and 6, a number of steppe aristocracies clearly did not trace common descent with their subjects, since descent from the ruling house was the basis of noble status. When it comes to the early history of the

Middle East, it is hard to find entities that look like tribes based on kinship, fictive or otherwise. Lapidus (1990, 29) remarks, "we commonly think of Arabian society on the eve of conquest as having been built around extended families or lineage groups, but despite the existence of this concept in the minds of Arabians, there is no evidence of large-scale genealogically defined tribes." She notes the importance of a certain interpretation of the fourteenth-century Arab historian Ibn Khaldun, who has been read as attributing successful state formation to the kinship solidarity of nomadic conquerors. But, she explains, "despite the authority of Ibn Khaldun, if we look empirically at Middle Eastern conquest movements, we find that kinship was a secondary phenomenon. Such movements as the Arabs, Fatimid, Almoravid, Almohad, Safavid, and other conquests were not based on lineage but on the agglomeration of diverse units" (Lapidus 1990, 29).

In the end, Khoury and Kostiner (1990, 5) concede that a definition of tribe is "virtually impossible to produce." And Tapper comes to view tribe and state as purely abstract models rather than real descriptive categories, noting, "there are elements of state within every tribe and of tribe within every state" (Tapper 1990, 68).[10] And yet Tapper, Hourani, and Khoury and Kostiner all continue to use the term "tribe" and employ it as an analytic category, mostly, it seems, for want of a better term. This was predicted by Godelier (1977, 90), who saw the concept of tribe as a product of the wider problems of outdated theories of kinship society:

> It is not enough, like Swartz or Turner, to ignore the concept of tribe by referring no longer to it; to appeal to prudence, like Steward; or to criticise its scandalous imprecision (Neiva); its theoretical sterility and fallacies (Fried); its ideological manipulation as a tool in the hands of colonial powers (Colson, Southall, Valakazi). The evil does not spring from an isolated concept but has roots in a problem which will necessarily produce similar theoretical effects as dictated by the scientific work put into it.

Godelier calls for a more thoroughgoing rethinking of the paradigm: "The most surprising thing in the history of this concept is that it has varied little in basic meaning since Lewis H. Morgan (1877). The innumerable discoveries in the field since have only aggravated and accentuated the imprecision and difficulties without leading to any radical critique, still less to its expulsion from the field of anthropology" (Godelier 1977, 89–90).

Indeed, the concept of tribal society as an evolutionary stage preceding state-organized society continues to have wide currency (e.g., Earle

1994, 944–945). However, the pejorative, colonial baggage of the term and its entanglement with nineteenth-century evolutionist theory caused most anthropologists to avoid it by the late twentieth century. Along with Godelier's objections, critiques such as Fried's 1975 *The Notion of Tribe* and revisionist works such as Vail's 1989 *The Creation of Tribalism in Southern Africa* helped establish the view that "tribalism" was a product of colonial classification and administration. A now common view, as Fried (1975, 114) put it, is to see the tribe as

> a secondary sociopolitical phenomenon, brought about by the intercession of more complexly ordered societies, states in particular. I call this the "secondary tribe" and I believe that all the tribes with which we have experience are this kind. The "pristine tribe," on the other hand, is a creation of myth and legend, pertaining either to the golden ages of the noble savage or romantic barbarian, or to the twisted map of hell that is a projection of our own war-riven world."

However, this critique has not seriously undermined the application of the model of tribal society to Inner Asia or indeed much of the Middle East, where the institutions of "the state" date back to the beginning of recorded history. Here scholars continue to apply parts or all of the tribal society model, although the analytical emptiness of the term becomes clear whenever it is seriously considered. While accepting that in sub-Saharan Africa modern tribalism does not represent indigenous political systems, in, for example, *The Dictionary of Anthropology*, R. B. Ferguson (1997, 476) reproduces the classical association between pastoralism and tribalism. "In the Middle East, unambiguous tribal identities are well known among PASTORAL NOMADS who have mobile bounded groups and a very long history of interaction with states."

The relative equality of tribal society is still central to this description, although the difficulty of sustaining this assumption in the face of the evidence of stratification is evident. "Most tribal leaders are noncoercive consensus managers, often working in formal councils. However, tribes of the Middle East and Central and South Western Asia have chiefs and even khans (Barfield 1993)" (Ferguson 1997, 476). The continued application of the notion of tribal society to "pastoral nomads" in Asia reflects anthropology's longstanding preoccupation with evolutionary kinship theory and its entanglement with notions of stratification and equality.

KINSHIP SOCIETY AND THE EGALITARIAN NOMAD

Structural-functionalist anthropology treated "pastoral nomadic society" as an ideal type with general characteristics to be discerned from the whole range of actual pastoral societies. This is discussed in greater depth in chapter 5. As Asad (1979, 421) notes, the segmentary lineage system model helped bolster the widespread assumption that, left to its own devices, pastoral nomadic society tended toward equality. Irons (1979, 362–372) summed up the received wisdom:

> Among pastoral nomadic societies, hierarchical political institutions are generated only by external political relations with state societies, and never develop purely as a result of the internal dynamics of such societies . . . in the absence of relatively intensive political interaction with sedentary society, pastoral nomads will be organised into small autonomous groups, or segmentary lineage systems. Chiefly office with real authority will be generated only by interaction with sedentary state-organised society. [11]

Dahl (1979, 261–80), for example, argued that the ecological constraints of pastoralism tend to prevent the accumulation of wealth necessary for stratification. Others, such as Burnham (1979, 349–360), saw the spatial mobility of the pastoral nomad as also being a political mechanism that inhibited centralization and class formation. As in comparable treatments of the "hunter-gatherer" ideal type (Lee and Devore 1968; Leacock and Lee 1982; Woodburn 1982), these approaches contained a strand of environmental determinism that deduced these characteristics "from first principles" rather than by close examination of particular historical cases. Surely, the argument went, nomads are bound to be egalitarian, as they could just move away from oppressive rulers. The counterarguments do not appear to have been seriously considered—that rulers might also be mobile and have political relations with neighboring power holders, that rolling steppes might appear empty but actually be divided between the various seasonal pastures governed by some powerful authority or other, or that there were numerous examples of historical pastoral societies with marked inequalities of wealth and power.

The segmentary kinship model was enthusiastically applied to Asian societies, with particular vigor in the case of groups thought of as "nomadic." Despite a notable lack of evidence, the practice that Andrew

Strathern (1983, 453) called the "background use of the segmentary model" retained a firm grip on ethnography of the region. In his treatment of Afghanistan, for example, Hager (1983, 83–86) advocates the "distinction between tribe, based on descent, and state, based on control of territory." As ideal types, he argues, "power in the state is monopolised by a central government, while in tribes such as the Pashtuns it may typically remain distributed among persons who adhere to the tribal law or who may occasionally be consolidated within various levels of latent tribal hierarchy." This theoretical distinction, however, appears unsustainable. State power operates through its distribution among persons adhering to state law, and state citizenship is also generally based on descent.[12] Hager (1983, 94) describes Pashtun tribal structure in segmentary terms as one of "progressively more inclusive groupings of lineage and faction." However, Glatzer (1983, 221) entirely rejects this idealized model. "Pashtun nomads . . . are organised socially not on the basis of a segmentary lineage or clan system, but on other bases." It is not descent but locality, interest, and political and economic structures that are the bases for social organization in Pashtun areas, he argues.

Descriptions of the purest segmentary or conical clan systems are generally found in accounts of historical "tribal" societies, rather than contemporary ethnographic accounts (e.g., Krader 1968; Garthwaite 1983; Barfield 1989; Geiss 2003). When such claims are made for a contemporary society, the clan system is usually in the process of being displaced or transformed as a political system by the state, and thus its characteristics are never fully found,[13] a strategy that Meeker (2002, 29) calls "anthropological reconstitution."

Ironically enough, one of the reasons for the persistence of this model of the pastoral nomadic tribe was that it happened to fit with arguments made by critics of the notion of the "pristine" tribe. Fried, for example, uses the long history of interaction between steppe powers and recognized states such as China as evidence that every group described as a tribe is in fact a product of the "secondary tribalism" generated by contact with states (see Fried 1975, 72). This is part of his argument, *contra* Sahlins, that small-scale aggressive societies are created by contact with states, and reflects his own notion of peaceful, egalitarian "prestate" society as a sort of human starting point, a notion that, he all but admits, is a matter of personal speculation and conjecture (Fried 1975, 71).

Fried reproduced Owen Lattimore's 1940 argument that Inner Asian pastoralists developed hierarchical formations as part of long historical relations with the Chinese state (see Lattimore 1940, 381). This provided an appealing reversal of the colonial trope whereby savage tribes were civilized by states. In Inner Asia, it seemed that some of the most famous predatory tribes, such as the Xiongnu, Mongols, and Manchu, were created by states. Jagchid and Hyer (1979, 261) reproduce this argument and even the otherwise well-informed Gledhill (1994, 43–44) is taken in by this appealing narrative:

> The nomad chiefdoms [of Inner Asia] were organised into a structure of clans whose segments were ranked. Although the powers of the chiefs was limited in peacetime, the hierarchical order of a chain of command was present in embryo in this political organisation . . . it enabled the nomads to achieve rapid consolidation of administrative control over the territory they conquered.

One of the reasons for the widespread reproduction of this vision of Inner Asian pastoral society is the work of Lawrence Krader, who is Sahlin's principal source on the subject. In his 1968 work *Formation of the State*, Krader gave a description of Mongolian pastoral society that fit the dominant model of tribal political organization perfectly: "An ordinary pastoral village in Mongolia is usually arranged in the form of either a circle, or an arc, of tents. The basis of village organisation is the extended family, composed of a patriarch and his sons, and their wives and children. Since families in the village are related, a kin community is formed. Typically the entire village is descended from a common founding ancestor" (Krader 1968, 86–87). Krader explains this contemporary social organization as the remaining, irreducible building block of the grander clan and tribal systems of the past:

> The history of the formation of these kin communities is directly related to the history of herding in Mongolia. . . . Villages were grouped into clans, and clans further into confederations, all still related by bonds of descent from a common ancestor. Thus all male members of a clan or confederation were related, even if only distantly; emperor and subject might be tenth or twentieth cousins in the male line. Each clan had a body of ritual which was special unto itself: ceremonies venerating clan ancestors, clan spirits, territorial spirits, the natural forces and phenomena of the territory.

In fact, Krader is mistaken in almost every detail of this description. There is no reason to suppose the relation between kinship and residence that he postulates, no evidence of different bodies of ritual special to "clans" (whatever he means by this term in the Mongolian context), and no genealogical scheme relating nobles with their commoner subjects.[14] Such a clan or lineage social organization was no more apparent in the early twentieth century, as the work of ethnographers such as Simukov (1933) and Vreeland (1962) make clear. In fact, as discussed in more detail in chapter 4, there is no reason to believe that anything like this structure of kin villages grouped into clans ever existed in Mongolia.[15]

Krader's next step, to claim that Mongol and Turkic clans grouped into confederations, could have been read directly from Morgan's original pattern for primitive society. "The plan of government of the American aborigines commenced with the *gens* [clan] and ended with the confederacy. . . . In like manner the plan of the government of the Grecian tribes, anterior to civilization, involved the same organic series. . ." (Morgan 1964 [1877], 63). In the conventional treatment of pastoral nomads, the confederation became the natural political aggregate formed by tribes.

THE NOMADIC TRIBE IN IRAN:
THE CASE OF THE BAKHTIARI

This Morganian approach is well illustrated by a description of the Bakhtiari "tribal nomads" of Iran by Garthwaite (1983). This apparently perfect example of the kin-tribe-confederation model turns out, on closer inspection, to raise a number of questions as to whether we can really see the political structure as forming from the "bottom up," by the mechanisms of kinship society, or from the "top down," by statelike processes of administration. Garthwaite (1983, 316–317) describes a "segmentary pyramid" starting with the descent groups that fit into a "sub-tribe" (*tireh*) of related descent groups, which in turn combined to form the "tribe" (*taifeh*) headed by an official appointed by the khans. These are grouped into one of eight *bab*, each of them with "a dominant lineage from which Khans are chosen." The *babs* are grouped into two "moities" (*il*), the Haft Lang and Chahar Lang, which together he describes as a "confederation." The impression Garthwaite gives is of a segmentary kinship structure that is only slightly hierarchical.

However, Garthwaite's source for contemporary ethnographic descriptions of the Bakhtiari is Jean-Pierre Digard, who directly rejected Garthwaite's segmentary kinship model, arguing it disguised the importance of class.[16] Although he does not explicitly reject the term "tribe," Digard cannot accept many of the distortions that Garthwaite's model of Bakhtiari society generates. He points out that "tribal confederations" in Iran such as the Khamseh were united "from above" in the nineteenth century by a family of powerful merchants from another region and that the subgroups had almost no connection before that time. Digard argues that the *tafia*, *bab*, or *il*, which he calls "large social units" rather than tribes, seem to have generated fictive genealogies so as to link their dominant lineages. The "confederation," then, did not grow from kinship relations between tribes of clansmen, but simply revealed "an anxiety to translate political affiliation, a posteriori, into terms of descent" (Digard 1983, 334).

The standard model of the "tribal chief" is largely encapsulated by Garthwaite's representation of the khan and closely matches the descriptions of nomadic rulers as nonexploitative "first-among-equal" tribal spokesmen by Krader (1968), Barfield (1989), and others:

> The khan's power was both personal and vested in their chiefly office: it was based on the benefits they were able to dispense, the respect they may have commanded because of their lineage, and their coercive capabilities within the tribe or confederation provided by armed retainers. Their chiefly functions included maintenance of order and adjudication of disputes; co-ordination of internal tribal affairs and migration, assignment of pastures, appointment of headmen and agents; collection of tribal levies, taxes and dues; and co-ordination of external relations, including representation of the tribe.
>
> (GARTHWAITE 1983, 318)

On closer inspection, however, the Bakhtiari khan begins to seem rather more like a hereditary governorship or vassal kingship within the Persian state than a confederation leader. The first recorded Bakhtiari khan, Ali Salih Beg, was given the title by the early eighteenth-century Iranian ruler Nadir Shah in return for his military support; he also received substantial estates in the rich agricultural district of Chahar Mahall. It is clear that the importance of noble or royal power is one of the few things that *is* known about Bakhtiari society at this time. His son Abdul succeeded him, extended his landholdings in Chahar Mahall, and is described in a 1780 document as governor of a large part of the Bakhtiari (Brooks 1983, 346). It turns out that "the Great Khans held executive power" (Garthwaite 1983, 319) and were part of the top echelons of the Persian court.[17] The closer the historical accounts are to the present day, the more hierarchical and statelike the descriptions of the political structure. Garthwaite (1983, 319) notes:

> During the late nineteenth and early twentieth centuries, Bakhtiari confederation leaders, the Great Khans, could have been removed only by a combination of the tribes and the state, thus limiting the tribes' independence of action and power. The leaders of the confederation acted as government surrogates in their role as administrators in the collection of taxes and conscripts, and the maintenance of order.

In fact, the pastoral nomadic lifestyle that appeared to define the Bakhtiari "tribe" seems to have been an innovation brought about by major economic disruption in Bakhtiari territory. Brooks (1983, 347) mentions in passing that "raids by Nadir's forces, the crushing of tribal revolts and the removal of thousands of families from the region made agriculture impossible. This [the eighteenth century] appears to have been the period when the Bakhtiari turned increasingly to the long-range pastoral nomadism which has characterised them since." He also mentions that at the time, the nobles were expanding their landholdings in non-Bakhtiari areas and "the distance grew between them and the bulk of the tribal population who were becoming nomadic" (Brooks 1983, 348). Since the time that they became "nomadic tribes," then, it is clear that the Bakhtiari were ruled by powerful and wealthy aristocrats.

Rather than "tribal solidarity" between kinsmen, historical records describe endless disputes between Bakhtiari khans, particularly in the early twentieth century, when the British controlled Iran. There is also ample evidence of class tension and the resentment of the khans by their Bakhtiari subjects at this time. A British political officer posted to Bakhtiari territory quoted one of his predecessors in his report: "In 1908 Col. Wilson wrote, 'The Khans are tolerated as a disagreeable necessity and feared and obeyed in proportion to their strength.'" (cited in Brooks 1983, 357).

As for the division between the Haft Lang and Chahar Lang described as "moieties," it turns out that these were administrative divisions.[18] Garthwaite (1983, 322) himself notes they "emerged as bureaucratic devices under the decentralised government of the late seventeenth century." The subsequent discussion shows that these units bore no resemblance to the marriage exchange groups of Morganian kinship theory.[19] Garthwaite hardly mentions the distinction between nobles and commoners, the class division that Digard felt was of such central importance, but on closer examination it seemed that the organization of commoners into groups under named heads is more likely to have been an administrative act than the result of some indigenous kinship structure. And instead of chiefs acting as representatives of their kinsmen, it seems that local nobles held a range of state-defined aristocratic titles and official prerogatives from as long ago as the eighteenth century, if not before. The continuities and connections between "the state" and the Bakhtiari nobles are much more striking than the evidence of a distinctive "tribal" society confronting it. As Digard (1983, 335) notes, this was no bounded social unit responding to "the state" as an "external stimulus." Rather, the state in Iran had long served the interests of "tribal" aristocracies such as those of the Bakhtiari. Instead of casting them as the confederated tribal "other" to the state, Brooks (1983, 362) shows the extent to which the Bakhtiari polity resembled it. He describes the Bakhtiari as a "failed state." Had the Bakhtiari khans managed to establish their own polity independent of Iranian suzerainty, we might be talking of the Bakhtiari state. The internal structure of Bakhtiari society was more indicative of political administration than kinship, but such was the influence of the segmentary lineage model that, at the time, it seemed plausible to describe it in these terms.

TRIBE AND CLAN IN INNER ASIA

Historically, the steppelands of Inner Asia have given rise to a series of imperial powers, including the Xiongnu, early Türk, Manchu, and Mongol empires. Scholars of Inner Asia have made much of the apparently incongruous phenomena of nomadic tribes periodically establishing vast and powerful states. Dominated by the notion of the pastoral nomadic society as an ideal type, these accounts commonly graft received wisdom regarding segmentary tribes onto their descriptions to fill the gaps left in the historical record.

Thomas Barfield (1989, 8), one of the best-known anthropologists of Inner Asia, summarizes the dominant view:

> Inner Asian nomadic states were organized as "Imperial confederacies"....
> They consisted of an administrative hierarchy with at least three levels: the
> imperial leader and his court, imperial governors appointed to oversee the
> component tribes within the empire, and indigenous tribal leaders. At the
> local level the tribal structure remained intact, under the rule of chieftains
> whose power was derived from their own people's support, not imperial
> appointment.

Barfield (1989, 24–26) offers a description of a timeless, essentialized, steppe
nomadic society that could have been written by Krader or Sahlins:

> Throughout Inner Asia historically known pastoralists shared similar prin-
> ciples of organization alien to sedentary societies. . . . Patrilineal relatives
> shared common pasture and camped together when possible. . . . Tribal
> political and social organization was based on a model of nested kinship
> groups, the conical clan . . . an extensive patrilineal kinship organization in
> which members of a common descent group were ranked and segmented
> along genealogical lines. . . . Political leadership was restricted to members
> of senior clans in many groups, but from the lowest to the highest, all mem-
> bers of the tribe claimed common descent. . . . When nomads lost their au-
> tonomy to sedentary governments, the political importance of this exten-
> sive genealogical system disappeared and kinship links remained important
> only at the local level.

Although it was clear to a number of scholars that the application of the
conical clan model was pure fantasy,[20] the lack of historical evidence for
the segmentary kinship system tended to be explained away by assuming that contact with, or conquest of, state systems caused them to decay.
In any historical description, the argument went, one would only expect
to find elements, remnants of the complete system of the past. The thirteenth-century Mongol state founded by Chinggis Khan (Genghis Khan),
for example, created a rich fund of historical materials, particularly Chinese, Mongolian, and Persian sources. It is clear from these that this was a
hierarchical society with a powerful pastoral aristocracy ruling common
subjects, and, as discussed in chapter 4, the richer historical sources of the
fourteenth century show that the *lack* of a segmentary lineage structure
dates back to at least this time.

Thus the essentialized tribal society is envisaged as existing before the
Chinggisid state, at a period for which we have almost no historical mate-

rial. Barfield (1989, 189) writes: "At the time of Temjuin's [Chinggis Khan's] birth the steppe was in anarchy. Segmentary opposition was the basic form of political organization: opposing tribes or clans would unite against a common foe, only to separate and continue fighting one another when | 61 | the common enemy was defeated."

Most of what is known about the pre-Chinggisid period that was not written by outsiders is provided by a single source: the *Mongqol-un niucha tobcha'an*, the *Secret History of the Mongols*, which was almost certainly authored by one or more members of Chinggis Khan's court in the thirteenth century.[21] *The Secret History of the Mongols* includes some genealogical data, and some of the named groups in it appear to trace descent from common ancestors. However, on closer inspection, these genealogies are not "segmentary."[22] There is no reason to suppose that the society was composed of territorial kin groups, and what little evidence we have on political alliances suggests shifting pragmatic alliances between powerful nobles with little or no respect for genealogical proximity, the most bitter warfare often breaking out between close aristocratic relatives.[23]

At the time of Chinggis Khan's birth, the steppes of what is now Mongolia were divided between a number of political entities (such as the Kereyid, Merkid, Tatar, Jürkin, and Tayichi'ut). In the dominant interpretation of the *Secret History of the Mongols*, these are described as tribes or clans. In fact, we know very little about the internal organization of these entities. What is clear, however, is that these polities were aristocracies with common subjects, and that the commoner-nobility distinction long predated Chinggis Khan's rise to power.[24] The term for groups defined largely (but probably not exclusively) through descent was *yasu* (bone), and nobles were referred to as of *chaqa'an yasu* (*chagan yasu*, "white bone")—this color contrasting with *qara* (*khara*, "black"), used for subjects. Documented traditions of aristocracy and hereditary overlordship in the Mongolian region stretch back as far as the Xiongnu of the second century B.C.E. The *Secret History* describes Chinggis Khan's ancestry in such a way as to include many with titles (often derived from both the Liao dynasty and the Orkhon-Turkish empire). Even some of the most distant matrilateral ancestors are said to be lords of large territories (Cleaves 1982, 2; Onon 1990, 3–11).

There is plenty of evidence, if one chooses to look for it, that these ruling houses or lineages were *not* related by descent to the people they ruled. The people known as the Jürkin, for instance, were one of several named groups living in Mongolia at the time. They have been described as a tribe (Cleaves 1982, 245) or a clan (de Rachewiltz 2004, 289), and from this it would appear they formed a homogeneous kin-based unit composed of clansmen. In fact, it is clear from section 139 of the *Secret History* that this political unit had originally been formed by a ruler (Qabul Khan) and that term "Jürkin" more properly referred to the ruling lineage/house only. "Chinggis Qa'an (emperor) made such arrogant people submit (to him) and he destroyed the Jürkin *obog* (*obug*, "family," "line," "lineage"). Chinggis Qa'an made their people, and the subjects (they ruled), his own subjects."[25] The conquest of other polities, such as the Tatar and Tayichi'ut, for example, are described in very similar terms, with the name of the polity attached most specifically to the nobility, who were clearly distinguished from their subjects.[26]

Instead of a map of a segmentary or conical clan kinship system, then, the *Secret History of the Mongols* describes sets of ruling lineages/houses with a large number of subjects.[27] The standard translation of terms, however, gives the impression that it describes a prestate society of clans and tribes.

There is no single term that corresponds to the way that the word "tribe" has been inserted in the translations of the *Secret History*. Instead, a series of different words—*irgen* (people, subjects), *ulus* (polity, realm, patrimony, appanage), and *aimag* (division, group)—have been translated as "tribe" in places in the text when the unit concerned is believed to be tribal. Similarly, there are two terms, *obog* (family, lineage, line) and *yasu* (bone, descent, lineage), commonly translated as "clan" depending on the context, and often the term "clan" has simply been inserted next to any group noun that the translator believes to be a clan.

Ratchnevsky (1991, 12) has a similar tendency. Knowing that the *Secret History* describes a clearly stratified society, he pushes the mythic nomadic kin-based era back to the turmoil before Chinggis is born. By the time of Chinggis, he writes, "the kinship group lost its homogeneous character." This is a strange comment to make, as Ratchnevsky uses Persian sources to show that both predecessors of Chinggis Khan (Qutula Khan and Ambagai Khan) ruled steppe empires, but presumably he conceives of these empires as consisting of homogeneous kin groups, much as Krader conceived of Chinggis's early empire.

The insertion of kinship has been accompanied by the deletion of stratification; the importance of aristocratic power and heritage has been consistently downplayed. At some points in the text, for example, the term *ulus* is commonly translated as "nation," which is the current meaning of the term (see Onon 1990, 11; Cleaves 1982, 11); elsewhere, translators have habitually translated it as "people"—for example, when the khan of the Kereyid tells Chinggis that he will help him reunite his scattered *ulus* (Pelliot 1949, 25; Onon 1990, 28; Cleaves 1982, 33; De Rachewiltz 2004, 30)—and this helped support the impression of egalitarian tribalism. In general a more accurate translation for the term in this period would actually be "patrimony" or "domain," as Morgan (1986, 95) and Jackson (2005, 367) suggest, and in Chinggisid states such as the Yuan and Ilkhanate it was consistently used for the appanages assigned to nobles. But it has been assumed that this usage was a state-induced distortion of an original, more "tribal" concept. The more probably accurate translation of the Kereyid Khan's offer, "I will reunite for you your divided patrimony," appeared rather too feudal, so most translators chose to render this in more romantic tones: "I shall unite for you your scattered people."

A clearer example of the way in which colonial-era models of tribal society were used to distort the historical evidence is provided by the treatment of Latin sources. The observant Franciscan Friar Giovanni Da Pian Del Carpini, for example, traveled to the court of Güyük Khan (Chinggis Khan's grandson) in 1246 and left the first detailed eyewitness account by a European of the Mongol polity. He describes a hierarchical and aristocratic society:

> The dukes [*duces*] have like dominion over their men in all matters, for all Tartars [Mongols] are divided into groups under dukes. . . . The dukes as well as the others are obliged to give mares to the Emperor as rent . . . and the men under the dukes are bound to do the same for their lords, for not a man of them is free. In short, whatever the emperor and the dukes desire, and however much they desire, they receive from their subjects property.
>
> (DAWSON 1955, 28; BEAZLEY 1903, 59)

Carpini used the Latin word *dux* for senior Mongol and European nobles alike, and early translators such as Hakluyt in the sixteenth century translated these as "duke" (Beazley 1903, 121, 59), as I have done in the passage above. However, nineteenth- and twentieth-century translators such as Rockhill (1900) and Dawson (1955) introduced an astonishing dual system whereby when *dux* referred to a European noble, such as the Russian nobleman Vassilko, it was translated as "duke," but where it applied to a

Mongol it was translated as "chief," thus confirming the tribal model of Mongolian society.[28]

The literary inertia of the tribal model continues to have an influential presence in the history of Inner Asia, despite considerable recognition of its flaws.[29] Contemporary specialists such as Peter Golden (2001a, 20), for example, are often cautious about the term "tribe," treating it as a matter of convention rather than a good description.[30] Nicola Di Cosmo (1999, 18) has to modify the meaning of the term to be able to use it with a clear conscience. He takes "tribe" to mean "a large group of people recognizable by one single ethnonym and *possibly* united by kin ties and kin relations" (my emphasis). In Inner Asian history, he says, this was "pre-eminently a political formation" replete with made-to-order genealogies but united in "a common political project."[31] Such specialists have largely abandoned the content of the term so that it really simply indicates a political formation of some kind. However, the "technical" meaning of a term cannot be so easily separated from its connotations and the contexts of its habitual application. The term "tribe" retains subtle echoes of its earlier meanings and its popular application to societies thought of as primitive. Never having been explicitly exorcized, the wider model of tribal society continues to haunt the scholarship on the region. Soucek (2000, 298), for example, describes Mongolia up to the advent of communist control in the 1920s and 1930s as "a confederation of tribal groups governed by a two-pronged aristocracy of lay tribal and Buddhist church leaders." This is rather like describing the Habsburgs as "tribal leaders," since the Borjigid aristocracy of Mongolia were quite as well established and socially elevated as the nobilities of Europe. But in the colonial era, it was understandable enough that the titles and terms used for the civilized world should not be sullied by universal application. However, this was not simply a matter of "the West" being marked off from "the rest": the discursive construction of the barbaric polity was also a significant feature in Chinese thought.

3

The Imaginary Tribe

Colonial and Imperial Orders and the Peripheral Polity

COLONIAL AND IMPERIAL NOTIONS OF
THE TRIBE IN INNER ASIA

The stereotypical representation of exotic peoples as barbarians is by no means a uniquely Euro-American phenomenon. As Hostetler (2001, 99) puts it, "the politics of representation encapsulated in the idea of 'orientalism' is not simply a feature of Western modernity, but of the colonial encounter itself, wherever colonial relations are played out. This capacity or inclination to 'orientalize' is not unique to the Western world." She demonstrates that Chinese representations of "barbarian" outsiders are susceptible to a comparable analysis. "The central issue is ... how centers of power with a monopoly on the production and dissemination of knowledge define peripheral groups and attempt in one way or another to dominate them. The struggle for control is not only a product of 'Western' hegemony" (Hostetler 2001, 96).

In Chinese literature, the tradition of representing those societies that are beyond the boundaries of the state as uncivilized stretches back to the earliest times (Rossabi 2004, 3). Since the Warring States Period (the third to fifth centuries B.C.E.), schemes were developed to describe the notional types of barbarians, such as that found in the *Li Ji*, one of the Confucian canonical works, which associates them with the cardinal directions—the Eastern Yi, Western Rong, Northern Di, and Southern Man. Such literary traditions remained influential until Qing times and formed part of the discursive construction of the Chinese state as standing for a "radiating civilization," as Di Cosmo (2002, 94) puts it. Barbarians were cast as not-yet-civilized people, distant from the "central state" (*zhongguo*). They were to be transformed (*hua*) by education (*jiaohua*) or royal power (*wanghua*) and brought inside the civilized fold (*guihua*). In this literary tradition, those entirely without the transformation worked by the civilizing state might be described as "raw" (*sheng*) barbarians, while those who had become partly civilized were "cooked" (*shu*), and Fiskesjö (1999, 162) notes "the uncanny similarity between the Raw/Cooked distinction and the nineteenth century 'savagery-barbarism-civilisation' schemes, devised in the heydays of European colonialism. . . . These, too, provide for three steps to civilisation, and similarly relegated barbarians and savages to the periphery in spatial terms, and to antiquity in temporal terms."

European scholars of the colonial period found a workable correspondence between their own categories and those of the Imperial Qing state when describing peoples on the peripheries or beyond the boundaries of their states, whose societies and elites were described as of a lower political order than their own. The widespread use of the term "tribe" to describe the societies on China's Inner Asian frontier was partly a result of translation, as this was the conventional translation of the Chinese term *buluo*. The first term, *bu*, means a class, division, or section, and was used for a division of a campaigning army. The character is based on the pictogram for "fief" and another form, which probably means "to divide" (Hucker 1985, 390). It was combined with *luo* to mean an aboriginal or native "tribe," but it could be more precisely translated as "indigenous division," and no kinship relations are implied by these terms. For colonialist discourse, however, the translation served well enough—both terms reflected the notion of a political division of the uncivilized and was consistently applied to societies at the periphery of empire.

The Mongol term *aimag* was conventionally translated into Chinese as *buluo*. In the Qing period, the *aimag* was the large administrative division into which the local principalities called *khoshuu* (*khoshigu*, or "banners," in English) were grouped and whose nobles met in assembly (*chigulgan/chuulgan*) to agree on policy under the Manchu supervision. In modern Mongolian, *aimag* means a section or administrative division—such the provinces of the state. But in historical documents, the word is commonly translated as tribe (e.g., Bawden 1997, 10), and in official Mongolian histories the term *aimag* became the standard term to describe "tribal" pre-Chinggisid political formations (Tseveendorj 2004, 376–380).[1] However, as Atwood (2004) notes, as long ago as the thirteenth century the term *aimag* was used in Mongolian documents for provinces of China and Tibet, and it would be more consistent to assume that the term meant an administrative division even at that time. None of the theoretical baggage that was attached to the term "tribe" is actually contained in the terms themselves, so their translations in early documents is a matter of convention based on particular models of steppe society at that time.[2]

There has been a good deal of persistent unease with the use of the term "tribe" by more critical scholars of Inner Asia. Lattimore sometimes placed the term in quotation marks to show the provisionality of its use and remarks (1934, 76), "a tribe is not so 'real' a thing as the genealogy of a princely family." He was also very conscious that the English word stood for the Mongol administrative terms *aimag* and *chigulgan*—units of regional government that formed part of the Qing state. When describing the Manchurian Tungus-speaking group the Oronchon, for example, Lattimore (1934, 165) describes them as having become "sufficiently 'tribal' to be organised in the modern Mongol style on a tribal-territorial basis." The "modern administration" that Lattimore is referring to was the system of local offices and *chigulgan* princely assemblies that characterized Qing indirect rule of the Mongol territories. Because these were in translation conventionally described as "tribal," Lattimore found himself describing "modern" governance in these terms. Similarly, when describing the Kitans, Wittfogel and Feng (1949, 428) are keen to note that "the term 'tribal' does not necessarily mean primitive" and stress the administrative complexity of the political divisions described by the term. Like Lattimore, they are conscious of the link between a *bu* (tribe) and the noble family to which it might be attached, remarking "a tribal name may derive from a noble—superimposed—leader, rather than from the inconspicuous and perhaps enslaved commoners" (Wittfogel and Feng 1949, 91).

NOMADIC TRIBES IN THE EUROPEAN COLONIAL
IMAGINATION

|68| In the late colonial period, popular representations of nomads portrayed them as simple people, fierce and free. Some of the best-known travel writing on Inner Asia in English was the work of Mildred Cable and Francesca French, two intrepid missionaries who traveled in the region in the late 1920s. "In nomad-land the spaces belong to the tribes, and the Mongol rides over them singing and shouting, free as the air he breathes, tied to no building and confined by no walls of city or of home. He belongs to the desert and the desert belongs to him" (Cable and French 1950, 267).

In fact, such accounts are rather misleading. From the seventeenth century, if not before, the territory of Mongolia was divided into administrative divisions (*khoshuu*), each ruled by a nobleman (*jasag noyan*). Later, after the Mongol nobles had sworn fealty to the Manchu emperor, some administrative districts were governed by Buddhist monasteries or Qing officials with similar powers. The default rank for noblemen was the title of *taiji* (prince), and there were eight classes of aristocratic title, from the greatest lords down to the generic title of *taiji* without a *khoshuu* to govern.[3] Each *khoshuu* prince had his own administrative staff, treasury, and offices, as well as personal retainers and numerous herds of livestock. His subjects were divided between subunits—the *sumun* of a notional 150 households, made up of *bags* of around fifty households, which were divided into *arban* units of a nominal ten. Pastureland was under the jurisdiction of the ruling lord or monastery who managed pastoral movement in their districts. There were vast inequalities in wealth, with rich aristocrats and monasteries owning thousands of livestock and the poorest herders having almost none at all and working for others to make a living. The Mongolian aristocracy had intermarried with the Manchu nobility since the seventeenth century and were frequently appointed to high imperial office, particularly in the military. They were generally highly literate and often multilingual, and they coordinated policy through the *chigulgan* regional assembles chaired by a rotating head.

One would hardly suspect any of this from the picture painted by Cable and French, who were writing at a time when, in the wake of the collapse of the Qing, the Mongolian nobility led by princes such as Gungsangnorbu and Demchugdongrob were negotiating an uneasy course between Chinese warlords, the Guomindang nationalist government, and expanding spheres of Japanese and Soviet influence.[4] Their account evokes visions of an ancient tribal life, and they frequently describe the prince as a chief or chieftain while hinting at a sort of exotic, barbaric lawlessness.

> We went to Etzingol . . . we learnt that the old Prince, at whose invitation we came, had recently died, and that the new head was a usurper who seized the Chieftainship, with all the tents and all the riches of the old Prince. Next morning we sat in the tent of this bold supplanter, and with the help of his Chinese interpreter we talked to him of many things. . . . The Chieftain's simple mind was bewildered by two irreconcilable assertions that simultaneously claimed his attention, and both of which were new and foreign to his thought. One concerned the Mongolian New Testament which we had sent ahead and of which he turned the pages as we talked. The first great proposition which faced him was the call from God to repentance "God commandeth men everywhere to repent." The other word was a denial of the existence of God, and a declaration by the strange lama [who had just returned from a journey into Soviet territory] that religion was the weapon of imperialism and the dope of the people. . . . That day, in the audience-tent, the destiny of the Etzingol tribes seemed to be outlined before our eyes. . . . Young boys would be claimed for school-life and their outlook cleverly biased, amplifiers carrying the voice of a Moscow broadcast might speak in the tent of Chieftains, and the conversion of fearless herdsmen into dashing cavalry could be easily effected. This might well be the future of the Etzingol nomads.
>
> (CABLE AND FRENCH 1950, 270–271)

Cable and French must have met the prince of Ejine gol *khoshuu*, who around 1930 would have been embroiled in the administrative consequences of the inclusion of his principality into the newly formed Ningxia province in 1928, within territory controlled by the Soviet-leaning Chinese warlord Marshal Feng.[5] Their description of him as a usurper is a little puzzling, as succession was governed by law, but the resulting hint of barbaric daring succeeds in making the account more exciting.

Lattimore (1951, 96) notes that this tendency among travelers to portray Mongolian nomads in romantic terms dated back to the previous century:

> Western travellers in the second half of the nineteenth century were attracted by the free spaces of the open steppe, the hospitality and noble manners of the aristocracy. . . . Abundant herds gave the impression of great wealth.

Only the sharper observers noted that the common herdsman consumed very little of the mutton and beef and milk that walked about the pastures under their charge, and that the poorer people were bitterly poor . . . few travellers were interested in deducing from the comparison between poor people and rich herds that the "free" life of the nomad was restricted even in freedom of movement and that ownership had passed from the herdsman to princes and ecclesiastical dignitaries.

Lattimore, however, remained sufficiently uncritical of longstanding European notions of the egalitarian nomad to displace the existence of nomadic freedom and equality into the pre-Qing and pre-Chinggisid period, for which there were fewer and less well-known historical records describing steppe society. Stratified political structures were explained away as "distortions" of the original kin-based nomadic society caused by contact with sedentary states.

In another of his entirely misleading flights of fancy, Krader (1968, 87) uses the notion of kinship society to try to explain away the starkly obvious importance of aristocracy in pre-Soviet era Mongolia:

> Nevertheless, this uniform kinship structure was divided into unequal estates, the nobility and the commoners. Both were estates related by descent from the clan founder; but in practice they were divided by differences in birth, wealth, accident, migrations, wars. Descent lines were not equal; the line of the firstborn was more highly placed than any other, having the right of seniority. . . . Leadership was a status that was not assigned by rote—it had to be achieved, and achievement was based on social recognition of leadership qualities.

Krader is, again, wrong in almost every respect. There was no established right of primogeniture in the imperial period.[6] Any of a ruler's sons might have his claim to the throne recognized, and this selection is presumably what Krader misleadingly describes as the "achievement" of leadership positions, unless he is referring to the process by which the prince selected his subordinate officials. The major status categories of *aran* [*haran*] (commoner) and *noyan* (noble) were entirely hereditary. Throughout most of Mongolia only the aristocracy kept genealogical records by the Qing period, and these show no shared descent with common subjects, let alone a neat ranking of different "lines" within a conical clan structure. The *khoshuu* districts were administrative units, not clans, and in most *khoshuus* the majority of commoners used no clan names. The areas in which such named descent groups and genealogical records were usual for commoners were those under direct Manchu or tsarist Russian administration, and, as discussed in chapter 4, in many cases such descent groups seem to have been introduced by the state.[7]

REEXAMINING TSARIST TRIBES—KAZAKHS AND KYRGYZ

The dominant vision of nomadic society was also applied to the Kazakh and Kyrgyz polities. Western and Soviet scholarship shared enough nineteenth-century social theory to make the segmentary kinship model of nomadic society mutually convincing, and the literature reflects this influence. Geiss (2003, 29), for example, sets out to study the "tribal people of Central Asia"—that is, the Kazakh, Kyrgyz, and Turkman—and draws on a good deal of Soviet ethnography. He writes:

> Genealogies played an important role in Central Asian tribal societies. They represented the backbone of the society, built a societal web. . . . Tribesmen formed a body of agnatic kin and traced their origin from common ancestors. In this way descent group names were inherited through the male line. Mutual relations were established according to the closeness and distance of shared ancestors. . . . Genealogies based on primogeniture could inform orders of seniority between groupings.
>
> (GEISS 2003, 46)[8]

As discussed in chapter 5, early Soviet-era scholarship had tended to describe tsarist and pre-tsarist Kazakh and Kyrgyz society in terms of feudalism, but later scholars—notably Tolybekov (1971) and Markov (1976)—argued that the earlier work must have been mistaken. Nomadic states, they argued, could not have been genuinely feudal, but rather were organized by kin relations. The segmentary kinship model matched Western studies of "nomadic society," and, since it precluded the existence of a clearly stratified class of "exploiters," it seemed—particularly to Western commentators such as Gellner (1988)—free of the taint of a Soviet ideology that must have imposed a model of class war on simple tribal peoples. The earlier Soviet language was generally dismissed by Western scholars, who liked to think of the notion of "nomadic feudalism" as an ideological, Marxist claim. The tribal model became deeply embedded in representations of Kazakh and Kyrgyz history; the standard description is of a kinship society composed of clans (in Russian, *rod*) coming together to form tribes (in Russian, *plemya*) grouped into a tribal federation. But is this rather ahistorical model of "traditional" kinship society well founded, and what happens when the effects of colonial administration are included in the analysis?

The Kazakh khanate[9] dates from the mid-fifteenth century. The Chinggisid conquests had generated a number of successor states on the Turkic steppes, such as the Golden Horde in the west and the White Horde and Shaybanid Horde in the east. The term "horde," which has come to have such exotic and barbaric connotations, was originally a rendering of the Mongolian word *ordo* (*ordu*), meaning "palace," and was used to mean a kingdom or royal house. Around 1450, Janibeg and Qarai, sons of Barak Khan of the White Horde, broke with their nominal Shaybanid overlord Abu'l Khair and established a khanate of their own (Groussett 2002, 479). The khanate expanded, and by the time of Qasim Khan (1511–1523) it had become a powerful state in its own right, occupying much of what is now Kazakhstan. By the end of the sixteenth century, the Kazakh khanate had conquered Tashkent, which became the seat of the Kazakh dynasty until 1723. The khanate was divided into three divisions, known as Jüz, meaning "hundred" (widely used as an administrative division in the Turkic tradition of statecraft)—the Greater, Middle, and Lesser Jüz (Ulu Jüz, Orta Jüz, and Kishi Jüz). Schuyler (1885, 30) notes that at the height of their power the Kazakh khans commanded over a million men and mustered more than 300,000 troops.[10]

Russian colonial expansion in the east led to tsarist power extending over increasingly large amounts of steppe territory. Russian control of Kazakh territory began around 1730, when Abilay Khan of the Lesser Horde swore fealty to the tsar, and other nobles later followed his lead.

There is no doubt that this was another aristocracy. For example, Alexis de Levchine, an early nineteenth-century eyewitness, comments: "We find among the Kirghiz the same hereditary distinctions that count for so much in Europe. Savages know, like us, how to take pride in the services rendered by others and to grant privileges in return for the merits of their ancestors" (Levchine 1840, 305). Twentieth-century accounts nevertheless represented the society as composed of segmentary clans, although it was recognized that the units termed "clans" were not actually consanguineous at all. Krader (1968, 101), for example, describes the polity as a "clan-confederation." Wheeler (1964, 33) follows the Morgan-Engels evolutionary scheme rather closely in charting a speculative development of sociopolitical structure, as usual placing real kinship society back before the era of good records:

> The so-called clan system, which was originally based on the union of a number of families related to one another and sharing a communal econo-my, had begun to change by the seventeenth century . . . the development of the clan system may be divided into three stages: the community, the community-family, and the family-community. During the last stage a Ka-zakh's loyalties would be first to the family, and the community would take second place. . . . During the seventeenth century the gradual breaking-up of the clans was accelerated, and in most cases the place of groups of fami-lies of the same clan was taken by *aymaks* or mixed communities made up of different clans. This was brought about partly by the needs of cattle-grazing and partly by the frequent wars between the sultans.

In retrospect, it seems strange that Wheeler imagined that processes as-sociated with cattle grazing and war should have only begun to operate in the seventeenth century. What, one wonders, had prevented these pro-cesses from breaking up clans in all those preceding centuries? The *aymak* "mixed communities" were in fact the *aimag* Chinggisid appanages or ad-ministrative divisions that one would expect to see allocated to the ruling houses of the aristocracy.[11]

Even the much better informed Khazanov, who makes a point of not using the word "clan" to describe what he terms the "subdivisions" of the Kazakh polity, can not entirely dispense with the segmentary model:

> The Kazakhs entered the historical arena in the fifteenth and sixteenth cen-turies, when their social organization was based on a stratified segmentary system. . . . The estate of the "white bone" traced its descent from Jenghiz [Chinggis] Khan and contrasted itself to all other Kazakhs, in both social and genealogical respect, cutting across the segmentary (local) groups. . . . A single khanate soon disintegrated into three Hordes (Juz), headed by elected khans who were descendants of Jenghiz Khan.
>
> (KHAZANOV 1984, 176)

Of course, as Radloff (1863, 322) noted, this election was not a form of pop-ular democracy but an assembly of ruling aristocrats to select an overlord.

Soucek (2000, 196) displays typical surprise at this stratification: "the prestige enjoyed by the steppe aristocracy of Genghisid [Chinggisid] ancestry may have been a factor in the peculiar vertical division of Qazaq society into two layers, the so-called 'White Bone' and 'Black Bone' (Aq Süyek, Qara Süyek)." Far from being "peculiar," the idiom of "white bone" to describe noble descent was found in all the Mongol polities and in other states, such as the ancient Korean-Manchurean kingdom of Koguryo.[12] But the notion that "tribal" society must somehow form itself in bottom-up processes of aggregation continues to dominate historical interpretation. Thus Soucek (2000, 195) writes that "by 1730 the Kazakhs, as we have seen, had asserted themselves as a distinct group of nomadic tribes . . . but lacking overall political unity. As a somewhat peculiar substitute for the latter, though, the tribes had coalesced into three confederations, the aforementioned Greater, Middle and Lesser Hordes." In fact, as Khazanov and the historical record show, quite the opposite process had been taking place, the fragmentation of a previously more centralized polity created by the political decisions of aristocrats.

Early colonial accounts, such as that of the Russian colonial official Alex de Levchine,[13] provided much of the raw material for the later misinterpretation of "nomadic" society. At first glance, Levchine seems to describe the fierce and free egalitarian nomads that seemed so plausible to nineteenth- and twentieth-century social theorists. Levchine describes the Kazakh political system as "anarchy." Following the Russian convention of the time, he uses the term Kirghiz (Kyrgyz) or Kirghiz-Kazakh to mean the Kazakhs.

> Certainly we don't employ the word anarchy here in its most rigorous meaning, as it is well known that nowhere in the world would a complete state of anarchy be durable; but the little solidity of the authorities that exists among the Kirghiz, their lack of definition or speciality, their weakness, the freedom with which they pass from the homage to one to the homage to another, which means that they disobey with impunity everywhere; the absence of laws, and finally their impunity for crimes approaches the state of society that we commonly call anarchy.
>
> (LEVCHINE 1840, 391)

But a closer reading of Levchine shows that this was not the egalitarian ordered anarchy of Evans-Pritchard's segmentary kinship society. This was an early nineteenth-century concept of anarchy much closer to Hobbes' notion of the state of war, a lawless and savage insecurity from which the ordinary Kazakhs might heartily hope to be saved by orderly

Russian colonial administration.[14] However, as Levchine (1840, 391–392) explains, the voluntary submission of the Kazakh nobility was not motivated by a genuine desire for "order and tranquility" but by the "ambition of their *chefs*"[15] to augment their powers by gaining powerful Russian protection and rich gifts from the tsar. Indeed, Levchine's attitude to the Kazakhs displays the loathing of a frustrated colonial administrator. He describes them as "savages" (Levchine 1840, 305) and in emphasizing their faults offers a justification for extending colonial control: "the ignorance, vulgarity, greed, rapacious and vindictive natures of the Kirghiz, all these things are the source of anarchy, the plundering and the murders perpetrated among them; but these crimes and vices only exist, multiply and cause misfortune because there is no force great enough to contain them, no authority that works invariably for the public good" (Levchine 1840, 404–405). His frustration reflects the failure of Russian colonial policies to transform a subject society.

> It has been more than 90 years since the Kazakh are thought to have come under the control of Russia, and for 90 years the Russian government has tried in vain to establish a certain organisation. The costs, pains, exhortations, the advice employed to establish exchange markets, schools and mosques; the houses built for sultans to accustom them to sedentary life; the establishment of the council of khans, the tribe jurisdictions and the frontier tribunals, the salaries allowed to the khans and the *chefs* of tribes, the mullahs and secretaries that Russia entertains to its cost, the authorizations to spend winter beyond the frontier of the empire, to this day everything has been useless. All these measures have not advanced the Kirghiz one step towards civilisation.
>
> (LEVCHINE 1840, 403)

That the Kazakh are in need of civilization is beyond doubt to Levchine, who is eager to compare the Kazakhs with the barbaric peoples of Europe's past (Levchine 1840, 402). He suggests that in their election of khans and the composition of their nation they faithfully resemble the German tribes described by Tacitus, and he also compares them to the tenth- and eleventh-century Russians.

However, it becomes clear that the instability of Kazakh society in Levchine's time was the result of the disruption of the earlier, more centralized political system of the khanate. According to Levchine, the Kazakh looked back on the "golden age" of Täuke (Tiavka) Khan, who ruled from 1680 to 1718. Although a code of law is now known to have been introduced by Qasim Khan in the early sixteenth century, Levchine credits Täuke Khan with the introduction of a law code that he described as "customary" (Levchine 1840, 398). Täuke Khan had been militarily defeated by the Zünghar in 1698, and his successor Pulad Khan (1718–1730) was defeated by them again in 1723, causing a severe disruption of the khanate (Soucek 2000, 172). It was in this context that nobles like Abulkhayr and Abilay Khan began to accept Russian (and sometimes Manchu) suzerainty or swear fealty to the Kokand khanate in the south.

The lack of law and order that Levchine laments was the result of the collapse of central authority, a situation frozen by Russian imperial expansion. The Russians encouraged the submission of rulers such as Abilai Khan with rich gifts and subsidies and backed one noble against another in a series of petty internecine wars. In the late eighteenth century, they also allowed raids by Ural Cossacks into Kazakh territories, which undermined the authority of the Horde khans such as Nurali Khan of the Lesser Horde. In 1801, the Russians created a new protectorate, the Inner Horde, soon to be known as Bukey's Horde after its sultan (r. 1801–1823). This was located in the region between the Volga and the Ural, and Sultan Bukey brought more than five thousand subject households into this territory. By 1845, the population of the Inner Horde had increased to thirty thousand households, who paid a regular yurt tax (Geiss 2003, 176–177).

The colonial administration set about undermining and, where possible, destroying the power of the Kazakh khans and the realms they ruled. In the case of the Middle Horde, when its ruler Vali Khan died in 1818 the tsarist authorities did not recognize the new khan. At the beginning of the 1820s, the tsarist authorities introduced new administrative structures. In 1822, Speransky's "Rules for the Siberian Kyrgyz" were applied to the Middle Horde administered from Omsk, and in 1824 the "Rules for the Orenburg Kyrgyz" was applied to the remains of the Small Horde. Both statutes abolished the status of khan and horde as political unities. The 1822 statutes divided the Horde territory into four *okrug* "county" districts and eighty-seven *volosti* subdistricts, governed by hereditary sultans who had to be confirmed in office by the Russian governor-general of Omsk.[16]

Many Kazakh nobles resisted. The grandson of Abilai Khan of the Middle Horde, Sarzhan Qasim-uli, organized military resistance against the Russians. After his defeat and escape to the Khokand khanate, his half-brother Kenisari Qasim-uli took up the fight and was elected khan by the nobles of the Middle Horde in 1841. He controlled much of the region until the Russians defeated his army in 1844. There were numerous revolts from the 1820s to the 1850s, and sultans such as Qayip Ali caused turmoil by repeatedly violating Russian colonial regulations. Small wonder, then, that Levchine, writing in the turbulent early nineteenth century, described the society as anarchic. Russian colonial policy was a variety of "divide and rule" (Bodger 1998, 3). Having decapitated the old Kazakh political system and broken up the hordes, the Russians ruled through a large number of petty sultans, but by all accounts the authority of this nobility "rapidly declined" during this period of Russian colonial rule (Geiss 2003, 180). The result was the partial breakdown of older political relations in a society subject to simultaneous integration into a colonial state and a cash economy. The local nobility had become partially dependent on the financial and military backing of the colonial administration and were finding it increasingly difficult to retain control over their subordinates when they had but a fraction of the money and military force available to the tsarist state.

Levchine (1840, 396) notes:

> The archives of the college of foreign affairs in St. Petersburg, as well as the archives of the frontier commissions of Orenbourg and Omsk, are full of the complaints of the Kirghiz khans and sultans on the insubordination of their subjects, and the weakness of their power, with convincing proof of the impossibility of their handing over the criminals who have violated the Russian border.

This is revealing with regard to tsarist interests and the representations of local nobles seeking to gain as much as possible from a colonial power while avoiding the wrath of tsarist officials. But it tells us much less about any supposed egalitarianism among the Kazakh. The senior nobility clearly faced difficulties in controlling at least some of their subjects, but the mention of "insubordination" reminds us that all hierarchies operate by continually remaking power relations. And it is worth noting that it could be convenient for sultans to claim that their subjects had broken Russian law without authorization, as they did after the failed 1773–1775 Pugachev uprising against tsarist rule (Bodger 1998, 10).

In the wake of the Russian dismemberment and partial integration of the Kazakh khanate, the problem for tsarist officials such as Levchine was not that the Kazakh aristocracy had no power, but that it was not *enough* power for the sort of orderly colonial administration they required.

Levchine clearly understands, as well as resents, the complaints of the sultans and khans who did not have the professional soldiery or bureaucracy that the tsarist state took for granted.

> What kind of order can we expect from the *chef* himself, when he commands a troop of men who only obey him because they are forced to, or because the interest of the moment attaches them to his cause . . . ? What could the most strict, the most fair, the most prudent, the most wise *chef* do if he has no troops or revenues to maintain a police force in good order, to watch subordinates and enforce regulations, or at least protect himself against violence resulting from his correct justice?
>
> (LEVCHINE 1840, 393)

Levchine is most concerned with the lack of power that the central authorities had over their subordinates and the petty nobility. Understandably enough, as a senior tsarist official, he is highly critical of the "unreliability" of Kazakh leadership and their impunity to colonial law. But his estimation of the power of the aristocracy is a relative one: he is struck by the notion that it is much less than in the neighboring "oriental" states that he describes as despotic (Levchine 1840, 390).[17] However, it is clear that although some may have had limited control, other local nobles did have real power over their subjects. Levchine (1840, 397) writes, "amid this anarchy we find *chefs* who hold the right of life and death over their subjects." Indeed, Schuyler (1885, 39), when describing the common Kazakhs with whom he traveled in 1873, notes, "one of their best traits is their respect for age and the authority of their superiors." Elsewhere, he writes "The Kirghiz [Kazakh] had great respect for their aristocracy, and the common people or 'black bone', were led by the 'white bone' (the Kirghiz for *blue blood*), or the descendants of the old khans and ruling families" (Schuyler 1885, 32). It is worth noting that the "black bone" (*qara süyek*) were not a uniform strata of commoners but were themselves divided into the "black bone" aristocracy and their subjects (Akiner 1995, 16). But it is clear that the "white bone" held the senior hereditary offices, in particular the positions of sultan and khan.[18]

Everywhere in Levchine's account we see the evidence of an older, pretsarist, aristocratic political order that was more, not less, ordered than the society he describes. And institutions that appear at first glance to be instances of tribal custom become on closer inspection to have been elements of the precolonial code of laws attributed to Täuke Khan. For example, Levchine mentions the system of vengeance by which raids and counterraids take place, and this might seem to resemble the tribal model of segmentary opposition described by Evans-Pritchard (1940) in *The Nuer*. But the system that Levchine describes shows this to be a highly circumscribed right, strictly regulated and subject to local authorities.

> If the condemned does not obey justice, or if the *chef* of his *aoul* [residential unit] intentionally avoids looking into the case, and in this way favours the criminal, then the claimant is allowed, in this case, by his *chef*, to carry out a reprisal (baranta); but on his return he is obliged to make a declaration, and the *chef* must ensure that the value of what the claimant was asking for and took himself by baranta was not greater than the contested object.
>
> (LEVCHINE 1840, 400)

Levchine's account has been read for evidence of a lack of "true" feudalism, usually conceived of in rather narrow Marxist terms, in which the appropriation of surplus value through land rent was regarded as a defining feature of feudal relations. Some of Levchine's remarks were taken as evidence of the lack of regular tributary relations between vassals and lords:

> Although the *chefs* of the Kirghiz have the right to require from their subjects a kind of tribute in livestock or other objects this tribute is paid without any fixed rule, and almost always is only done in the case that the need for protection is felt. As for the fixed tax, the Kirghiz just do not pay; it is in vain that the most wise *chefs* of the tribes try to preach to their people the Koranic chapter on the *zekate* [Islamic concept of tithing and alms], confirmed by the most ancient law of the Kirghiz; but only the absolute necessity of force will remind them of this obligation.
>
> (LEVCHINE 1840, 393–394)

Taxation, like full control of their subjects, had clearly become difficult for the Kazakh nobility faced with incorporation into the tsarist state. On the other hand, we might treat these claims with a certain amount of caution, since in Levchine's time the Kazakh nobility had come to rely on salaries paid by the colonial state, and it becomes understandable that both they and officials such as Levchine might feel the need for greater allowances from the tsarist administration and underrepresent their ability to raise independent revenues by taxing their own subjects.

But in any case, Levchine makes clear that regular taxation had existed in the precolonial period "by the most ancient law of the Kirghiz." Later in the text, he describes the annual tax on all those of military age in the laws attributed to Täuke Khan. "All men able to bear arms must pay each year to the Khan and *chefs* of the nation a tribute of one twentieth of their goods" (Levchine 1840, 401).[19] So contradictory was this to the tribal model that the passage was somehow twisted to mean the exact opposite. Olcott (1995, 14) states that evidence that the Kazakh khans did not have feudal powers and regular taxes can be found in Täuke Khan's law code, which "records the levying of an extraordinary tax of one-twentieth of an individual's wealth to pay for the provisioning of men to bear arms."[20]

Rather than the "self-forming" tribal model by which kinship society constitutes itself by clans coming together to form larger political aggregates, Levchine's account of the foundation and composition of the Kazakh polity makes it entirely clear that the "tribes" were actually administrative divisions or appanages created by a top-down process of political demarcation:

> Whatever the differences in the origins attributed to them, the tribes that compose the Kirghiz nation were all merged into one people who live in the same country and used to be ruled by a single *chef*. . . . Tradition confirms this, they add that on the death of one of their khans who ruled the entire nation, his three sons divided it between themselves and that these adopted, according to the respective order of the birth of their *chefs*, the names of the Great, Medium and Small Hordes; the difference in population between the parties resulted in some war and varied success, with further growth the parties again subdivided into many races which took the name of their *chefs*, or kept names of their ancient forebears such as the Naimanes, the Kiptchaks etc. The races subdivided in their turn into tribes, these into sections and branches into parties.

(LEVCHINE 1840, 301)

Levchine notes that it is next to impossible to note all the subdivisions, but he gives an example of the many subdivisions of one of the units within the Lesser Horde. These are so numerous that at first glance it might seem that this was a top-to-bottom description of society and that the smallest groups must be on the order of a few households—the sort of size one might expect of the minimal lineage in classical structural-functionalist descent theory. However, this would be to completely misunderstand the scale of the Kazakh polity. Levchine estimates the Lesser Horde contained a population of a million, and the Kazakh nation as a whole between two and 2.4 million—about the same as the entire population of sixteenth-century Tudor England (Rigby 1995, 81). It becomes more understandable then that he should find it next to impossible to list all the petty noble families of such a large society. The smallest subdivisions of the Lesser Horde that he names would seem to have contained, on average, something like fifteen hundred to three thousand people, a very respectable size for a European manorial estate (Levchine 1840, 304, 300).[21]

What is described here is quite the reverse of the Morganian vision of an organic process by which small descent units came together to form progressively larger tribal units and ultimately a confederation. Levchine describes an original political allocation of that khanate's subjects to noble houses, followed by a progressive fragmentation of the appanages of the ruling nobility. But so firmly entrenched are notions of tribal political units being formed by grassroots processes that Geiss (2003, 114) has to explain away the historical account that the Kazakh themselves gave of the origin of the hordes. "The animistic Weltanschauung of the tribesmen tended to perceive the origin of the hordes as being founded by three sons. . . . Nevertheless, the division of the hordes emerged from the tribesmen's political orientation to secure their winter and summer pastures."

As Martin (2001, 174) notes, "anthropologists have sought to identify the kinship structure of the Kazakh nomads as a 'conical clan,' described by Thomas Barfield as a 'model of nested kinship groups.' "[22] But the evidence simply does not support this characterization, and certainly Levchine's account offers no support for the notion of the classical model of lineage structure. As Khazanov (1983, 132) pointed out, his account of residence does not suggest it matched unilineal descent groups.[23] Levchine describes the larger divisions and subdivisions of the Kazakh polity, but these are not linked to a kinship genealogy, and their formation and combination seem to be political acts.[24] Indeed, he complains in a footnote (Levchine 1840, 301–302) that Kazakhs could not agree on their genealogical branches and sections, and some were completely ignorant of them.

Khazanov makes the point that only the aristocracy kept genealogies, noting "Grodekov (1889, 12) wrote of the Kazakhs and Kyrgyz that, in contrast to aristocracy, ' . . . the poor do not know, apart from the names of their direct ancestors and their clan [rod] and tribe [koleno], anything about the distant branches of kinship.' Levchine (1832, III: 11) also made this point some fifty years earlier" (Khazanov 1983, 143). As usual, these discrepancies are explained away with the notion that the "tribal structure" was in decline at the time it was observed.[25] Geiss (2003, 40) writes, "most of the reports were done during tsarist rule, when Russia has already introduced its administrative order. . . . Consequently, tribal affiliations and genealogies lost their political significance." It is worth adding that by the late nineteenth century, when Grodekov was writing, the *rod* was used as a census unit within the administrative district (*volost*), since the population had been divided into units with a recognized leader who had jurisdiction over each *rod* (Grodekov 1889, 13). Knowing one's "clan" and "tribe" meant knowing the administrative units one belonged to, and it was understood that these were not exogamous or consanguineous units of kinship.[26]

At first glance, it seems incomprehensible that Soviet scholarship should continue to describe the prerevolutionary Kazakh subdivisions as clans (*rod*), since they were not consanguineous kinship groups. But, like the English terms "chief" and "tribe," this terminology had its roots in the history of colonialism. The Russian empire incorporated its Asian colonial territories by integrating and reworking the indigenous political relations. The legal basis of this rule was codified by Count Michail Speransky, the famous statesman. Speransky was a reformer who had attempted to limit the power of tsarist autocracy and introduce a constitutional system for Russia based on district assemblies and a series of elected chambers (*dumas*). His attempts met with very limited success in Russia, but when he became governor-general of Siberia in 1816, he was able to start work devising a reformed administration of native peoples there. His new regulations became law in 1822. Speransky was very much concerned with promoting the European "civilizing mission" while at the same time preserving "native customs" (Whisenhunt 2001, 25; Martin 2001, 34–45).

Speransky's "Rules for the Siberian Kyrgyz" organized the steppe into *okrugs* (counties), *volosti* (districts), and *auls* (villages). The *aul* of fifty to seventy households was headed by an *aksakal* theoretically elected for three years. The *volost* consisted of ten to twelve villages and was ruled by a *bii* as well as a hereditary sultan. Twenty to forty *volosti* were included in an *okrug*, ruled by a senior sultan elected by the *volosti* sultans and confirmed by the Russian governor. The *biis* were judges at "native/people's courts" (*narodnyi sud*) used for minor matters within the *volost*. The *aul* leaders also had policing functions.[27] The empire had previously governed its colonial subjects in Siberia using units called *uprava* (administrative clans). In fact, these did not imply any particular kinship relations between members (Dobrova-Iadrintseva 1925, 30). However, Speransky's 1822 statutes enshrined the position of the indigenous elite using the paternalistic language of kinship. The statute declares that a native prince (*kniaz*) is "the governor of a clan" and "is accepted as an elder *as if* this clan is a single family" (Ssorin-Chaikov 2003, 54, emphasis added). This terminology by which the language of kinship was used to express political relations helped fuel the Morganian vision of naturally democratic kinship society. Geiss (2003), for example, paints a picture of pre-tsarist nomadic society composed of descent groups led by leaders chosen for their personal abilities. He writes: "Thus Kazakhs formed changing alliances headed by leaders who were influential and enjoyed authority due to their wealth and generosity, their age and experience, their sense of justice and their prominence in a numerous family which supported them" (Geiss 2003, 117).

But this impression of nonaristocratic leadership was, in part, created by a Russian administration. Local elections were not some ancient expression of democratic kinship society; they were a colonial introduction that sat uneasily with the powers of the aristocracy. Following Speransky's system, administration was carried out through elected native officials who received a salary and local nobles, *biis*, now recast as judges, who had no salaries but received "gifts" from subjects.[28] But these new electoral procedures were alien to the region and something of a fiction in practice. Akiner (1995, 16) notes, "the 'black bone' aristocracy was in theory an elected ruling elite, but in practice was often hereditary." Carrère d'Encausse (1967, 154) notes, "villages were supposed to elect a salaried elder (*aqsaqal*) for three years; in practice, though, he would almost always, as in the past, be appointed as a result of his belonging to the ruling group."[29]

Administrative reforms were introduced in 1865 through 1868, with the explicit aim "to distance the local aristocracy from power" (Akiner 1995, 24). Schuyler, writing in the 1880s, notes:

> Some years ago an effort was made to abolish, as far as possible, the tribal distinctions of the Kirghiz [i.e., Kazakh] aristocracy, and for the purpose of a better government the so-called reform was introduced into the Orenburg steppe in the year 1869. By this . . . each district was placed under the command of a Russian military governor, district prefects, and the *volost* or *aul* elders. The district prefects were of course appointed by the Government, while the rulers of the *volosts* and *auls* were elected by the inhabitants. It was perhaps carrying the system of elective government too far to introduce it into the steppe among people who were accustomed to nothing

else than hereditary and arbitrary rule, for the khans, when they were still elective, were chosen by the aristocracy only, and the result was very great discontent, which broke out into open insurrection.

(SCHUYLER 1885, 33)

It is clear that far from the Kazakhs having a precolonial *tradition* of choosing their leaders as representatives of the local communities, these were forms that the tsarist administration struggled to introduce so as to undermine the aristocracy.[30]

ARISTOCRATIC ORDER AND THE KYRGYZ

Although they were commonly termed simply "Kirghiz" (Kyrgyz) in historical documents, the peoples who had once been subjects of the Kazakh khanate were eventually designated "Kazakhs" during the Soviet period.[31] There were also, however, Kyrgyz vassals of the khanate of Khoqand, which had its capital in the Fergana Valley. These did not come under full tsarist colonial rule until the late nineteenth century, after Russian annexation of the Khoqand khanate in 1876. They continued to be called Kyrgyz in the Soviet period, and the territory they occupied is now largely included in the present-day Kyrgyz Republic.

The Kyrgyz hereditary nobility held the titles of *bai* (or *bii* or *biy*, variant of the Turkic *bey*, meaning "lord") and *manap* (prince), who ruled political divisions referred to by the terms *uruu* and *uruk*. Soviet ethnography, however, pictured Kyrgyz society in familiar tribal terms: *uruu* and *uruk* were translated into Russian as *plemya* (tribe) and *rod* (clan), although not in a consistent way. Abramzon (1971, 180), for example, writes "Kyrgyz tribal organisation was preserved through a clearly expressed division into tribes and clans." In this he follows Tolstov, who describes prerevolutionary Kyrgyz society in similar terms. However, Tolstov et al. (1963, 171n1) was rather more aware of the misunderstandings that this use of these terms might generate:

For a long time already, tribe and clan divisions had not corresponded to tribal organisation, peculiar to primitive communism. They were not consanguineous unions, which Engels wrote about. Headed by *manaps* and *bais*, greater or smaller size groupings kept the old form of tribes and clans, which were united with each other by real or legendary genealogical relationships as parts strictly regulated by tribal structure.

But on closer examination, the genealogies that Tolstov refers to seem to be those of the Sarybagysh, Bugu, and other ruling houses.[32]

The Kyrgyz hereditary aristocracy predated Russian colonial administration. We know that in the seventeenth century, "each tribe and even the large subdivisions of the tribe had hereditary leaders, *biis*. According to Chinese sources 'Each bii rules his own land and has his own followers. In might and power they are equal to one another and in no way does one submit to another. When a bii dies his son and brother are set up as bii, others cannot occupy this place.'" (Khazanov 1983, 175).

But this evidence of an ancient Kyrgyz aristocracy does not sit well with the kinship society model, and it has been downplayed or even rejected. Geiss, for example, does his best to explain away the importance of nobility among the Kyrgyz.[33] For him, like Morgan, tribal society could not tolerate real hereditary aristocracy, so he implies that the *biis* were elected by their "tribesmen" and argues that, despite appearances, the senior title of *manap* (roughly equivalent to prince) was a recent development and could not have really been any more powerful than the *biis*.[34] He concludes that "there did not exist ruling endogamous hereditary lineages similar to those of the Kazakh khans and sultans." (Geiss 2003, 112).

Advocates of this tribal model picked up on an account by a tsarist commentator in the late nineteenth century, who represented *manaps* and *biis* as representatives of their tribal peoples. General Grodekov, the Russian governor of the nearby Syr Dariya region, quotes his friend Mulla Asan, who states that *manaps* owed their position to their bravery and leadership, and although they were not elected, they would be if there were elections (Grodekov 1889, 6). But Mulla Asan was himself a *manap* and thus might be expected to represent the Kyrgyz aristocracy as holding their positions on the basis of popular support and ancient law; since the Speransky reforms, popular election was the measure of legitimacy for more junior native leaders. Such late tsarist-period comments, however, are quite different from the earlier accounts that describe Kyrgyz and Kazakh society in the mid-nineteenth century. Chokan Valikhanov (1835–1865), himself of Kazakh origin, provided a wealth of ethnographic description in his short life. The son of an aristocrat who was sent away to receive a Russian education, Valikhanov shared the common nineteenth-century European preoccupation with a lost form of kinship society of the distant past. But he describes Kyrgyz society as so clearly stratified that he describes it in terms of caste. "As on estates, the people are divided into two castes: possessors (manaps) and simple people (kara-bukhary). Manaps, as direct descendants of the most ancient ancestor of a horde, originally had patriarchal rights as father of the family, but gradually over the course of time this power increased and turned into, in the end, despotic relations of the possessor and slaves" (Valikhanov 1985, 38).

Friedrich Radloff (1863, 322) describes the position of the Kyrgyz aristocracy in administrative rather than kinship terms:

> Each of these biis have direction of a certain number of families over which they exercise administrative and judiciary functions. They can meet in assembly, but only to treat the business which concerns the subjects of the different biis, or that of general interest. These assemblies are presided over by the Aga manap (the chief manap), who, according to national law, has no authority himself and can do nothing without the assistance of the biis and manaps. The nomination of all these is sanctioned by the Russian government, which gives them, after several years of service, either medals or officer's rank in the cavalry. The Aga manap is ordinarily a major.

Like Valikhanov, Radloff is quite clear on the powers of the aristocrats over their subjects. He notes that "manaps . . . have almost despotic power over their people." This account suggests aristocratic assemblies with a relatively weak institution of overlordship, very reminiscent of the Mongolian *chigulgan* councils of nobles that were also endorsed by the imperial power that controlled the region—in this case, the Qing. In the Kyrgyz case, there were a series of ranked noble titles, from the *aga manap* (great *manap*) down to the *cholok manap* (minor *manap*), and *biis* and common subjects were also stratified (Gullette 2006, 55; Israilova-Khar'ekhuzen 1999, 94–95).

The parallels between this political order and European feudalism were too clear to be ignored; early Soviet archive documents describe prerevolutionary society as feudal or feudal-patrimonial (Kuranov 1937) and historians such as Vinnikov (1956) also described Kyrgyz society as feudal. Yet late twentieth-century scholarship was keen to see the Kyrgyz as a kin-organized society. Aristocratic rule was recast as an evolutionary stage somewhere between clan and feudal society. Abramzon (1971, 157) writes:

"Using the great endurance of patriarchal-clan traditions, *manaps* and *biis* not only widely used them for masking feudal relations . . . but also actively promoted the preservation of these traditions." This fitted the notion of a "traditional" society still preserving ancient forms of kin society despite the hierarchical structure into which it had been forced. But there was no disguising the statelike administrative prerogatives of the Kyrgyz nobility. Commoners were subject to a series of taxes and levies, including a tax for the use of pasture (*otmai*), a levy for the *manap*'s table (*soyush*), a charge for driving a herd through the land of the *manap* (*tuyakat*), and a levy covering the expenses of a *manap* for hosting guests (*chygym*) (Gullette 2006, 56).

NOBLE VALUES—ARISTOCRACY AND BLOOD PRICE

One of the most visible expressions of aristocratic privilege in both the Kazakh and the Kyrgyz political orders was the institution of *qun*—the unit of blood price payable as compensation for the killing of a person. Nobles were quite literally worth more than commoners, and the compensation payment was set higher. Up to seven *qun* were payable for the killing of a sultan or *khoja* (a member of senior Islamic religious lineages); slaves were valued at half a *qun* (Riasanovsky 1965 [1937], 193, 201; Geiss 2003, 36). This system of liabilities was not a remnant of a preexisting lineage society regulated by segmentary opposition, as Geiss (2003, 49–51) implies, but were parts of a legal code, probably derived from similar Mongol codes (see chapter 6). Riasanovsky (1965, 311–312) notes the similarities between the law attributed to Täuka Khan and the Mongol-Oirat code of 1640 (discussed further in chapter 7) and their probable common origin. The units of blood price in the Kazakh law have a distinctly aristocratic tone. The unit (*qun*) was a hundred horses, two servants, two camels, and two suits of armor.

Nobles had a very different political importance from subjects, and their blood price might be a matter of some discussion. Petr Semenov, a Russian who traveled to both Kazakh and Kyrgyz regions in 1856 and 1857, described the way in which the amount of compensation was calculated in the case of raids or war.

According to Kirghiz customary law, the basis of such a score is, first of all, the calculation of the losses of each side in sheep, cattle, horses, camels and, finally, in people, both "commoners" and of "blue blood." All these losses were converted into a number of sheep, which served as monetary units when doing calculations at that time. In doing such calculations, the ascriptions of this or that value to an ox, cow, horse, camel or even a "common person" in relation to a sheep, did not present any difficulty, as it was determined by custom; and only the loss of a person of "blue blood", or someone acknowledged by public opinion as a "batyr", was subject on each occasion to special evaluation by mutual consent . . . the redemption of "common people" was accomplished according to a fixed indisputable statutory price.

SEMENOV (1998, 195)

Semenov provides an insight, albeit from the perspective of a tsarist official, into the unmistakably aristocratic order of steppe societies on the edge of Russian colonial expansion. He describes the "aristocratic Kirghiz type," the "refined manners of a man of blue blood" (Semenov 1998, 137), and "the dignity of a girl of blue blood" (Semenov 1998, 133). He became particularly friendly with one nobleman, Sultan Burambai of the Bogintsy. The sultan ruled his own subjects and had noble vassals who owed him fealty. Semenov describes one *bii* as "bearing the same relationship to Burambai as the appanage princes did to the grand princes in ancient Russia" (Semenov 1998, 145). At the time of Semenov's visit, Burambai was engaged with defending his territories against rival lords, and Semenov (1998, 144) describes the way in which he located the households of his subjects in a strategic manner, leaving some in tactically important locations to better defend his borders.[35] Some of Semenov's turns of phrase could mislead the casual reader. At one point, he writes of "the old patriarch of the Bogintsy tribe" (Semenov 1998, 144), which evokes the vision of kinship society. However, it turns out this "old patriarch" is none other than the decidedly aristocratic Sultan Burambai, and his "tribe" is described unambiguously as "Burambai's subjects" (Semenov 1998, 145).

IDEOLOGIES OF TRIBE AND ARISTOCRACY

Faced with the evidence that nothing much like a "tribal structure" could be found in terms of actual social organization, Tapper (1990, 56) argued that the tribe was primarily an ideological construct—the dominance of the idea that social groups ought to be politically organized by the principles of genealogical relatedness. This is taken up by others, including Geiss

(2003). Since it is clear that residence groups did not coincide with descent groups, he supposes that the Kazakhs, Kyrgyz, and other tribal societies must at least have had an ideology that they were. "The tribal paradox consisted in the materiality that tribes were residence groups based on consent and friendship . . . and that they *were not* descent groups. They were *perceived* as descent groups, however, since they dominated the latter" (Geiss 2003, 65–66, original emphasis). This view is based on the ethnography of Irons (1975), which is examined in chapter 5, but for reasons discussed in that chapter the idea that residence and descent groups coincide even ideologically is unconvincing (see, for example, Khazanov 1983, 135).

The notion that Kyrgyz society was defined and ordered by genealogy has become embedded in contemporary ideologies of the Kyrgyz state (Gullette 2006). But the elaborate historical genealogies that have survived seem to only concern the ruling houses and tell us almost nothing about the wider organization of society. The Sarybagysh, for example, was one of the pre-Soviet political divisions of the Kyrgyz. The published Sarybagysh genealogy traces descent from a man named Tagai, whose great grandson was Manap—a lord who established not only control over a large part of the Kyrgyz polity but also, like Caesar, gave his personal name to the office of ruler. Manap's great-great-grandson was Tynai, and his great-great-grandson was Shabdan (1840–1912), a famous *manap* that ruled a large part of the Belo Piket area. It was Shabdan who recorded the genealogy, and in his time—the mid-nineteenth century—the Sarybagysh seem to have numbered some fifty thousand people (Valikhanov 1985, 42). But the genealogy contains only about thirty names of people of Shabdan's generation, and given the huge difference in scale between the "descent group" and the Sarybagysh social unit, it cannot be taken as evidence of wider genealogical organization. Furthermore, the genealogy is not segmentary in structure—and still less "conical"—since figures that we know held high office do not appear as eldest sons or part of a "senior" branch (Attokurov 1995, 119–23).

Tapper and Geiss suggest that tribalism is a type of ideology, but what were indigenous notions of political and social order like before Russian administration? One rather untapped source is *Manas*, the great Kyrgyz oral epic, thought to date back to the fifteenth century or earlier. It has been compared with the *Iliad* in terms of its richness and depth, and it might be expected to offer some insights into pre-tsarist Kyrgyz culture. The *Manas* epic describes a thoroughly aristocratic society. The protagonists are almost all khans, princes, princesses, noblemen, and ladies. These nobles do not lead named clans, lineages, or descent groups, but rather groups of numbered retainers and "companions" (*choro*) who do not seem to be their kin. Groups of people are not described in terms of clans—bodies of warriors are talked of in thousands, for example. No clan identity is given for the superhero Manas, but he comes from a line of kings—the epic begins by noting that his father was Jakip-khan, the son of "born-brave Kara-khan, son of high-born Böyön-khan" (Hatto 1990, 7), and his son Semetey "became a khan ruling his people." (Hatto 1990, 347).

There is no recounting of the "seven forefathers" (the notional depth of the exogamous descent group according to Geiss 2003, 28) in the epic. The longest genealogy mentioned seems to be that of Manas himself, and this stretches back just three generations, to Manas's great-grandfather, Böyön-khan. Descent groups are noticeable by their absence, and characters are not introduced as members of such and such a clan, but generally as the son or daughter of someone, often a khan. Political and social groups are not spoken of in the idiom of kinship, genealogical distance, or descent groups, but in terms of kingly and lordly power. When the ailing Kökötöy Khan sends word to all the neighboring peoples to invite them to a feast, for instance, the neighboring peoples are usually described as "the people of" such and such a khan or noble (Hatto 1990, 165–167). There is no mention of named descent groups, the supposed "building blocks" of segmentary tribal society, only princely rulers and their subjects—who are described as commoners.[36]

Kyrgyz hierarchy is not an entirely historical phenomenon. Nazif Shahrani's 1979 work *The Kirghiz and Wakhi of Afghanistan* presents a detailed study of a group of Kyrgyz families who had moved into the Wakhan corridor of northern Afghanistan as a result of the closure of the Chinese and Soviet borders. Shahrani shows that wealthy herders dominated production, and they did so largely through the control of livestock rather than land, as some might have expired. The rich had a form of competitive advantage over poor households since they could distribute their herds, parceling them out to households in different areas and consequently having greater security against livestock loss due to poor conditions in any given locality. This was part of a process that supported the preeminence of a single powerful figure, Haji Rahman Qul, termed "the khan," who came to dominate the 135 Kyrgyz families. The result was an "increasingly more centralized, mildly authoritarian and 'feudal' structure in which the khan figures prominently" (Shahrani 1979, 184). Interestingly, Haji Rahman

Qul's commanding position did not depend on appointment by a central state, and his concentration of (livestock) wealth really only emerged after the movement of the Kyrgyz group to the Wakhan corridor. It is a striking example of the way in which mobile pastoralism can be the basis for concentrations of wealth and power without the apparatus of the centralized state.

4

The State Construction of the Clan

The Unilineal Descent Group and the Ordering of State Subjects

In 2004, thousands of Mongolian citizens rushed to choose a new sort of name for themselves, a surname, or *obog ovog ner*. The hurry was caused by government deadlines: new state regulations stipulated that all citizens must have a registered surname so that they could be issued with new identity cards. The conventional Mongolian method was to use the patronymic or matronymic in an analogous way to a surname, so that a full name such as Tsevegiin Naranbat would be made up of the personal name Naranbat plus the parental identifier "of Tseveg," rather like the Icelandic system. But the identity-card legislation required a new sort of *obog ner*, a family name that was handed down from one generation to the next unchanged, as American or Chinese surnames are.

The representation of this episode in the Western media is revealing. Since *obog* can also be translated as "clan" and "family," the episode was represented in terms of revived tradition. Mark Magnier of the *Los Angeles Times*, for example, wrote the story up in the following way:

> Mongolia once had family names. Local historians claim that the country was among the first to adopt them, and cite clan-name entries in "The Secret History of the Mongols," a 13th-century text.

This tradition was ended, however, when Mongolian Communists swept to power in the early 1920s. Clan names initially were banned in order to improve tax collection. So many people at the time shared the same last name, said Lonjid, a Mongolian State University historian, that using your first name—and occasionally your father's for clarity—was seen as a way to make names more distinct.

Once in place, however, the surname ban stuck, in part because it suited Mongolia's often-brutal communist regime, historians say. By wiping out old clan names and destroying historic baggage, the revolutionaries hoped to stifle resistance by the former aristocracy, so-called "golden relative" clans that traced their lineage to Genghis.

Mongolia first passed a law requiring surnames in 1997, but it was largely ignored until this year when the names became necessary for a new government identity card. Now, more than 90 percent of Mongolia's 2.5 million people have adopted them, experts say. Holdouts tend to be herders and nomads in the country's more remote areas.

"This isn't a fad—it's Mongolians finding their roots," said Leyton Croft, director of the Asia Foundation's Mongolia office. "There's a feeling that this is their historical right, and they're now going to exercise it."[1]

This treatment is highly misleading. Historically, Mongol personal names have never included clan or family names. The *Secret History* lists many *obog*s, but their names were not generally combined with personal names to form identifiers. Similarly, Qing- and Bogd Khaan–era documents used only personal names and titles. In this sense, the notion of Mongolian clan surnames is an entirely contemporary innovation, but it is not the first time that the state felt the need to introduce a surname of some sort. The new government of the Mongolian People's Republic found it necessary to have something more than just personal names for registering the population. In 1925, the problem was discussed at the Twenty-fifth Government Assembly, and the Interior Ministry issued the following decree:

> All Mongolian people should be registered irrespective of men or women, young or old. Those who know their *obog*s should retain them, and if they don't know their *obog*, they should adopt the names of their fathers or mothers, grandfathers, great grandfathers, or any people of generations above that. Or they can adopt whatever surnames which suit them. Their names should not exceed two words.

(BULAG 1998, 121)

It was because, as Bulag notes, most people did not have an *obog* identity that the patronymic/matronymic form became the rule.

The exception, of course, were the members of the Borjigin nobility, who kept detailed genealogical records, often stretching back several hun-

dred years and including thousands of male names. As the revolutionary government targeted the aristocracy, Borjigin descent became a liability, and members of once noble families had to take patronymic or matronymic "surnames" rather than retain the once glorious Borjigin name. It was this process that was misrecognized as a communist "ban on surnames" in the journalistic accounts.[2] Something similar seems to have happened in other parts of Soviet Central Asia. Adrienne Edgar (2001, 288) argues that "kinship was class—the closest thing to class Turkmen society had to offer—and eliminating the one while promoting the other was next to impossible."

The legislation introduced by the Mongolian state in the 1990s actually reflected the emergence of a public discourse of genetics and the dangers of inbreeding. In the first few years of the decade, public attention began to focus on the danger that the number of Mongolian children with hereditary diseases apparently was growing, and the dominant explanation was that this was the result of accidental inbreeding (Bulag 1998, 107–121). The government launched a campaign to use clan names and compile family trees to prevent the weakening of genetic stock by accidental inbreeding. Guidebooks were published to help people choose an appropriate *obog* name, since most families had never had one. In the post-Soviet context, the notion of aristocratic descent had become attractive once more, and over 50 percent of those who registered chose Borjigin as their *obog* (Sanders 2003, 242). Only a minority of these can have actually traced descent from Borjigin ancestors, since just 5.7 percent of those included in the 1918 census were nobles (Otgonjargal 2003, 15). However, most people continue to use the patronymic/matronymic as a surname in everyday life, and the new clan names are rarely used. Rather than a process of rediscovery in which Mongolians "found their roots," the production of contemporary clan identity has been a creative and thoroughly administrative development, driven by a state concern with the condition of the national gene pool. But this is not the first time that forms of kinship have been produced by the state in Mongolia. An analogous process took place during the Qing period, as we shall see.

An official guidebook has been published to help people choose suitable *obog ner* names, and it lists hundreds of names, organized by province so that readers can choose from among those listed in the area where their family might come from. The lists were compiled using census materials from the nineteenth and twentieth centuries, but, as the authors explain, the names derive from a variety of sources: "Firstly, there are ancient aristocratic (*survaljit*) *obogs* (*ovogs*); secondly derivative *obogs* formed by splitting off from an *obog* or *yas* (*yasu*, bone, lineage); thirdly, former *otog* (administrative division), *sum*, and *bag* military-administrative units that were made to conform to the *obog* form" (Ochir and Serjee 1998, 8).[3] The great majority of the names listed are of this third category. For example, apart from the Borjigid, twenty-three of the thirty-seven other *obogs* listed for Gov'sümber province are actually the names of administrative units (*sums* or *otogs*) found in a single banner (Borjigin Janjin Beiliin Khoshuu) that occupied much of the territory of the current province, and a further four are clearly derived from these unit names—*Ikh Tavnan* (Greater Tavnan) and *Bag Tavnan* (Lesser Tavnan), for example, where *Tavnan* was the name of an *otog*.[4] This *khoshuu* did not occupy the whole territory of Gov'sümber province, and it is safe to assume that some, if not all, of the remaining ten names derive from *otogs* or *sums* of neighboring banners. What have been taken as the names of "clans," then, are names of administrative divisions that were not necessarily consanguineous at all. This is not as strange as it may seem, however.

In the seventeenth century, Mongolia became part of the Manchu empire, largely by diplomatic means. The Manchu attempted to impose a system of lineages upon the their Mongolian subjects, using any convenient terms that could be made to stand as clan names. Szynkiewicz (1977, 32) notes:

> Nurhaci (the founder of the Manchu state) based his organisation on kinship groups in the conquered areas. . . . Following established practice, the Manchu began with registering the kinship groups in the conquered areas. They succeeded in putting on record 233 groups of the *obug* [*obog*] type in southern Mongolia (Lebedeva 1958), a very modest number in comparison with the potential number of lineages in the entire society. . . . Quite a few of them were presumably somewhat artificial constructs put on the list—as argued by Mergen Gegen.[5]

Many of these census groups were simply sets of people identified by some characteristic, as can be seen by names such as Taijnar ("the princes"), Khyatad ("the Chinese"), and Achit Lamynkhan ("the people of Achit Lama")

(Ochir and Serjee 1998, 26–29). During the Qing period, the administrative nature of the *obog* made it easily identifiable with the pre-Qing unit called the *otog*—the people and territory ruled by a nobleman and the basic unit of Mongol sociopolitical life in the fifteenth through seventeenth centuries (Atwood 2004, 430; Bold 2001, 117). These were certainly not consanguineous units and might have contained several thousand households at that time. For commoners, membership of such units was hereditary, unless they were transferred by their lord to another noble's holding. The *otog* was retained as an administrative subunit in some banners, particularly for ecclesiastic estates, and in others it was replaced by the *sum* and *bag* units. The two units were sufficiently analogous that Badamkhatan (1972, 10) hyphenates the terms and talks about the *obog-otog* tradition (*ulamjlal*).

Evolutionist social theory had pictured the clan or lineage as the natural social building block of societies without the state. In the classical model of steppe society, nomadic families lived in patrilineages, kin communities that grouped together on the basis of common descent to form clans, or "maximal lineages," to use the anthropological term, if descent to the ancestor was traced (Krader 1968, 87; Barfield 1989, 5). Firsthand accounts, however, made it clear that in the early twentieth century, if not before, actual Mongol social organization was nothing like that.[6] The pastoral encampment, the *khoton* (often described as *khot-ail*), was a fluid residential group of about one to eight *gers* (yurts). These would often come together temporarily, for a season or more, before the constituent households would combine with others to form a new *khoton*. A study by A. D. Simukov in the early 1930s showed that only a minority (41 percent) of the one hundred *khotons* he studied were linked by patrilineal kinship between household heads, compared to 56 percent with other links (Simukov 1933, 29). A much more common basis for coresidence was unequal wealth, since the head of each *khoton* tended to be relatively rich, Simukov noted, and wealthy households preferred to have two or three poor households in their *khoton*, since herding work was shared between the households and thus the richer households would benefit from a relatively greater proportion of the total amount of labor being devoted to looking after their livestock. Administratively, households were usually grouped into a series of nominal units of ten (*arban*), fifty (*bag*), and 150 (*sum*), within the *khoshuu* (banner) of the ruling lord.[7] All of these were administrative units subject to periodic reorganization, not clan or lineage structures. Genealogical relations were generally traced back to grandparents and occasionally great-grandparents, and the network of kin (i.e., birth relatives, *törül sadun, töröl sadan*) would commonly meet on ritual occasions such as the lunar New Year. But these sets of relatives were traced bilaterally, formed networks rather than discrete descent groups, and were not ordinarily residential, so that relatives were often widely scattered (Vreeland 1962, 155).

It has been widely accepted that in the nineteenth century, if not before, genealogical knowledge past three or four generations was rare in both Khalkha and Inner Mongolia (Atwood 2004, 314).[8] But the absence of extended lineages and clans (apart from the nobility) was assumed to be a result of a decline from a putatively more elaborated "kinship system" in the past. Thus even Vreeland (1962, 57) implies that kinship was in decline when he wrote, "by 1920 most persons had difficulty in tracing their patrilineal connections in their own generation beyond 1st and 2nd cousins." However, detailed studies pushed the era of comprehensive clan or lineage organization further and further back historically. Szynkewicz (1977, 31) noted, "towards the end of the Yuan dynasty . . . the lineage organisation, composed of a network of maximal lineages going back to the forefather of the clan and subdivided into segments, can be assumed to have ceased to exist. The few surviving maximal lineages may have comprised the aristocracy." Rinchin (2001, 57–59) suggests that the *obog* lost its character as an exclusive descent group very early, and that it started to become a unit of local relations (*gajar nutug-un kharichagan-u nigech*) sometime before the twelfth century. Gongor (1991 [1970], 6) noted that very little was known about the early history of the *obog* and that historians were restricted to examining the breakup of the "clan system" (*obug baiguulal*) and transition to class society.

But such findings had little influence on the orthodoxy that "tribal" society was bound to be organized into clans. The Mongols may have partially lost their traditional tribal structure during their imperial period, the argument went, but it probably revived with the demise of empire, and in any case, it had survived in neighboring societies such as the Manchus. This was plausible enough, because the classic 1915 ethnography by Shirokogoroff had described the Manchu as organized into archetypal clans (*mukun*), each with a distinctive name (*hala*). For a long time, this was seen to be a form of basic tribal organization, later adapted for the purposes of state administration after the Qing came to control China.

However, as Crossley (1990, 1997) remarks, before the establishment of the Qing dynasty, the *mukun* were probably not descent groups at all, since they were constantly formed and reformed by economic and environmental circumstances" (Crossley 1997, 29).

> Etymologically the word for clan, *mukun*, suggests not kinship but a hunting or herding collective. Its Jurchen antecedent indicated a moving group, Qing glosses on History of the [Jurchen] Jin Dynasty (*Jin Shi*) cite the Solon word *mouyouke*, "village". . . . Pre-Qing clans were not, as the clans of the dynastic period generally were, unexceptionally blood-bound. . . . Individuals claiming no clan affiliation were assigned to functioning clans at the time of incorporation.
>
> (CROSSLEY 1990, 34)

The Jurchen antecedent that Crossley mentions was itself another product of administration. By the early twelfth century, the Jurchen used the *meng-an mou-ke* administrative system, a series of units ruled by hereditary lords that closely resembled the decimal structure of the later Mongolian and Manchu empires. As Elliot (2001, 60) explains:

> The *meng-an mou-ke* originated as a way to rationalize management of the Jurchen population, but as the Jin state grew it also used the *meng-an mou-ke* system to attract and then integrate Chinese, Khitan and other non-Jurchen groups into its military and civil structure. The smaller unit, the *mou-ke* (related to the Manchu word *mukun*, "clan, lineage"), nominally consisting of three hundred households which made it approximately comparable to the *niru* [the Manchu subunit of the banner]; seven to ten *mou-ke* combined to form a *meng-an* (Ma. Minggan, "one thousand") . . . the *mouke-ke* themselves were also subdivided into units of fifty households, called *pu-li-yan*, commensurate perhaps to *tatan* [the Manchu subdivision of the *mukun*]. As in the Eight Banners, military service was obligatory for all males in the *mou-ke*, and offices were hereditary.

In the case of the Manchu *mukun*, it was not until the later period that genealogies were drawn up, but even these do not match classical kinship theory very well. Many did not trace descent from a single ancestor, but rather had a number of founders (Crossley 1990, 36). A corporate group with hereditary membership is not necessarily a clan in the technical sense, and in the end Crossley could only find one aspect of Shirokogoroff's treatment to be really well founded: his comment that "the clan cannot exist without a name and this is an important character of the clan" (Crossley 1990, 36). She explains, "names were the starting point for Nurgaci's revival of the clans in the early seventeenth century and were integral to his claim that his people were the direct descendants of the Jin Jurchens. Around the names he organized registration, company structure, and integration into the Khanate" (Crossley 1990, 36). This clan name (*hala*) was "most often a toponym of ancient or recent vintage," which is another reason to take seriously the early identification of the *mukun* with the village.[9] Although the Qing later placed greater administrative emphasis on the *niru* (the "arrow" political subdivisions that were the template for the Mongolian *sum*), they also became increasingly concerned with compiling genealogical records of the "clans." A number of official works of this sort were compiled for the Qing court, such as the *Comprehensive Genealogies of the Clans and Lineages of the Eight Banner Manchus* (*Baqi Manzhou Shizu Tongpu*) commissioned by the Yong-zheng emperor and published in 1745. Far from decaying under the influence of the Qing administrative system, genealogical kinship became increasingly important, as is clear from the retrospective insertion of a detailed section on "clans" into the second edition of the official history of the Manchu banners published in 1799 (Crossley 1990, 37).

In short, like its Jurchen antecedent unit, the original *mukun* looks far more like an administrative division than the clan of putative kinship society. *Mukun* were usually named after a place rather than a person, they had subjects allocated to them who were not kin, they were subject to hereditary rulers, and the word itself seems to have been related to the term for a village or herd (Crossley 1990, 34; Franke 1990, 418). There is no doubt that it was used as a registration unit from well before the establishment of the Qing. A 1610 Manchu document records the registration of hundreds of captured households, noting their affiliation to *mukun* and to subunits called *tatan* (Elliot 2001, 66). Similarly, the Dagur descent groups (known by the Manchu name *hala*) seem to have been newly created at the time of their incorporation into the Manchu administration. When the Dagur moved from the Amur to the Nonni River in the seventeenth century, the groups that later became *hala* were named after rivers and were probably territorial groupings at that time rather than preexisting kinship groups.[10] But since membership of units was hereditary and carried legal obligations and rights, these administrative units began to resemble descent groups, since an enormous bureaucracy had developed as the Qing administration expanded to keep track of the genealogies, eligibilities, and rewards of *mukun* members.[11]

The increasing emphasis on genealogy and descent groups in the Qing period also reflected Confucian traditions of administration that sought to institute and regulate the patrilineage as a basis for orderly governance. The Cheng-Zhu school of Neo-Confucian thought had developed during the Song (Sung) dynasty (960–1279) and came to dominate Chinese philosophy until the end of the Qing era. The most influential of these thinkers were Cheng Hao (1032–1085), Cheng Yi (1033–1107), and in particular Zhu Xi (1130–1200), who had grouped together the four great Confucian texts for the first time and elucidated them with extensive commentaries. After his conquest of the Song in 1279, Khubilai brought leading Neo-Confucian scholars such as Chao Fu (1206–1299) to teach at the Mongol court, and the Cheng-Zhu school became the basis of Confucianism in Yuan China (Chan 1982, 214). Much of this scholarship was concerned with orderly government and affairs of state, and genealogy was presented as a mechanism for orderly government. Zhu Xi argued: "In order to control the minds of the people, unify one's kin, and enrich social customs so that people will not forget their origin, it is necessary to clarify genealogy, group members of the clan together, and institute a system of heads of descent" (cited in Deuchler 1992, 130).

Patrilineal descent groups were advocated as institutions that would structure society and guarantee the uninterrupted continuation of the political process. This was a response to the familiar problem of succession: without a clear rule as to the selection of a lineal heir, the noble houses that supplied the senior officials of state were liable to fragment. The answer was the "agnatic principle," by which descent was strictly patrilineal. As Deuchler (1992, 130) put the doctrine: "If the agnatic principle is established and the high officials of the land preserve their houses, they develop loyalty and righteousness, and the state's foundation is firm."

This was elaborated into a scheme for an idealized agnatic lineage structure that ranked senior and junior lines of descent and used ancestor worship to generate loyalty and solidarity. Under this scheme, only the eldest son by the primary wife could succeed his father, and he was known as the "major ritual heir." He inherited the ritual obligations of his father as well as his fief and rank, while his younger brothers were called "minor ritual heirs." The line of the major ritual heir became the superordinate descent group, while his younger brothers founded subordinate descent groups. These were replicas of the superordinate branch but had less genealogical depth, since the senior line was traced back indefinitely while the junior ones extended only to the generation of great-great-grandson and split up in the next generation (Deuchler 1992, 132).

This bears a striking resemblance to the "conical clan" of Kirchhoff (1955), and indeed the Krader and Barfield descriptions of idealized Turko-Mongol social organization looks rather like the Neo-Confucian model. But the scheme was not a description of an existing "kinship structure" but rather a plan for one, based on the study of classical texts. Such a system had never existed as such in Chinese antiquity and the Song Neo-Confucians failed to establish it in their own times (Deuchler 1992, 134). It was, above all, a vision of state, designed as a strategy for orderly government, and it shaped legislative and administrative practices in China. As Ebrey (1986) showed, genealogies were one of a set of elite strategies for constructing descent groups and forming them into corporate "building blocks" of society in a way that they had not been before. In the Song and Yuan periods, she writes, "I have found little sign that membership in a descent group was so basic to social life that it restricted other social activities" (Ebrey 1986, 55). But after the collapse of Mongol rule in China, the early Ming initiated a drive to form common descent groups and create genealogies among the elite, which Dardess (1996, 112) describes as part of "a determined effort to identify an upper class and to justify its existence in the light of the moral values of Confucianism." These descent groups were progressively transformed by the Neo-Confucian state so that by the sixteenth and early seventeenth century they had become "large and corporate lineages with special endowments of buildings and property, and institutions for the control and discipline of their memberships" (Dardess 1996, 112). The result of these changes was to create what Dardess (1996, 137), following Brook, calls an *aristogenic order*—"a corporate, kin-based upper class."

The effects of Ming administration on kinship structures was not confined to the aristocracy. Commoners did not form wealthy patrilineages in the same way as the elite, but, as Szonyi (2002) shows, the nature of the Ming taxation system forced groups of patrilineally related kin to organize themselves to ensure their obligations were fulfilled. The Ming *lijia* system for the registration of households created units of tax assessment and legal obligations that were inherited patrilineally by commoner households. This system was inherited by the Qing, who continued to apply Neo-Confucian policies designed to strengthen the role of lineal descent. Thus in the late seventeenth century the Kangxi emperor introduced reforms such as the "allocating tax households to the descent-line" (*lianghu guizong*) policy, which reinforced the administrative importance of patrilineal descent (Szonyi 2002, 76). Rowe (2001, 533) notes:

> Lineage organization was seen by both elites and the state as a powerful tool of social control. In many areas which had undergone bondservant rebellions and other forms of class-based disorder in the dynastic transition era, kinship organization was seen as a deterrent to recurrence. Local leaders expanded them and strengthened their compulsions in the later seventeenth century. The early and mid-Ch'ing [Qing] saw a virtual frenzy of promulgating regulatory codes.

This is exactly the reverse of the classical theory of social evolution by which kinship society preexisted the state and was gradually replaced by an administrative order. As Szonyi (2002, 57) put it, "it was not the absence of the state but rather its presence that drove the construction of kinship organization in the Ming and Qing."[12]

The influence of Chinese notions of lineage organization had an even more striking effect on the Korean Choson dynasty (1392–1910). A standard view, as Deuchler (1992, 6) puts it, is that the "hallmark of Korean society in the late Choson was a kinship system that rested on highly structured patrilineal descent groups. These patrilineages comprised groups of agnates who derived their common descent from a real or putative apical ancestor (*sijo*) and identified themselves with a common surname (*song*) and a common ancestral seat (*pon'gwan*)."

This vision is misleading, however, in a number of ways. First, lineage organization was actually confined to the hereditary aristocracy. "Lineages represented the social organization of the Korean upper class. Called *yangban*, the elite of Choson Korea constituted a relatively small segment, perhaps not more than ten percent, of the total population; but, drawing on descent and heredity, it monopolized the political process, economic wealth and Confucian learning" (Deuchler 1992, 12). Unlike their masters, commoners (called *yangin* or *sangmin*) were subject to taxation, military service, and corvée labor, and since "commoners did not form lineages, their kinship system was less complex and less ritualized. Moreover, commoners did not keep genealogies and thus lacked recognized charters of descent" (Deuchler 1992, 12).

Deuchler shows that the aristocratic patrilineage was itself a striking feat of social engineering initiated by the Choson state. The setting for this innovation, however, was a society in which genealogy and descent had long been of central importance to the elite. Aristocracy was ancient in Korea, and in the Koryo dynasty (918–1392) the great families traced their ancestry back to the state of Silla, which had unified the peninsula in the seventh century.

> In the hierarchically structured Koryo society, certified descent meant attested membership in a descent group that looked back to an illustrious ancestry. It was a Koryo aristocrat's key to elevated politico-jural status. . . . But how was such membership certified? This could be done practically only through systematic genealogical recordings. At the beginning of the dynasty it was reportedly not customary to keep family records (po); therefore the names of antecedents (kison) got lost and only their origin from Silla was vaguely remembered. Judging from funerary inscriptions of the elite, around the middle of the twelfth century genealogical recordings became more precise, and two or even three generations of agnatic antecedents began to be listed. . . . The actual tracing of ancestral lines undoubtedly ran counter to native genealogical consciousness, but it became a prerequisite for the capital elite that monopolized political office. As the equation between well-established social status and political participation came to be variously challenged by social newcomers during the second half of the dynasty, ancestral reckoning became even more important and consequently grew more elaborate. To depict an individual's ancestry, a sophisticated construct was developed . . . pushing the ancestral reckoning back to the sixth ascending generation.
>
> (DEUCHLER 1992, 39–40)[13]

In the thirteenth century, the Koryo state was invaded by the Mongols and eventually forced to recognize Chinggisid suzerainty. By the fourteenth century, the power of the Koryo royal house was in decline: eroded by almost a century of Mongol rule, the central administration had become weak. Korean scholars had studied Neo-Confucian ideology under the Yuan, and sections of the aristocracy began to advocate wholesale reforms in line with Cheng-Zhu thought. Confucian-style ancestor worship was officially instituted in the last years of the Koryo dynasty, but the measures came too late for the dynasty, which had largely lost control to the military by this time. In 1392, the military hero Yi Song-gye ascended the throne and, with the support of Neo-Confucian scholar-officials, founded the Choson dynasty. The new administration set out to establish the Confucian ideal in Korean society by edict and example.

This transformed the notion of descent and the institutions that depended on it. In the Koryo era, a person's kin in the widest sense were designated *chok*. "Anyone who was related to a person through either a parent or an affine belonged to that person's *chok*." This made it "an imprecise and elastic term for any kind of kin" (Deuchler 1992, 38). The group was neither exogamous nor endogamous, and marriages between *chok* members, even half siblings, appears to have been common, as were marriages with members of other *chok* (Deuchler 1992, 58). Under the Choson, however, the descent group became an exclusive, patrilineal, and uncompromisingly exogamous institution for the first time. The official form of ancestor worship established the seniority of the eldest primary son, who became responsible for the rituals of the senior line of ancestors. Legislation was introduced that distinguished primary sons from other offspring and gave them senior status. Inheritance law changed to increasingly favor the eldest son and destroyed what had been an equal division of the patrimony, originally between surviving siblings as well as offspring. These processes created a ranked order within elite families, forming the nobility into hierarchically structured descent groups with clear heads, as the Neo-Confucian scholars had intended. Again, lineage society had been created by the state, albeit only among the aristocracy.

In the Mongol case, the Qing state largely failed to create anything approaching the Neo-Confucian model. The Borjigid did not really observe primogeniture as a rule, let alone produce the full lineage structure of the Chinese and Korean elites. However, patrilineal descent groups other than the Borjigid certainly are found in parts of Inner Mongolia—in Hulun Buir, for example, among the Barga and Daur Mongols.[14] Interestingly, however, these groups do not use the term *obog* or *yas* for these descent groups, but the Manchu term—*hala*. The apparent "loss" of kinship structures among the Khalka has tended to be viewed as an anomaly, and explanations have been sought in the influence of state administration, monastic Buddhism, or other historical factors (Bulag 1998, 122–125; Sneath 2000, 197–206). But given the Qing's administrative interest in promoting descent groups, it seems more reasonable to assume they were simply never formed in the regions least subject to direct Manchu administration, such as Khalka. Qing-era Mongol literature suggests that the ecclesiastical elite, as well as the Manchu state, wished to promote patrilineal descent groups. Eighteenth-century Mongol chroniclers attribute (and much quote) a saying to the Fifth Dalai Lama: "if one does not know one's own *obog*, one is like a dragon made out of turquoise; if one does not read scripts narrated about one's own ancestors, one is like a lost child" (Munkh-Erdene 2006, 66). The Mergen Gegeen, for example, stressed the importance of patrilineal genealogy for orderly rule and was very disapproving of those tracing bilateral descent.[15] Such exhortations suggest that some Mongols, perhaps most, did not know their *obog*s or the scripts narrated by their ancestors, but that the ecclesiastical elite was concerned that they should. Certainly this was the sort of process of kinship construction that occurred in China. On this point, Ebrey (1986, 40) quotes Watson (1982, 618): "it is difficult for many anthropologists, given their frog-in-the-well view of Chinese society, to accept that lineage and related social forms . . . emerged as a consequence of an ideological transformation among the national elite."

But, as discussed in chapter 2, there certainly were Mongolian lineal descent groups, at least among the aristocracy, and these were more numerous in the era before Borjigin dominance. This was taken as evidence of a basic tribal organization composed of exogamous patrilineal clans, and although scholars have doubted this model from time to time (e.g., Bulag 1998, 122), there was no major attempt to rethink it. In fact, the actual material we have on the *obog* and *yasu* in this early Chinggisid period is rather sparse (Rykin 2004). Foreign-language sources, as one would expect, do not generally retain the original terms *obog* and *yasu* and so are of little help. The *Secret History of the Mongols* remains perhaps the most useful source for indigenous Mongol terms for descent groups, but such has been the dominance of the clan model that the two terms *obog* (family, lineage, line) and *yasu* (bone, descent, lineage) were both commonly translated as "clan" depending on the context, and often the term "clan" has simply been inserted next to any group noun that the translator believes to be one.[16] De Rachewiltz (2004, 3) provides a typical example (§15) when translating a passage describing a meeting of two men on the steppe: "Dobun Mergen asked him 'To which clan do you belong?' The man said 'I am a man of the Ma'aliq Baya'ut, and I am in desperate straits.'" However, the reconstructed Mongol text actually reads *"ya'un gü'ün chi kä'än,"* which literally just means "of-what you (addressed familiar/junior) who?" and this could as well mean "what principality are you from" as anything to do with clans.[17] The reply is *"bï Malig Baya'udäi"* (literally, "I with/of Malig Baya'ut"), and, as in the original question, no actual kin term is used at all.

Other primary historical sources have suffered from the same treatment. One of the most influential primary texts on the early Mongol period is the *Compendium of Chronicles (Jami'u't-tawarikh)* written by the Persian historian Rashid ad-Din (1246–1318), vizier to Ghazan Khan of the Il-Khanate of Persia. It describes the divisions of the Turkic and Mongol peoples and gives a detailed history of the background to, and expansion of, the Chinggisid empire. Rashid ad-Din reads, in translation, in a way that supports the tribal model. He introduces, for example: "The Turkic nations that are now called Mongols but in times past were separate nations, each with its own language and name: Each of these nations had a leader and a commander, and from each of them branched off tribes and clans, like the Jalayir, the Oyirat, the Tatar, etc. . . . " (Thackston 1998, 37). It seems that tribes and clans must be the "building blocks" of the societies described here. Similarly, the "clans" of the core Mongols are each described. The entry for the Tayichi'ut, for example, starts:

> The clans of the Tayichi'ut consist of numerous branches. Their origin and lineage are as follows. Qaidu Khan had three sons, and the eldest was named [Bai] Singqor, from whom stems the branch of Genghis [Chinggis] Khan's forefathers. The third son was named Cha'ujin, and from him descend the two clans of the Ärigin [Härigan] and Sanchi'ut. The middle son was named Charaqa Lingqum, and all the Tayichi'ut clans are descended from him.

But in fact, Rashid ad-Din does not use any term that corresponds to clan or tribe. He uses a single term, *qawm*, for all groups of people, which can mean a group of any size and contains no inherent kinship content. Thackston (1998, xvii), the translator, explains, "when the English terms 'nation,' 'tribe,' and 'clan' are used, they are dictated by sense and by the necessity to introduce some variety into the text." Thackston's selection of terms was informed by, and so reproduced, the tribal model, and there is enough ambiguity in the original term *qawm* for this to be possible. The passage noted above, for example, talks of various Tayichi'ud groups as descended from named noblemen, and it seems at first glance that there could have been many such descendants—enough to populate a whole "tribe," perhaps? But from the *Secret History* (§47) it is clear that when Ambagai Khan and Senggüm Bilge's descendants took the name Tayichi'ud this was only about four generations before Chinggis Khan's own time.

The biological descendants of Senggüm Bilge can simply not have been very numerous in absolute terms, although they were clearly politically powerful. On closer inspection, Rashid ad-Din is describing the branches of the aristocracy. The distinction between the nobles of Tayichi'ud descent and their subjects is made explicit in the *Secret History*, in the passage that describes Chinggis Khan's eventual victory over them (§148). "Chinggis Qa'an plundered the Tayichi'ut. He wiped out the men of the Tayichi'ut bone (lineage)—A'uchu-ba'atur, Qoton-orcheng, Qudu'udar and others. . . . The people of their nation he brought (with him)" (De Rachewiltz 2004, 70; Onon 1990, 63; Cleaves 1982, 76).

There is no doubt that noble descent groups such as the Jalayir, Qonggirad, and Tayichi'ud existed and acted as important political entities in this period, just as various originally Borjigid descent groups, such as the Manggud and Suldus, were prominent in the imperial period; the Choros and Galwas were ruling lineages among the Oirats, and different branches of the Borjigid, such as the Urad and Khorchin princes, formed noble houses of long standing.[18] The *Secret History* mentions a number of nobles who founded *obog*s that had names derived from the personal names of the founders or supposed characteristics of the *obog* members. Section 42, for example, describes the descendants of the five sons of Alan Qo'a, who jointly established a realm by conquest. "From Begünütei stemmed the Belgünüt *obog*, from Bügünütei the Bügünüt; from Buqu Qatagi, the Qatagin; from Buqatu Salji, the Salji'ut; from Bodonchar, the Borjigin."

But these early *obog*s do not seem to have been exogamous, patrilineal clans. The Borjigid, for example, are clearly counted as an *obog* but were not exogamous in the early period; they married partners from other named descent groups within the Borjigin category, such as the Barulas, Baarin, and Mangghud (Atwood 2004, 45). The constitution of *obog*s appears to have been more political than genealogical. Most of the ancestors and their descendants do *not* give rise to named clans or lineages; recognition of descent from a common ancestor alone did not generate a sociopolitical grouping in the way that the classic segmentary lineage model would suggest. At least one *obog* was created by a king as an appanage for his son. The Jürkin *obog*, for example, came about in the following way:

Qabul Qan [Khan], saying that Ökin Barqaq was his eldest son, chose men for him from among his own people and, having chosen them, gave him strong and mighty men who had

> Gall in their livers,
> Thumbs good for shooting,
> Lungs filled with Courage,
> Mouths full of fury
> And, all, men of skill.

Because they had fury and gall, and were proud and inflexible,[19] that is the reason that they were called Jürkin.

(DE RACHEWILTZ 2004, 61)

This had happened in the relatively recent past. The founder of the Jürkin *obog* was Chinggis Khan's great-uncle, and his descendants alone cannot have been very numerous. However, the Jürkin, and the subjects they ruled, were clearly a force to be reckoned with at the time of Chinggis Khan's struggle for power, and it seems that recruitment may have been at least partially by choice. We know that at least one nobleman who was not a descendant of Ökin Barqaq was a member of the *obog*.[20] Indeed, in a recent study of the use of the term *obog* in the *Secret History*, Rykin (2004, 196–197) concludes that there are no grounds to assume it was a kinship group and that the primary evidence suggests it was used to indicate both the rulers of a group of people and the group itself.

Some scholars, particularly those working with the original texts and aware of difficulties with the clan model, reconciled the historical evidence with Marxist theory by assuming that—once again—the kinship system was in breakdown by the time of historical records (Markov 1976, 69). Zhou Qingshu (2001, 1), the Chinese historian of the Yüan, for example, notes than in pre-thirteenth-century Mongolian society descent groups (*xing shi*) included many who were not related by blood. Rinchin, the Inner Mongolian historian, wrote that sometime before the twelfth century "*obog* institutions also lost their blood descent (*chisun udum*) character, and gradually became a unit of territorial relationships (*gajar nutug-un kharichagan-u nigech*)" Rinchin (2001 [1977], 57–58).

The term *obog* is not the only term used for politically significan groups in the *Secret History*, and the term *yasu* (literally, "bone") appears no less important. This seems to have been used to describe a noble lineage or line, sometimes overlapping with *obog*,[21] and it may have been that *obog* was a rather more inclusive term (Rykin 2004), indicating the sociopolitical entity headed by the descendants of the founder, while *yasu* was used as a more exclusive term to indicate the patriline. In any case, there is evidence that non-kin could become members of a *yasu*. A number of funerary inscriptions in both Mongolian and Chinese have survived from the four-teenth century. One such stele was set up to memorialize the good deeds of a man named Jigüntei, who was originally a subject given as part of the "human dowry" or *inje*[22] of the Princess Sengee, when she married a Qonggirad prince named Dimubala Ong [Wang], who governed the prin-cipality of Lu in northern China. Jigüntei acted as a steward, overseeing the pasturing of the prince's horse herds. The inscription reads: "Dimubala Ong, greatly loving him, cared for [him] he made [him] a Qunggirad in his own family (*yasun*)" (Cleaves 1951, 67). The adoption of infants might be accommodated into the standard model of the patrilineage, but the inclu-sion of adults (possibly by marriage but probably without marriage, since no such alliance is mentioned) poses a rather more serious challenge.

Eyewitness reports do not support the notion of large exogamous patri-lineages. John de Plano Carpini, the Franciscan who left the first detailed European account of the Mongol court in 1246, reports that Mongols "are joined in matrimony to all in general, even to their near kinsfolk except their mother, daughter and sister by the mother's side." He also notes that, like the members of aristocratic Korean *chok* descent groups at this time, they "may marry their half-sisters." William of Rubruck, who visited the court of Mönke Qagan in 1254, noted that with respect to exogamy, Mon-gols only "keep the first and second degrees of consanguinity"—that is, marriage was forbidden between those related by common grandparents (Beazley 1903, III, 197). Evidence of large patrilineages does not appear in Mongolian textual sources either. One of the earliest Mongolian language dictionaries, the *Dictionary of Twenty-One Volumes* (*Khorin Nigetü Tailburi Toli*) was complied in the early eighteenth century. The dictionary does not give a picture of distinctive descent groups that might count as "so-cial building blocks." The definitions of terms such as *obog*, *urug*, and *törül* (*töröl*, "kindred," "sort") tend to be overlapping and vague. It notes, for example, that "one *törül* is one *obog*," but defines *törül* by stating "the *akha de'ü* of an *obog* are a *törül*" (*Khorin Nigetü* 1979, 676). The literal meaning of *akha de'ü* is "elder and younger siblings" but the phrase is used to mean both family and close friends in contemporary Mongolian, rather like "kith and kin," and there are passages in the *Secret History* that suggest it could have been used in such an inclusive way at that time too.[23] The dictionary adds that a *törül* can also be a *süreg*, a term that generally means a herd of livestock but when applied to humans can simply mean a crowd.[24] The |III| later dictionary *Khorin Naimatu Tailburi Toli* was compiled from many earlier ones. It notes that the "[people] who are originated from a grandfather are called a *töröl*" (*Nige ebüge-eche ürejigsen-i inu törül khememüi*) (Namjilma 1988, 1614), and this suggests that the *törül* and therefore the *obog* were small bilateral groups that we would call families (rather than lineages or clans), tracing descent back to common grandparents, as in William of Rubruck's account of the exogamous group in the thirteenth century.[25]

Taken together, all this makes the existence of large exogamous patrilineages unlikely and suggests a good deal of flexibility in the membership of the groups described as *obog* and perhaps even *yasu*. This need not contradict the central importance of tracing descent for the noble families of that time. Deuchler (1992, 290) notes that in both Tang China and Koryo Korea aristocratic descent groups were "loosely structured, but nevertheless placed great value on descent."[26] In the wake of Schneider's critique, we may question the primacy of kinship in the classical sense as the basis for these groups. The nineteenth-century conception of kinship society had tended to contrast horizontal relations between kin with vertical relations found in states. But the recognition that steppe polities such as those of early Mongol society were aristocracies makes it easier to conceive of descent groups as primarily political forms rather than as self-forming kinship structures with political "functions."

One need not reject anthropological kinship studies entirely to find an alternative to the lineage model of the descent group. In their 1995 work *About the House*, Janet Carsten and Stephen Hugh-Jones revived a relatively little known theme in the work of Claude Lévi-Strauss, the notion of "house societies" (*sociétés à maison*). Lévi-Strauss coined the term to describe the principal grouping of the Kwakiutl, which Boas had found fitted none of the classical kinship categories of gens, sept, clan, or sib, and those of the Californian Yurok studied by Koeber (Lévi-Strauss 1983, 163–170). He compared these to European noble houses, which:

> combined agnatic and uterine principles of succession, as well as sometimes adopting in heirs, often through marriage. Their wealth consisted of both tangible property and less tangible names, titles and prerogatives, and

their continuity was based on both kinship and marriage alliance. Alliances could be both endogamous (to keep the house from losing wealth) and exogamous (to accrue further property or status). The bringing together of "antagonistic principles"—alliance, descent, endogamy, exogamy—was governed by political considerations and is a central feature of the house in these societies.

(CARSTEN AND HUGH-JONES 1995, 7)

This concept is particularly helpful in the light of Schneider's critique of classical kinship theory, in which he shows that in the Yap case the "house" (*tabinau*) is a fundamental social institution of relatedness, one that he originally misrepresented as a patrilineage. It also sits well with Bourdieu's treatment of Kabyle society, in which the house is the fundamental institution in the constitution of the social order, and with his rejection of structuralist and structural-functionalist treatments of kinship on the grounds that practice should not be seen as the expression of abstract norms[27] but rather as the results of strategizing behavior of households seeking to pass on symbolic capital.[28]

I do not seek to simply replace the concept of "clan society" with that of "house society," or to propose social typologies of this sort to try to fill in the blank spaces left in the historical record. But there are a number of reasons why the house might serve as a better comparative term for aristocratic descent groups than the clan. First, as a comparative category, the house has not been built into dominant models of kinship society and may serve as a relatively open term that does not imply particular practices such as segmentation, exogamy, endogamy, unilineality, and so on. Second, it does not presume the primacy of classical constructions of kinship in the Schneiderian sense, so it could accommodate the interpretation that it was essentially a field of power relations expressed in the idiom of descent. Third, it is a readily recognizable term that is not uncommonly used by historians to describe noble descent groups in Inner Asia and elsewhere.[29] Finally, the underlying associations of the term are those of aristocracy, not imagined kinship society, and this makes it easier to conceptualize a society in which ancient aristocratic descent groups existed alongside commoner families who may not have traced descent back more than a couple of generations.

This last possibility becomes more plausible in the light of the idioms of descent used in neighboring parts of Inner Asia, such as Tibet. In the

Tibetan case, the term *rü* (*rus*) means "bone" and is also used as the term for the descent group. In most of Central Tibet, *rü* indicates patrilineal links within the immediate family only, with bilateral descent traced back only a few generations, and does not indicate extended clans or lineages with specific names. Social groups are generally based on residential and administrative units. Among the elite, however, *rü* was a principle of patrilineal inheritance for religious and political office, often involving records of descent stretching back many generations (Aziz 1976). Some of the most famous of these *rü* claim to trace their origins back to the ruling families of the sixth- to ninth-century dynastic period and even earlier, to the ruling houses of the petty kingdoms incorporated into the emerging Tibetan state. In the Tibetan case, a single idiom of descent ("bone") is used to describe patrilineal kin ties within a wide range of very different descent forms, from ramified aristocratic lineages to local extended families recruited bilaterally or even matrilineally among commoners (Diemberger and Rambal forthcoming). This seems comparable to the Mongolian case, and it raises the question as to why commoner households without aristocratic claims to office would generate extended genealogical knowledge, much less seek to organize themselves socially and politically on this basis, even if this were permitted by their rulers.

This is not to say, of course, that nonaristocratic Mongol subjects did not trace descent or organize collective action on the basis of kinship relations at all; it would seem almost certain that they did to some extent. But there is no reason to suppose that they formed patrilineal clans or lineages of the sort supposed by classical theory, and the evidence we have suggests that whatever descent groups there might have been did not form the "social building blocks" of putative tribal society, since administrative units appear as old and fundamental groupings. The first census that Chinggis Khan undertook in 1206 recorded subjects not in terms of clans or lineages, but in decimal administrative units, the *arban* (ten), *ja'un* (hundred), and *minggan* (thousand). This has generally been explained away either as a result of a sort of "Chinggisid revolution" that had destroyed the clan structure and completely reorganized steppe society along decimal lines or by claiming that the decimal organization only applied to the organization of the army.

But neither of these explanations is convincing. First, there is no indication of such a complete reorganization of society in the historical sources. The *Secret History*, for example, describes the reordering of subjects into units that already seem readily understandable to contemporaries and includes nothing that suggests the abolition of older social structures. It records simply that Chinggis Qa'an decreed: "For those who went with me in establishing the *ulus*, I shall, forming thousands, appoint lords (*noyad*) of the thousands and speak words of favour."[30] The usual translations render the term *minggad-un noyad* as "commanders of a thousand" (De Rachewiltz 2004, 133; Cleaves 1982, 141) to try to accommodate the theory that these were purely military units, but the term *noyan* (plural *noyad*) was considered equivalent to the Arab and Persian *emir*, and the *minggan* were civil as much as military units ruled by their *noyans* in peacetime as well as war (Atwood 2004, 139), so "lord" seems the better translation. Most of the nobles mentioned in the list as lords of *minggan* appear to have been confirmed in existing positions, and, indeed, the process described by the *Secret History* seems largely to be the official recognition of existing lordly domains and their integration into a uniform *minggan* administrative system.

In any case, we know that the Jurchen, who at the height of their power controlled much of what subsequently became Mongol territory, had been administering their subjects in nominal "thousand" units (*minggan*) since well before the time of Chinggis Khan, and that these "thousands" were also civil and military institutions composed of *mouke* units of a nominal three hundred households, each with the duty of supplying one hundred regular soldiers. At the time of his decree on *minggans* in 1206, Chinggis already governed his own subjects using the nominal thousand and hundred (*ja'un*) units, so at most he was extending an existing system for the registration and management of commoner households, one that must have been known since Jurchen times. There is no evidence that commoners were organized in a different way between the Jurchen and Chinggisid eras, and if so, what the social units concerned were like. But the decimal administrative system was certainly not invented by the Jurchen.[31] Both the institutions of aristocratic power and the decimal civil-military administrative system are described in the earliest detailed accounts of Inner Asian steppe society records that we have.

Sima Qian (145–90 B.C.E.), the author of the *Shiji*, described the great steppe polity of his time, the Xiongnu empire, which was ruled by an aristocracy composed of three families: "The high ministerial offices are hereditary, being filled from generation to generation by the members of the Huyan and Lan families, and in more recent times by the Xubu family.

These three families constitute the aristocracy of the nation" (Watson 1993, 136). The polity was organized into two vast wings, with the left wing forming the eastern division and the right being the western portion, as if the empire was a gigantic army at rest, facing south. The Xiongnu emperor was named the *chanyu*, and below him stood the "wise kings" and senior officials of the left and right wings. Just below these stood twenty-four great lords. Of these, Sima Qian wrote, "the most important ones [command] ten thousand horsemen, the least important a few thousand; altogether they are referred to as the twenty-four high dignitaries" (Di Cosmo 2002, 177). These kings, officials, and lords ruled a number of divisions and subdivisions of the empire. Whatever the nature of these units, it seems that, in the case of large ones at least, "each group had its own area, within which it moves" (Watson 1993, 137). The administrative system was decimal. "Each of the twenty-four leaders [*zhang*] in turn appoints his own 'chiefs [*zhang*] of a thousand,' 'chiefs [*zhang*] of a hundred,' and 'chiefs [*zhang*] of ten,' as well as his subordinate kings, prime ministers, chief commanders, household administrators . . . and so forth" (Watson 1993, 137).[32] There is no indication that this decimal organization was an exclusively military system, and Grousset (1970, 21) concludes that the entire nation was permanently organized as an army, even in peace.

This is so strikingly similar to the Chinggisid imperial organization that it is strange that more has not been made of the comparison in the standard treatments.[33] But both aristocracy and a numerical administrative system are so incompatible with the tribal model of pastoral nomads that they tended to be explained away as phenomena of contact and conquest. Even when it uses very nominal units, a decimal administrative system, for example, operates on entirely different principles from the descent groups of the kinship society model. Decimal units fit together to form larger aggregates on the basis of their number, not kinship relations, and since genealogies, however fictive they might be, could hardly be made to justify a series of ten, hundred, thousand, and ten thousand, the relationship between the constituent units cannot be defined by descent. Membership of an administrative unit may, of course, be hereditary, as it was in the case of the medieval English *tithing*, but the unit is not in any way an element of a "kinship system," since its role and relations are defined by an administrative rather than a genealogical order. In the Xiongnu case, it appears that the registration of subjects within administrative units seems to have been a definitional feature of commoner status, at least in the Chinese sources. The Chinese term used for Xiongnu commoners meant, literally, "registered households" (Honey 1990, 21).

| 116 | Apart from the aristocracy, what little evidence there is on Xiongnu kinship does not suggest a society based on "clan identity." As in contemporary Mongolia, it seems that the Xiongnu had nothing resembling clan or lineage names. Sima Qian notes: "They have no family names or polite names but only personal names" (Watson 1993, 130). This does not sit well with the model of kinship society and Watson, the translator, decided that it must be an error, only adding this comment in a note. It seems, then, that the baseline Xiongnu cultural practice was not to have clan or descent group names, except in the case of the aristocracy, whose noble houses were described as *xing* by Chinese commentators, and this name was used to compose the full names of aristocrats, at least in the Chinese sources. But even these aristocratic houses do not seem to have been strictly patrilineal in the tracing of decent. The Han emperor Gao Zu sent a princess of his own house (Liu) to marry the great Xiongnu emperor Modu, for example, and the descendants of Modu took the (affinal) name Liu themselves (Honey 1990, 17).

This is not quite as strange as it may seem. In ancient China, surnames (*xing*) were at first only possessed by the leading aristocratic families who played political roles, and rulers created new *xing* by bestowing surnames on those they favored. Sima Qian notes, for example, that the Zhou Emperor Shun gave the surname Ji to a court official in charge of farming named Qi (Watson 1993). We cannot be certain that all those without surnames were not organized into descent groups at all, but it seems unlikely that at that time they formed lineages of the sort indicated by the term *xing*. Only later, in Han times, does it appear to have become a term applied to common subjects.

But whatever the social organization of Chinese commoners might have been, the meaning of the term *xing* is important because of the way it is used to describe steppe societies. Historical Chinese descriptions of the structure of the Türk empire describe its subdivisions in terms of *xing*—often in a numbered group such as the *Jiu Xing* (Nine Surnames) of the Türk and early Uighur states, the *Shi Xing* (Ten Surnames) of the Left Wing of the Western Türk empire, and the probably more inclusive *Shanshi Xing* (Thirty Surnames) of the Türk (Mackerras 1990, 320; Golden 2006, 31). In these descriptions, the usual practice was to translate *xing* as "tribe" or "clan," in line with the dominant tribal model. But to those writing early Chinese texts, the term *xing* could indicate an aristocratic descent group. Indeed, the *xing*s that they mention by name—such as the Ashina, Yaglaqar, and Ädiz—were undoubtedly powerful noble and royal houses. A quick look at the numbers of people involved reinforces this view. The Arab traveler Tamin Ibn Bahr, who journeyed to the ninth-century Uighur capital, estimated the Türks could raise about a quarter of a million warriors (Minorsky 1978, 1:283–285). If these nine or ten surnames were inclusive of the whole population, each would average over 100,000 members or so—surely too huge for an exogamous clan unit. Without the influence of the tribal model, then, the historical sources suggest political divisions based on aristocracy, not grassroots kinship structures. And again, even among the aristocracy, *xing* membership was not always based on genealogical descent. Taking a particular "surname" could be an entirely political act indicating succession to high office. The ninth-century Uighur ruler El ögäsi, for example, simply acquired the surname of the royal house of Yaglaqar when he usurped the throne, although he had originally been of the house of Ädiz, and this was noted without surprise by the Song chronicler Sima Guang (Mackerras 1990, 318).

It seems probable that where exogamous lineage-style descent groups did appear they were linked to the project of rulership. This certainly seems to have been the case among the neighbors and contemporaries of the Uighurs, the Kitans, who established one of the largest steppe powers that preceded the Chinggisid Mongol state. Based in what is now Manchuria, the Kitans founded the Liao dynasty, which ruled most of Mongolia and northeastern China from around 924 until 1125. At first glance, the pastoral Kitans seem to conform to the classical clan model of Inner Asian tribes—a set of kin groups united by common descent from ancestors. Historical sources refer to an ancestral pair whose eight sons became the founders of the eight original Kitan tribes (Franke 1990, 406). However, yet again, on closer inspection we find nothing like the clan-society model but rather a description of aristocratic houses or lineages. As Wittfogel and Feng (1949, 17) note, well before the establishment of the Liao the Kitans had a "fixed nobility and a relatively stable ruling house." The aristocracy had a privileged legal status, without the obligation of labor service imposed on common subjects and facing much milder punishments for crimes (Wittfogel and Feng 1949, 193).

The nobility did not trace shared descent with their subjects, and the commoners seem to have had no clans at all. Franke (1990, 403–405) notes that "originally there existed no clan groups within the tribes. . . . The Chinese exogamic clan-system was adopted under the Liao only for the ruling Yeh-lü [Yelü] clan and the Hsiao [Xiao] clan of the imperial consorts; as a consequence the Kitan commoners and tribesmen had no family names." This pattern seems to predate the Kitan period. The predecessor power in Manchuria was the Bohai state of the eighth to the tenth centuries. Crossley (1997, 19) notes that in the rigid Bohai class system the elites tended to be affiliated with large families and had surnames, but there is no evidence that commoners did. Despite the influence of the notion of kinship society, specialists have been troubled by the lack of evidence for it in the Kitan case. Wittfogel and Feng (1949, 206) remark upon "the 'clanless' nature" of the society as a whole, noting the "instability in their organization of kin" (Wittfogel and Feng 1949, 204) and the general lack of ancestor worship and proper exogamy by Chinese standards.[34] They note that "extended genealogies remained the concern of the powerful families" and suppose that "poor families and weak ones might only remember the genealogies of their immediate ancestors" (Wittfogel and Feng 1949, 205).

A central feature of Kitan society was the *ordo*, an institution that appears in many Inner Asian languages and remained fundamental to steppe polities throughout the Mongol period. The *ordo* was the palace or court of a ruler. "Each ruler had his own ordo which functioned as a bodyguard in peacetime and elite corps in war. The number of warrior households attached to a single ordo might be as high as 15,000" (Franke 1990, 404).[35] Similarly, rather than being self-formed social aggregates, the Kitan "tribes" (the Chinese original being *bu*, meaning division/section) were clearly formed and reformed by numerous administrative acts of their rulers, there being at different times between eight and fifty-four such divisions (Wittfogel and Feng 1949, 86–100).[36] As with the decimal administrative system, this suggests that "social building blocks," if we can talk in these terms, were formed by the vertical relations of aristocratic power rather than by horizontal bonding on the basis of descent. In each of the cases examined in this chapter, we see genealogy-keeping corporate descent groups formed by aristocratic elites; the more segmented, exclusive, and strictly patrilineal forms seem to be linked to the ideology and bureaucracy of the state.

The *ordo* remained a central institution in the Chinggisid Mongol world. It passed into European languages as "horde," and the current connotation of this term—a barbaric, undisciplined mass—provides another telling example of the influence of the tribal model in misrepresenting "nomadic society." Its association with primitive society was such that evolutionist anthropology chose the term "horde" for the groupings formed by the social type they considered most archaic—hunter-gatherers. It is hard to think of a less appropriate use of a term meaning the palace of a great ruling house, such as the Golden Ordo of Batu Khan, the vast and disciplined headquarters of a small empire. But the idea of the horde as the primitive social unit was plausible enough at the time because the association between barbarism and nomadism was deeply rooted in the Western intellectual tradition. Although peripatetic courts were common in medieval Europe, the routine use of mobility had come to seem so exotic in European eyes that the notion of nomads as a distinctive and somehow less fully evolved social type remained dominant throughout much of the twentieth century, giving rise to the model of nomadic society as an ideal type. This model had a formative influence on treatments of steppe societies; to understand it, we need to excavate the concepts and debates upon which it drew.

5

The Essentialized Nomad

Neocolonial and Soviet Models

In his monumental study of world history, Toynbee describes nomadic society as one of several "arrested civilisations." Along with the Eskimos and Polynesians, "nomads" represented "cases in which civilisations have remained static" (Toynbee 1946, 193). This was an essentialized vision of nomadism as a social form that had remained unchanged for countless generations, like the societies of ants and bees. Toynbee's treatment set the scene for ecologically determinist accounts of nomadic pastoralism. He emphasized the "formidable environment which he [the nomad] has succeeded in conquering" (Toynbee 1946, 169), arguing that the adaptations required for survival had trapped them in a timeless stasis. "The Nomads and the Eskimos have fallen into arrest through an excessive concentration of all their faculties on their shepherding and hunting" (Toynbee 1946, 327). The numerous conquest states founded by "nomads" were explained away as historical cycles of expansion and collapse that left the essential nomadic way of life unchanged. "Once the conquest has been achieved the nomad conqueror degenerates because he has passed out of his own element" (Toynbee 1946, 173). Like a fish out of water, then, the nomad cannot long survive in the sedentary world.

Toynbee was, of course, following a well-worn path. Nineteenth-century evolutionist social science had pictured pastoralism as a sort of developmental dead end. In Engels' scheme, for example, the evolutionary stages that preceded "civilization" began with "savagery" and progressed to "barbarism." Each of these stages were characterized by a certain technological level: savagery by fire, hunting, and fishing; barbarism by pottery and the domestication of plants and animals.

|122|

> In the Eastern Hemisphere the middle stage of barbarism began with the domestication of animals providing milk and meat, but horticulture seems to have remained unknown far into this period. It was, apparently, the domestication and breeding of animals and the formation of herds of considerable size that led to the differentiation of the Aryans and Semites from the mass of barbarians . . . having accustomed themselves to pastoral life in the grassy plans of the rivers, these barbarians of the middle period would never have dreamed of returning willingly to the native forests of their ancestors.
>
> (ENGELS 1986 [1884], 54–55)

These pastoral nomad barbarians were thought of as essentially preagricultural. Having branched away from the technological and social development that led to agriculture and successively higher forms of civilization, pastoralists had become stuck at this early stage.

This may have been a plausible enough scenario in Engel's time, but twentieth-century archaeology has shown it to be quite mistaken. It has become widely accepted that Eurasian pastoral nomadism developed long after the advent of agriculture, probably as a more specialized offshoot of the mixed farming that had developed in areas such as southwestern Asia between the fourth and eighth millennium B.C.E. (Cavalli-Sforza 1996, 54–64). Mobile pastoralism emerged no earlier than the middle of the second millennium B.C.E. (Khazanov 1983, 92–94), probably on the southern Russian steppe, and a number of studies suggest that the fully mobile equestrian form is an even later development than previously thought (see Allard and Erdenbaatar 2005, 560–561). Indeed, recent archaeological discoveries have suggested that even in steppe regions agriculture is much older than this, with millet being cultivated as long ago as the sixth millennium B.C.E. in the eastern fringes of the steppe and around Lake Baikal—indeed, millet probably spread to Europe along the steppe corridor (Jones et al. forthcoming). Rather than an earlier, more primitive lifestyle, fully mobile pastoralism seems to have developed long after agriculture on the Eurasian steppe.

The earliest Eurasian pastoral societies appear to have been less "purely" nomadic than some of the later societies for which we have historical records. The first detailed accounts of a mobile steppe society are ancient Greek descriptions of the Scythians. Herodotus describes a stratified polity with the ruling strata, the Royal Scythians, "who deem all other Scythians their slaves [*douloi*]." These slaves or subjects included numerous agriculturalists, some of whom are described as distinct subject peoples and some simply as "Scythian tillers of the land, who sow corn not for eating but for selling" (Godley 2000, 219). The Scythian ruling aristocracy controlled much of the southern Russian steppe in the eighth to third centuries B.C.E.[1] In describing Scythian "society"—that is, the politically defined social entity ruled by Scythians—it is clear that it included subjects engaged in both agricultural and pastoral livelihoods.

The Greek conception of the "nomad" (the term meaning those who pasture livestock), did not associate it with an earlier or more primitive way of life. Indeed, Herodotus (4.46) describes mobile pastoralism in terms of discovery and innovation.

> But the Scythian race has in the matter of which of all human affairs is of the greatest import made the cleverest discovery that we know. . . . For when men have no established cities or fortresses, but all are house-bearers and mounted archers, living not by tilling the soil but by cattle-rearing and carrying their dwellings on wagons, how should these not be invincible and unapproachable?
>
> (GODLEY 2000, 247)

This was not an ecological adaptation to allow bare survival in a harsh environment, as imagined by Toynbee. For Herodotus, mobile pastoralism was a political and military development that allowed invincibility in war, and it was simply facilitated by the environment. As Herodotus (4.47) puts it: "This invention they have made in a land which suits their purpose . . . " (Godley 2000, 247).

The Scythians bore very little resemblance to the stereotype of tribal nomadic society that became so widespread in the twentieth century. The Scythian kings were enormously powerful monarchs, deeply embroiled in courtly politics with neighboring polities such as the Greek city-states. Some, such as King Scyles, could certainly read and speak Greek (Herod.

4.78; Godley 2000, 279). The wealth and power of Scythian rulers is evident from the archaeological excavations of their huge "kurgan" burial mounds, such as the Chertomlyk mortuary complex on the Dniepr, which includes hundreds of solid gold plaques, vessels, and works of art in such abundance as to rival the tomb of any great monarch of antiquity.[2] Their kingdom was subject to systematic administration and is described by Herodotus as divided into pasture districts (*nomoi*) ruled by governors (*nomarches*). These districts were grouped into provinces or "governments" (*archai*) under the central authority of the Scythian king and are described using the same terms as those applied to Greek and other sedentary states (Herod. 4.62, 4.66; Godley 2000, 261, 265).

But the Scythians were not allowed to challenge the notion of the essential nomad. The sophistication of their monarchs was explained away as a result of Greek and Assyrian influence, and since they ruled agriculturalists, they were thought of as deviating from the "pure" nomadic form. Indeed, the nineteenth-century notion of nomadism as an early evolutionary stage, arrested and "outside history," was given powerful new impetus by Soviet ethnographers working within an explicitly evolutionist Marxist tradition.

SOVIET ETHNOGRAPHY AND
THE NOMADIC FEUDALISM DEBATE

In Soviet scholarship, Marx's five stages of history (primitive communism, slave-owning society, feudalism, capitalism, socialism) were taken as axiomatic, and a key problem seemed to be how to classify pastoral nomads in these terms. It was clear from the outset that they were not primitive communists—there were marked differences in wealth and status among pastoralists, and they were ruled by monarchs and often had slaves. Vladimirtsov, the great Russian scholar of Mongolia, set out his views in his book *Social Order of the Mongols: Nomadic Mongol Feudalism*,[3] published posthumously in 1934. Although completed in the Soviet era and entirely compatible with Marxist typology, this was not a doctrinaire Marxist work. It was largely the result of prerevolutionary scholarship and represented the first comprehensive study of relations between social strata in the Mongol world. For Vladimirtsov, the resemblance between European and Mongol aristocracy was quite sufficient for the term "feudalism" to be applied to both, although in the Mongol case it had a particular "nomadic" form. Since the Kyrgyz, Kazakh, and other steppe peoples also had aristocracies, the notion of "nomadic feudalism" also seemed a fair description of their political structures. In the same year as the publication of Vladimirtsov's work, another Soviet scholar, Tolstov, published an article on "the genesis of feudalism in pastoral nomadic societies," in which he applied the notion more widely.

But there was some reluctance to abandon the Engelian evolutionary scheme and allow nomads to "catch up" entirely with agricultural aristocracies. It was clear that pastoral nomads were ruled by aristocrats, but were these noble ruling kinship societies composed of clansmen, or feudal societies composed of rent-yielding serfs? The classification of societies within the Soviet Union had important political implications at the time, since the Kazakhs and Kirghiz were undergoing the wholesale social engineering project of Stalin's collectivization drive. Gellner (1988, 99), in his summary of the debate, quotes Tolstov on this point:

> This problem is by no means of academic significance ... its solution allows us to sharpen our weapon of a correct Marxist understanding ... it is relevant to the immediate practice of the political struggle, the practice of class war both in the Soviet East and abroad, in the colonial Orient ... the correctness of the practical work of the socialist reconstruction of the nomadic and semi-nomadic *aul* [residential group] of the Soviet East depends on the correct theoretical solution of this problem.

As colonial subjects, pastoralists within the tsarist empire had been governed in administrative "clans" (*rod*) and thus could be rather easily represented as not having quite passed the stage of kinship society. So Tolstov (1934) described the Kazakhs as being only in the early stage of nomadic feudalism, having retained remnants of a kin-based society. Viatkin (1947) invoked the ultimate Soviet authority on this matter, noting that Stalin had described the pastoral nations of the USSR as "patriarchal-feudal." The solution was, then, to class them halfway between kin-based patriarchal society and feudalism, and this typology was widely used by Soviet scholars such as Potapov (1954).

However, some went further than this. In the post-Stalinist era it became possible to tentatively question the universal applicability of Marx's five-step scheme for historical development (Bold 2001, 16).[4] Tolybekov developed the view that as a form of tribal, kinship society, pastoral nomadism could not possibly generate the class society required for feudalism.

This was hardly a break from the Marxist canon, however. Tolybekov followed Engels directly in holding that nomads were not capable of social development. As Gellner (1988, 106) puts it, nomadism "constitutes a sociological cul-de-sac, or, to use the expressive Russian word, a *tupik*."

Markov followed Tolybekov in treating pastoralism as a sort of simple, natural economy of subsistence. He quotes Marx in commenting on the nomad's lack of technical progress (Markov 1976, 285) and argues that such societies could only develop under the influence of neighboring sedentary societies, such as Russia. He was somewhat less categorical than his mentor; as Gellner (1984, xxiv) puts it: "Whereas Tolybekov asserts with firmness, and perhaps a touch of bitterness, that nomads *could not* develop further than they did, Markov contents himself with asserting that they *did not*." But his conclusions were the same: "nomads were not feudal in the full sense of the term, but were located only in the transition to a feudal state" (Markov 1976, 293). Both argued for what Gellner (1983a, xxii) describes as "recognition of the basically stagnant or oscillating nature of pastoral nomadic society."[5] Elements of feudalism might appear, but they could not be the product of internal social development, only the result of colonizing forces. The progressive development of nomads required their sedentarization (Markov 1976, 287).

For a number of reasons, Western scholars such as Gellner found the Tolybekov-Markov position much more attractive than the Vladimirtsov-Potapov one. First, it seemed to correspond better to the generalizations being made regarding pastoral societies by structural-functionalist anthropologists in the West. Second, the debate seemed to reflect cold war politics. Potapov and other defenders of the nomadic feudalism thesis could be pictured as apologists for the Stalinist liquidation of the Kazakh and Kirghiz elites on the grounds that they were indeed a feudal ruling class, while Tolybekov and the advocates of the kinship society model appeared as their courageous opponents, reaching beyond the confines of narrow Marxist scholarship to show that no such exploiting class could have existed. Gellner (1988, 104) speculates on the possible subversive effect of such a finding: "One can imagine a Kazakh herdsman in his pastoral collective, scratching his ear with a bit of stubble . . . wondering 'Now if we Kazakhs really had no classes to speak of before the revolution, who exactly was it that we liquidated during the recent decades?' "[6]

But in fact, both sides of "the feudalism debate" wrote in a solidly Soviet mode. Tolybekov (1971, 232), for example, made a point of citing Lenin in his argument and accused Vladimirtsov of reproducing Dühring's "reactionary" theory of force (*nasiliya*) in putting the case for nomadic feudalism (Tolybekov 1971, 224). Dühring had argued that political power precedes the economic relations of exploitation and produces them (as Clastres 1977 does), and he had been criticized at length for this by Engels in his 1877 work *Anti-Dühring*. Vladimirtsov, it seemed, had made the error of implying that the coercive power of the Mongol nobility had given rise to the economic exploitation of their subjects, whereas a more proper Marxist reading revealed this to be incorrect. So Tolybekov rejects Vladimirtsov's notion of nomadic feudalism on general theoretical grounds, citing examples from Aztec Mexico and the Peruvian Inca to argue that since nomads had an even less developed means of production, they could not have had a form of property rights over land that qualified for the Marxist definition of feudalism (Tolybekov 1971, 216–218). In the end, Tolybekov's position is that feudalism is a category only properly applied to sedentary societies (Markov 1976, 292).

In general, it seems that Vladimirtsov's critics were more influenced by Marxist and Leninist theory than Vladimirtsov himself, who had done much of his work in the pre-Soviet era. Neither were Tolybekov and Markov's views any more potentially subversive of Soviet policy. If Vladimirtsov's notion of nomadic feudalism could be used to justify the Stalinist liquidation of the Kazakh elite, the implications of the Tolybekov-Markov position was that the huge Soviet sedentarization and collectivization programs were necessary, since without settlement the "nomads" could not develop further.

Indeed, the critique of Vladimirtsov depended on a rather particular Marxist definition of feudalism, by which exploitation takes the form of rent on land, the ownership of which is monopolized by the ruling class (Vainshtein 1980, 233–234). While there was no doubt that Kazakh, Kyrgyz, and Mongol nobles controlled land, sometimes reserving amounts of prime pastureland for their exclusive use (Abramzon 1971, 157; Khasanov 1968, 11, 124; Sneath 2000, 36), there was sufficiently patchy historical evidence concerning their rights over land for Tolybekov and Markov to argue that in their "pure" state nomads could not possibly have properly "feudal land relations." What evidence there was for such relations was explained away as either a result of impositions by the tsarist administration or, in the case of indisputably indigenous institutions, as temporary devices superimposed on kinship society in the interests of military centralization. Gellner (1983a, xxiii) summarizes the position: "Inequality amongst nomads is not very great, and when it does emerge, is a consequence of war and trading rather than the normal functioning of the economy, within which leaders, members of the privileged stratum, have no interest in depriving their fellow tribesmen of access to the means of production." While granting that the role of "chiefs" could be considerable, in "temporary military and imperial situations," the argument went: "the leaders did not form a closed stratum and did not retain stratum privileges when they lost their leading position. The kinsmen of Ghengiz Khan did have a few privileges, but it did not amount to much. Members of the white bone amongst the Kazakhs (supposedly kinsmen of Ghengiz Khan) had no great power, even if they attained chiefly status" (Gellner 1983a, xxiv).

It is a tribute to the influence of the egalitarian nomad model that such astoundingly counterfactual statements could seem so plausible. The Chinggisid aristocracy, both the Mongol Borjigin and the Kazakh Aq Süyek, not only monopolized high office, but they existed in an entirely different political and legal category from their common subjects. Although not all the Borjigid were able to rule appanages or hold imperial offices, for example, all members of the nobility remained partners in the project of government, exempt from corvée service and taxes and subject to fewer laws and much lighter punishments. Similarly, without the notion of a timeless subsistence nomadism it would be difficult to conceive of a "normal" functioning of society that excluded such fundamental activities as trade and war. The ample evidence of stratification and marked differences in wealth and power within pastoral steppe societies could always be explained away as a result of contact with sedentary societies, particularly as most written accounts of steppe societies dated from periods of intensive engagement.

Gellner (1983a, xv, original emphasis), for example, concedes that:

Mongols appear subject to complex nuances of unsymmetrical rights and duties between various ranked layers of the population, in a manner which certainly suggests a "feudal" society. . . . The leaders of the decimally organized military units had to be located in prescribed places so that the Emperor could mobilize them, and the ordinary Mongol in turn had to graze his flocks in the area assigned to his superior military officer. This can be made to look like the granting of land in return for military service. In general the central charge that can be levied against the feudalizing thesis is that it takes its evidence from the periods when either the Mongols were conquer*ing*, or when they were conquer*ed* and incorporated in the Manchu empire.

But even if they were intellectually sustainable, Gellner's excuses are historically unconvincing, since for much of their history, and certainly from the thirteenth to the twentieth centuries, most steppe polities were engaged in some sort of conquest or had become subject to one or another imperial power. The documents that do survive from periods such as the mid-sixteenth century, in which the Chinggisids reached an accommodation with their rivals the Oirats, suggest that aristocratic privileges were as strong as ever at that time.

Nevertheless, following Tolybekov and Markov, Khazanov also conceives of feudalism as based upon the differential relations of social strata to the means of production. So, he argues, the Chinggisid polity was "not nomadic feudalism . . . but a society of another type. In this society the main differences between the different strata and classes consisted not in their relation to key resources, but in their relation to power and government. Those direct obligations which rulers imposed on the ruled were not the cause but the consequence of the emergence of the rulers" Khazanov (1983a, 240).

However, non-Marxist characterizations of feudalism are more inclusive and much less exclusively concerned with rights over some notional productive base.[7] Weber applied the term rather broadly to non-European contexts, including Japan, Turkey, and Russia. He identifies the key characteristics to be the division between commoners and nobility, enfiefment, and a political system that tied commoners to land administered by the enfiefed lord (Weber 1923, 61).[8] Following Weber, Gellner (1981, 187–188) suggests that the essential characteristic of feudalism is a hierarchical, stable power structure supporting an enfiefed aristocracy through the corvée labor of their subjects—a description that would fit the Mongol case rather well.[9]

Indeed, even Marx did not define feudalism solely in terms of class control of resources. He writes, "feudal organisation was . . . an association against a subjected producing class. . . . Labour is here again the chief thing, power *over* individuals" (Marx 1964, 125–127). It was not simply the relation to key resources that characterized a feudal ruling class, but their relation to coercive powers over people. Khazanov's characterization of the Chinggisid polity does not seem so incompatible with this conception of feudalism.[10]

But, in general, there was little attempt to really consider the applicability of the term "feudalism" seriously, since nomadic society seemed bound to be based on clans and tribes. Some charismatic leader might establish a temporary dominion over them by conquest, but this would be unstable. The notion of an imperial structure imposed on kinship communities seemed entirely plausible; after all, this was the essence of Marx's notion of the Asiatic Mode of Production, except in that model the structure was stable to the point of ossification, whereas for "nomads" it was thought of as fragile and temporary.

In retrospect, the feudalism debate in the Soviet literature largely reflected the limitations of the nineteenth-century evolutionist categories for social types that it had inherited. Lattimore (1962, 546–550) noted the peculiarly narrow Soviet definition of feudalism and rejected it on the grounds that its advocates "are so much obsessed with . . . asserting *a priori* that land is the determining kind of feudal property, that they neglect the significance of mobile four-footed property." He writes, "there are those who hesitate to call the Mongolian social order 'feudal,' but I do not see how the term can be avoided: aristocratic rank was hereditary and identified with territorial fiefs, and serfdom was also hereditary and territorially identified" (Lattimore 1976, 3).[11]

In part, Lattimore's view reflected that of indigenous Mongolian historians who affirmed the use of the term "feudalism" to describe the aristocratic order, particularly from the sixteenth century onward. Natsagdorj (1967, 1978) and Sanjdorj (1980), for example, argued that the means of production should be seen as the combination of both livestock and pastureland, and in this case there was little doubt that the aristocracy's rights over the "means of production" matched those required by the Marxist notion of feudalism. Sanjdorj (1980, 1), for example, writes: "In the sixteenth and seventeenth centuries . . . Mongolia was a nation where feudal relationships were strong and highly developed. The land—the most important tool for production—was the property of the feudal classes. . . . Ownership of livestock, which was an important asset in the livelihood of the herdsmen, became, together with the land, the economic basis for political rule." The general Marxist evolutionary scheme remained dominant for historians in both the Soviet- and Chinese-controlled regions of Mongolia. This was reconciled with the historical evidence by pushing the "prefeudal" period back to before the Chinggisid period—when the lack of historical materials allows fairly free speculation as to what society was like. The Inner Mongolian historian Rinchin (2001 [1977]), for example, provides a variant of the standard Marxist narrative in which early Mongol society begins as a primitive communist kinship society, but this is taken to have broken down before the historical period, as feudal relations developed.[12] Similarly, Zhou Qingshu (2001, 8) the Chinese historian of the Yüan, reproduces Marx's evolutionary stages and locates the emergence of feudal relations among the Mongols at some point before the thirteenth century.[13]

More recently, however, Mongolian historians such as Bold (1992, 2001) have questioned the applicability of the term "feudalism" in the wake of the collapse of Marxist intellectual hegemony. "The concept of feudalism was formulated on the basis of an assumed universality of the special economic, political and social system that was created by the resolution of the contradictions of Byzantine and some European peoples" (Bold 2001, 24). In this view, there is simply no need to force Mongolian history into the Marxist model of feudalism or some other supposed historical stage.

THE CURIOUS CASE OF MILITARY DEMOCRACY

Soviet ethnography revived another nineteenth-century concept to try to classify the nomads—the notion of "military democracy." As Markov (1976, 307) put it, since "Marxist theory helps clarify the characteristics of nomadic social relations," it should guide us in selecting a suitable category for the nomad political form. Military democracy, he explains, was an epoch in which clan relations had broken down but true class relations had not yet developed. In view of the famous egalitarian and warlike qualities of nomads, this must have been their basic political organization. The influence of this argument can be seen in the work of a number of authors (e.g., Bold 2001, 83).

Military democracy was another Morganian notion that was adopted by Engels and passed into the lexicon of Marxist evolutionism. Morgan first used the term in *Ancient Society* (1964 [1877]) to describe a form of political organization that lay somewhere between kin-based society and the state. Appropriately enough, it was a concept that Morgan used to try to explain away the importance of hereditary power in ancient Greek society.

As noted in chapter 2, the problem for Morgan was that one of the earliest terms for a group of people, the *phyle* (translated as "tribe" and thought by Morgan to be made up of *gens*—"clans"), was ruled by a *basileus*—a "king." This was a grave difficulty for Morgan's scheme, in which early social organization ought to be based on egalitarian kinship relations. On these grounds, Morgan rejected the translation of *basileus* as "king" for this early period, arguing that at that time the term meant a "general military commander" (Morgan 1964 [1877], 210), who must have been elected, or at least confirmed in office, by the people. In this he differed even from Grote, his main source for speculation on ancient Hellenic civilization, whom he accuses with monarchical bias (Morgan 1964 [1877], 214). Rather than kingdoms or princedoms, then, "basileia may be defined as a military democracy, the people being free. . . . The basileus was their general, holding the highest, the most influential and the most important office known to them" (Morgan 1964 [1877], 215).

Needless to say, this view is not taken seriously by classical historians, but it was retained in the Marxist canon to be taken up by Markov to solve the same dilemma that Morgan faced: how to explain away institutions of lordship among peoples supposed to be egalitarian. As representatives of prestate society, fierce and free nomads must have chosen their chiefs for success in war, the argument went, and this might *look* like institutions of hereditary lordship from the outside, but the wider study of kinship organization and political evolution teaches us that they must *really* have been "first among equals." This was entirely plausible for many anthropologists trained in the West.

STRUCTURAL FUNCTIONALISM AND THE SEGMENTARY KINSHIP MODEL

In Western anthropology, the Morganian tradition lived on in the lineage theory of Fortes and Evans-Pritchard. The publication of *African Political Systems* in 1940 laid out the new manifesto of the structural-functionalist school. Inspired by Weberian sociology, Fortes and Evans-Pritchard sought to present a typology of African systems of government that would cover the range of political forms described by ethnographers. Fortes and Evans-Pritchard took as axiomatic the nineteenth-century characterization of prestate society as organized by kinship, and state society as organized by territory, and cite Maine as an authority on this point (Fortes and

Evans-Pritchard 1940, 10). They used these principles to divide the African polities they surveyed into two types, group A and group B, which they described as "organised on totally different principles." Group A contained "primitive states," in which society must be organized by territory, since "the head of state is a territorial ruler." The other group, B, were nonstate societies based upon "the segmentary system of permanent, unilineal descent groups." In segmentary lineage societies, they explained, there were "no sharp divisions of rank, status or wealth" (Fortes and Evans-Pritchard 1940, 5–10).

The model had never seemed very convincing to some Africanist anthropologists, including Audrey Richards, who in her review of *The Nuer* pointed out that in her experience, "nothing is more remarkable than the lack of permanence of particular lineages or 'segments'" (Richards 1941, 51; cited in Kuper 1988, 196). Nevertheless, the model was widely taken up for application elsewhere, particularly in the case of pastoral nomadic societies, as it seemed as if such societies must face the problem of organizing themselves in the absence of the territorial state, a problem for which segmentary opposition had been offered as the solution. In retrospect, this seems strange, since Fortes and Evans-Pritchard (1940, 8) had themselves warned that "mode of livelihood" did "not determine differences in political structure." Still, the model seemed well founded on African anthropology, and since it was still assumed that in societies without states kinship must form the basis of political organization, it was logical to suppose that something like the segmentary kinship system would be common among "nomadic tribes." This seemed to be confirmed by studies of Bedouin Arabs such as the Al Murrah (Cole 1975) and Rwala (Lancaster 1981), which suggested that the segmentary model was, if not a perfect fit, then at least a useful guideline for understanding these societies.

There were good reasons, however, for the apparent applicability of the segmentary kinship model to Middle Eastern pastoral society. Evans-Pritchard's original model of segmentary kinship society was itself derived from theories of Arab society put forward by Robertson Smith in the nineteenth century. Evans-Pritchard admitted as much: "It was reading Robertson Smith's writing [on the Arabs] that first made clear to me the kinship and political systems of the Nilotic Nuer" (Evans Pritchard 1938, 123; cited in Dresch 1988, 63).

Robertson Smith attempted to reconstruct the social structure of early Arabia based on historical sources, and he proposed a scheme in which social and political units were defined by patrilineal descent and connected by principles of genealogical segmentation in which the same organizing principle was used for successively larger units. Smith also stressed the importance of blood feud in uniting and dividing different segments.

However, as Dresch (1988, 53) notes, the grand segmentary Arab genealogy that Smith describes was a product of a political project undertaken in the mid-eighth century, about a century after the Prophet's death and a long time after most of the ancestral figures included in it had passed away. Smith (1885, 5–6; cited in Dresch 1988, 53) writes:

> The elaboration of this genealogical scheme . . . is probably connected . . . with the system of registers introduced by the Caliph Omar I for the control of the pensions and pay distributed among believers from the spoil of the infidel. The pension system, as Sprenger has explained at length, afforded a direct stimulus to genealogical research, and also, it must be added, to genealogical fiction, while the vast registers connected with it afforded the genealogists an opportunity, which certainly never existed before, to embrace in one scheme the relations of a great circle of Arab kindreds.

As Dresch points out, this was a state system of entitlements, now organized using the principles of descent. "The first segmentary, total genealogy, whose form was later taken as typical of certain 'stateless' societies, was thus the product of a growing state" (Dresch 1988, 53). As in the ancient Greek, Chinese, Manchu, and Korean cases, kinship structures once taken as original "traditional" political forms appeared as products of particular historical circumstances and are linked, in each case, to the expanding state.

NOMADIC PASTORALISM AS AN IDEAL TYPE

The explicit model of pastoral nomadic society as an ideal type emerged as part of a wider interest in typology in the social sciences: the identification and sorting of societies into evolutionary stages or structural forms. The notion of a pastoral nomadic social type was understandably popular among those who studied eligible societies. Their work not only offered understandings of the society in question, but it became widely applicable and promised insights into the nature of pastoral nomadic society as a general form.

In this model, the social type was defined by its putative productive base. Goldschmidt (1979, 15), who proposed a general model for pastoral social systems, describes "a class of societies categorized on the basis of their productive technology. Essential to this productive technology are two elements: the attendance upon and husbandry of ruminant animals (hence pastoralism), and the utilization of natural grasses as fodder (hence nomadism)." This creates "certain degrees of homogeneity in the general character of the societies." The result was a model of a rather classical structural-functionalist form, whereby a table of characteristics was drawn up (see Goldschmidt 1979,19), including a head-spinning kaleidoscope of different features extracted from their proper contexts and presented in tabulated form. Under the subheading "social nexuses," for example, we are given "segmented patrilineages (Obok) [*obog*], age-sets, stock linkages, inheritance, brideprice, wergeld, clientship, dydadic contracts." From these were distilled general features such as, in the case of this set, the terms "patrikin" and "contractual."[14] Although it is sometimes unclear how these characterizations were arrived at (it is difficult to conceive of a contractual age-set, for example, and many mobile pastoralists are matrilineal), the intention was to outline general trends that might reveal social adaptations generated by this particular means of livelihood.[15]

Central to this characterization was the persistent notion of the egalitarian nomad. When Irons (1979, 362) stated, "among pastoral nomadic societies, hierarchical political institutions are generated only by external political relations with state societies, and never develop purely as a result of the internal dynamics of such societies," he was simply making explicit the implicit characteristics that both structural-functionalist and Soviet anthropology had already attached to the ideal type and which reflected the longstanding stereotypes of the "fierce and free" pastoralist. He offers this as a hypothesis for testing, but since all pastoralists have had some sort of contact with "state societies," it is difficult to see how this could really have been done.

Many arguments were put forward to explain why nomads ought to be egalitarian. Some declared that the ecological constraints of pastoralism did not allow for the accumulation of wealth needed for hierarchical strata to develop. In the case of the East African Boran, for example, the simple technology, the risks to livestock, and the maximum size of a herd provided "limits to the possible accumulation of wealth and obstacles to the transmission of undivided wealth over generations. These obstacles lie in the pastoral dependence on household labour and the need to disperse animals geographically" (Dahl 1979, 279). Huge herds, the argument went, were not ecologically viable in the semiarid climates of the nomads, and there was a limit to how many livestock even an extended family group could herd. Instead, redistributive mechanisms would tend to spread animals out between households, offering long-term security to nomadic families in the face of herd loss. Although in retrospect it might seem strange to assume that ownership among pastoralists would be limited by the size of herds kept by domestic groups, the assumption was that as nonstate "tribal" societies, nomads could not have the sort of wider property relations thought to be characteristic of states. Any ownership beyond a household's personal control must be somehow conditional, a potential "redistributive mechanism" that might end up transferring herd wealth to those less well off.

Others emphasized the political, rather than economic, constraints generated by mobility. Burnham (1979), for example, argued that rights over people and objects are weaker, and institutions for dispute settlement less elaborate, when people can use mobility to avoid trouble or oppression. Mobility, then, is cast as a political mechanism that inhibits centralization and class stratification, and for this reason nomads tend to retain it even when faced with state sedentarization schemes. Although Burnham's ethnographic experience was in Africa, where this argument might be convincing, rather than in Eurasia or the Middle East, this analysis was taken as applicable to pastoral nomads as a general type.

Irons uses a loosely functionalist approach, mixing environmental determinism with a sort of political utilitarianism to explain the model of the egalitarian nomad.[16] "Under the conditions of low population density and high mobility characteristic of pastoral societies, segmentary lineage societies represents a better solution to the need to organise large political units than do stratified forms of organisation" (Irons 1979, 369). Hierarchy was self-evidently a necessary evil, the argument went, which would only develop if the society as a whole had some sort of need for it. Since in this perspective political office was a solution to the social problems of dispute settlement and defense, the proper question was: how could nomads get what they needed with a minimum of government? Segmentary lineage systems, it was supposed, offered an alternative method of conflict resolution, removing the need for "chiefly" office, so for "pastoral nomads, who need only form large groups temporarily for military purposes, such a segmentary lineage system is ideal" (Irons 1979, 369). The analysts began by attempting to deduce the "needs" of the social organism, and it is taken for granted that political forms represent some sort of optimal adaptation to the perceived needs of the collectivity. Historical events have no real place in this sort of analysis, and neither does the idea that stratification might, for some, be an end in itself. Instead, it seems as if the nature of society can be divined through reasoning from some sort of social "first principles." Salzman (1979, 441), for example, advances a similar sort of thought experiment. "The greater the dependence upon pastoral resources and the less upon agricultural resources, the more likely that the means of production will be distributed throughout the society, and the less hierarchical and oppressive the society is likely to be."

Of the fourteen pastoral societies Tapper surveyed by 1979, almost all of them deviated from the segmentary lineage model in some significant way (see Tapper 1979, 49–58). Either they were too hierarchical with hereditary rulers (as in the cases the Shahsevan of Azerbaijan, the Pashtuns of Afghanistan, the Kababish and Rufa'a Hoi of Sudan, the Jaf Kurds, the Bakhtiari and Qashqai of Iran, and the Al Murrah and Shammar Bedouin), or their residential and territorial divisions did not seem to be clearly based on lineages (such as the Humr Baggara of Sudan), or the political units did not seem to operate according to the principles of segmentary opposition (as in the case of the Saadi Bedouin and the Basseri of Fars). About the only society that appeared to match the model reasonably well was the Yomut Turkmen studied by Irons (1975).

By the 1970s, the ideal type of a segmentary, egalitarian pastoral nomadic society began to draw criticism on both theoretical and empirical grounds. Telal Asad found that the notion of the egalitarian nomad contradicted his own ethnographic experience. His 1970 study of the Kababish Arabs showed clear hierarchy and hereditary rulers, and he formulated a Marxian critique of both nomadic pastoralism as an ideal type and the notion that pastoralists tended to be egalitarian:

> The assumption seems to be that inegalitarian nomadic societies represent a deviation from the norm. Such deviations are usually explained in two ways: it is proposed that certain processes essential to the structure and functioning of pastoral nomadic systems have been blocked or distorted (due to internal or external pressures); or it is pointed out that the society in question is not a pure pastoral nomadic society (i.e. because it is not subject

to a purely pastoral regime, but combines sedentary practices and institutions). . . . Are we justified in talking about "pastoral nomads" in this way? Could we not consider political and economic inequality among sedentary populations as being due to the fact that processes essential to the operation of sedentary cultivating societies are blocked or distorted by internal developments or external events? Indeed, this is precisely what people who have adopted Chayanov's theory of "the peasant economy" do argue. The important economic point about nomads, surely, is not that they move about in order to care for their animals, or that animal husbandry is subject to a range of biological and environmental constraints, but that their political and economic organization may be based primarily on production for subsistence. Modern ranchers also live by animal husbandry and move about to care for their herds, but they are structurally in the same category as farmers who employ wage labor and produce commodities for the market. On the same principle, free peasants applying family labor to land primarily for subsistence, selling only a small portion of their produce in order to buy consumption goods, and yielding up another portion to the state in the form of tax, are in the same category as pastoral nomads who do the same. An undue concern with rehearsing the biological and environmental constraints of animal husbandry not only fails to tell us anything about such crucial differences and similarities; it also gives the misleading impression that technique in the narrow sense is an independent variable, always determining and never determined by social relations in the development of social formations.

(ASAD 1979, 419–420)

In drawing attention to the political economy within which pastoralism is found, Asad pointed to the way that classical treatments have tended to offer depoliticized accounts of pastoral societies: they are represented as "natural" in that their principal constraints are environmental and demographic. Rather than discrete social systems, Asad argued, pastoral nomads lived as part of wider "total systems" that include agricultural, urban, and pastoral sectors, within which they can be seen as analogous to a class.[17] Since the wider system within which pastoral nomads exist and reproduce themselves varies radically in space and time, there cannot be an essential pastoral society.

The more anthropologists studied societies they designated "pastoral nomadic," the more clear it became that they were diverse and different.

That they all happened to employ mobility in raising livestock simply reflected the grounds for their inclusion in the category and implied very little about their wider social orders. Reindeer-herding peoples such as the Evenki of the Siberian taiga, for example, had been subject to Russian colonial and state administration since the eighteenth century; though herders of single-species herds of reindeer through forests, they have long relied on the fur trade to supplement their income (Vitebsky 2005; Anderson 2002; Ssorin-Chaikov 2003). Socially and economically, they have very little in common with the equestrian pastoralists of Mongolia, with their long history of indigenous statehood and a range of movement techniques for raising sheep, goats, cattle, horses, and camels and yaks in some regions. Apart from herding some of the same livestock and employing mobility, Mongolians have very little in common with the village-based Hindu pastoralists such as the Raika, who cultivate crops but also engage in some specialist mobile herding of livestock such as camels along clearly demarcated routes between other agricultural areas. The Raika also form an integral part of the wider Hindu society of Rajasthan (Ikeya 2005). None of these "pastoral societies" have much in common with the now largely motorized sheep- and camel-oriented pastoralists of Islamic Bedouin societies such as the Harasiis of central Oman, who employ movement between widely spaced water sources in almost continuous trade relations with oasis settlements (Chatty 1996, 87). These forms of livelihood are clearly very different again from the cattle-oriented pastoralism of East Africa, the Nuer, Karamojong, Dodoth, and Jie, for example, who mostly live in homesteads raising crops but move their cattle out to cattle camps in the dry season (Evans-Pritchard 1940; Hutchinson 1996; Baker 1975). Each of these nominally pastoral peoples were clearly so different, even with respect to their employment of mobility as a technique for raising livestock, that at the very least they had to be classified as subtypes of the broader pastoral nomadic type (Khazanov 1983, 40–69).

But the ideal type itself became increasingly implausible, as noted by Dyson-Hudson and Dyson-Hudson (1980, 116–117):

> Recent studies clearly demonstrate that among groups who are principally dependent on livestock, and for whom spatial mobility is regularly employed as a survival strategy, there is an enormous variability in herd management strategies, in social organization, in land tenure, degree of dependence on

agricultural products, interactions with outside groups, differentiation of tasks by sex and age, etc.

As Spooner (1973, 3) acknowledges: "there are no features of cultural or social organisation that are common to all nomads or even that are found exclusively among nomads." By the 1970s, the notion of "pastoral nomadism" as an ideal type had been all but abandoned by anthropological specialists. Dyson-Hudson and Dyson-Hudson (1980, 55) remark:

> Most of the anthropologists writing during the 1970s apparently are no longer constrained by the romantic stereotype of the "pastoral nomad." Although the phrase "nomadic pastoralists" was often used in titles of recent studies of people who depend on livestock and use mobility as an adaptive strategy, these then proceeded to analyze some aspect of a particular livestock herding system, or a group of such systems, without any attempt to apply "nomadic pastoralism" as an analytic category. . . . If this trend continues, in 1990 it will not be possible to write a review on "pastoral nomads," not because all "nomads" have disappeared, not because all livestock herders have become sedentary, but rather because anthropologists during the 1980s will increasingly recognize the value of focusing on variables rather than types. . . . The typology "nomadic pastoralism" which locks together livestock herding and mobility into a single arbitrary category will then cease to define a subject suitable for review.

The Dyson-Hudsons were largely correct in their prediction. Ingold (1980, 228) went on to argue, like Asad, that pastoralism should be treated as a mode of production rather than as a social type. The new consensus, as Galaty (1981, 19) expressed it, was to reject the assumption that "the conceptual ideal types of 'nomadism' and 'pastoralism' converge and characterize whole societies,"[18] and where the substitute term "mobile pastoralism" was used typographically, it was usually treated only as a regional type, as Chatty (1996) does in her treatment of Arabian mobile pastoralists.

The model may have been sunk, but its wreck continued to pose the risk of entanglement for those attempting to navigate the waters of pastoralist studies. A particularly enduring piece of the original structure repeatedly resurfaced. As Asad (1979, 421) had put it, "the idea has somehow persisted among anthropologists that the segmentary lineage system is particularly identified with 'nomadic society,' and that it constitutes the principle at once of integration and of equalization in such societies." So while Roy

Ellen (1994, 212) concedes that "no one social form is common to all pastoral nomadic peoples," he goes on to write, "socio-political organisation is usually agnatic, segmentary and acephalous; it is focused on the lineage and quintessentially tribal."

And since the critiques of the segmentary kinship–egalitarian nomad model were largely concerned with contemporary societies, their observations had rather little effect on historical representations of pastoral societies—particularly those of the Eurasian steppe—taken to be the heartland of the archetypal nomadic society. Thus Barfield (1989, 24–26) remarks that "pastoralists shared similar principles of organization alien to sedentary societies" and "tribal political and social organization was based on a model of nested kinship groups." Indeed Geiss (2003, 22–23) explicitly applies the Fortes and Evans-Pritchard model of segmentary lineages to "tribal" Central Asia as characteristic of "acephalous political communities."

So although it became accepted that the segmentary lineage model might not hold for all pastoral nomadic societies everywhere, it seemed at least a good description of some, such as the Yomut (Iomut) Turkmen studied by Irons (1975), and these "good examples" represented rare survivals of precolonial forms of social organization. Irons's ethnography is held up by Salzman (1999, 5) and Geiss (2003, 4) as a rare and valuable study of traditionally egalitarian and "acephalous" Turko-Mongol pastoralists. Geiss explains: "Since a significant amount of retribalization occurred, after Riza Shah's (1825–41) centralisation policy had declined in the 1940s, Irons was still able to observe some independent tribes in the Gurgan plain in the 1960s." Although there had been a century of Iranian state administration before the 1940s, such was the appetite to describe the nomadic tribe in its pristine state that this history was rather wished away: administrative changes must have been turned back by "retribalization" (Geiss 2003, 62).

Khazanov (1983, 175) also presents the Turkmen as the least hierarchical and least centralized Eurasian nomads:

> In some areas where the Turkmen lived large subdivisions had no permanent leaders at all, in other areas there were chiefs without any permanent real power. In the words of one observer of the Yomuts living near the Caspian Sea: "Anyone with a little extra wealth calls himself a khan" (Galkin 1867, 31). Amongst some groups the elevation of separate lineages was ob-

served and sometimes a title was handed on by succession; but all of this was only temporary.

One might wonder, in passing, how permanent the Turkmen leadership could be expected to be, given their tumultuous situation at the time of Galkin's account—sandwiched between Persia and an expanding tsarist empire. But in any case, it seemed that the Yomut Turkmen represented the closest match to the ideal typical model of the nomadic tribe that ethnographers of Eurasia could find.

THE TURKMEN:
REEXAMINING THE TRADITIONAL, SEGMENTARY TRIBE

Irons was writing in the heyday of descent theory and he made it clear that he saw his task as an anthropologist was to understand "the role of kinship in organizing human social relationships" (Irons 1975, 1). At the time of his study, there were about 140,000 Yomut Turkmen living in the Gurgan Plain, on the Iranian side of the international border with the USSR, to the east of the Caspian Sea. About ten thousand of these people were pastoralists, herding mostly sheep and goats, as well as some horses, camels, and cattle, with agriculture and carpet weaving as secondary sources of income. These pastoralists were administered by the Iranian state, but, Irons stressed, they had retained much of their traditional political structures, and this is what really interested him as an ethnographer.[19] However, the Yomut had experienced a good deal of change in the twentieth century, having largely fled to the USSR to avoid the control of Reza Shah's Iran in 1920s and then having fled back into Iran to escape Soviet collectivization in the 1930s. There they had then become tenants of the king and subject to compulsory sedentarization campaigns. After an interregnum during the Soviet occupation of northern Iran in 1941 through 1946, they had become once again subject to systematic Iranian state administration.

Irons (1975, 2) presents a society organized into "a segmentary system of territorial groups which functions in a manner similar to that described for stateless segmentary society in other areas of the world (Evans-Pritchard 1940; Fortes and Evans-Pritchard 1940; Middleton and Tait 1958)." Thinking of segmentary lineage society as a documented social type, Irons seems to have done his best to make his material fit it, and he writes of the kinship system as virtually synonymous with social organization. "The indigenous political institutions of the Yomut consist of a hierarchy of descent groups and a hierarchy of residence groups," and although he concedes that "these two types of groups do not have the same composition," he goes on to claim that "each residence group has a numerically dominant descent group which can, and usually does, control and group action by the residence unit" (Irons 1975, 39).

The smallest residential units were camps of two to ten yurts, but these do not appear to have constituted territorial kinship segments, as the segmentary lineage model would predict. Irons can only write that they *tended* to be made up of close patrilineal kin, and it turns out that "group composition is constantly changing" and "closely related groups often join with other similar shallow patrilineages [a group of brothers whose father is deceased] with whom they have no close agnatic ties to form a single camp group" (Irons 1975, 46).

Above this, structurally, Irons places the *oba*, which he describes as a community sharing common rights including access to land. Irons is not very interested in the current administration of the *oba*; instead, his description focuses on what it must have been like "before the establishment of effective government control" (Irons 1975, 47). Again, however, the membership of the *oba* was *not* defined by descent. People could and did decide to change from one *oba* to another. The most Irons can claim is that he found a "tendency" for the descent and residence groups to "correspond approximately" (Irons 1975, 49).

Since it was clear that descent groups did not themselves constitute political-territorial units, the claim became that dominant lineages in each political unit related to each other in opposition or alliance in line with genealogical distance, as predicted by Evans-Pritchard's model. On closer examination, however, the evidence for this is rather questionable. First, the identification of the "dominant lineage" of a political unit can be accomplished by moving up the genealogical scale to successively more inclusive groups until one fits the model. This is what Irons did in the case of the single *oba* whose composition he studied in any detail, which he called Aju Qui.

In Aju Qui there were not one but eight different "lineages" (that is, sets of households tracing descent from a common ancestor), the largest of which included just 20 percent—twelve of the fifty-nine households—of the *oba*. None of the ancestors of the eight groups of related families in the *oba* had any genealogical links to one another that could be traced, and all that Irons was left with was that five of these groups recognized some sort of descent from the ancestral figure Dath (Daz), although they did not trace specific genealogical links to him. So Irons claimed that in this *oba* the dominant descent group was Dath. However, the Dath were apparently also the dominant descent group in at least sixteen other *obas*, so this pattern was not even remotely segmentary, since the "dominant" group in Aju Qui did not make up a segment of the more inclusive category. Although Irons suggested that there were properly segmentary structures in the other Dath *obas*, he presents no evidence for this, and there was certainly nothing of the sort in Aju Qui. It also becomes clear that the groups of related families in Aju Qui are not corporate descent groups, since the majority of the households descended from a given ancestor turn out to have lived in different *obas* and so could not share in any sort of regular joint work.

Indeed, Irons is wrong to refer to the Dath and other apparent descent groups as "lineages," since it is clear that their members did not trace the specific genealogical connections that linked them to their ancestors. In standard anthropological terms, these would be termed "clans" (Keesing 1975, 148). And eighteen of the fifty-nine households did not trace Dath descent, whether we consider them a clan or not. The case is not strengthened by the imprecision of the Turkmen terms for descent groups. So although Irons states with confidence that "numerous levels of segmentation can be identified, dividing the Turkmen into progressively smaller and more closely related groups until ultimately the level of small groups consisting of ten to forty households is reached," he goes on to add that "all of these descent groups can be referred to in Turkmen as 'taypa,' regardless of the level of segmentation" (Irons 1975, 40). The very smallest groups of ten to forty households, he adds, were usually called *tire*. This does seem a little odd, as one would expect that units and subunits that were as politically significant as the model suggests would have distinctive names—as the territorial units undoubtedly did.

The territorial unit above the *oba*, in terms of scale, was the *il*, which Irons translates as "tribe." At the time of his study, there were 248 *obas* on the Gurgan Plain, divided into eleven *il*. At first, it seems that these *il* match the genealogies that Irons presents, but it turns out that five of the eleven *il* are not associated with a single lineage; instead, "separate descent groups are joined together to form a single tribe" (Irons 1975, 56). These joinings seem to have no regard for genealogical distance. Indeed, the closer one looks at the structures, the less segmentary they appear. Irons admits that at each level of segmentation "a similarly irregular relationship between descent and residence emerges" (Irons 1975, 55).

One of the arguments that had been advanced by advocates of the segmentary model of tribal society was that the system represented an ideology. It was to be expected that reality deviated from the ideal—for example, in the coincidence of descent groups and residence. But the important thing, the argument went, was that "tribal" people organized their political groupings and relations using the idiom of shared descent, and, if necessary, they would retrospectively generate fictive kinship connections so that their political realities could match their supposed ideology (see Tapper 1983; Geiss 2003). But this does not seem to occur in the *il* described by Irons. He notes that four of the sixteen descent groups supposed to belong to the Dath "lineage" were not related by descent at all and shared no common ancestor with the other descent groups in the Dath. Instead, they were said to have been absorbed into the unit through long residence (Irons 1975, 43, 58). But this raises the question as to why these categories of people were considered members of the Dath at all, since they were very clearly not genealogically related, and why fictive kinship had not been employed to try to fit them into a unified genealogy.[20] It seems that, strictly speaking, the Dath, the group Irons knew best, was not a group defined by descent. At one point, Irons concedes that he is describing a "segmentary political system" rather than a segmentary kinship system, noting that "the segmentary political system of the Yomut . . . differs from a segmentary lineage system . . . because it is only partially based on a genealogy" (Irons 1975, 58).

Indeed, for a society supposedly organized by genealogy, the Turkmen that Irons studied seemed to have a remarkably patchy knowledge of it. The impression Irons gives is that all Turkmen knew their patrilineal genealogies back to a depth of five to seven generations (Irons 1975, 44).[21] But the genealogies he presents for Aji Qui show nothing of the sort. Only one group of twelve households recalled a common ancestor more than four generations senior to a living relative; a further eleven households recognized a common ancestor four generations back. The majority, some thirty-seven households, are not shown as tracing descent more than three generations beyond a living relative—a great-grandfather. Irons (1975, 15) blames this lack of genealogical information on the poor trust between himself and the local community, assuming that the people concerned knew their distant ancestors but chose not to give him this information.[22] He does not seem to have considered the possibility that only some families might have kept extended genealogies.

Descent groups, if that is indeed what they should be termed, did not seem to act in a very segmentary way. In the classic model of segmentary opposition, blood feuds should lead to descent groups and subgroups forming alliances with one another based upon genealogical proximity. But Irons (1975, 62) notes that among the Turkmen responsibility for blood vengeance was largely felt by immediate relatives of a murder victim rather than the wider agnatic set of kin, regardless of the genealogical distance between the killer and killed. He also remarks (Irons 1975, 71) that one of the most frequent outcomes of disputes was the movement of one or more affected families to another *oba*, which further undermined the correspondence between descent groups and residential units.

But although the political system did not really match the segmentary lineage model very well, Irons nevertheless presents a picture of an egalitarian society, without hierarchy, governing itself by tribal custom. The *oba*, for example, is portrayed as a traditional community, based on common resources, formed by a sort of "bottom-up" social process. The *oba* is described as "a corporate group which shares a joint estate" and a "group of households associated with a definite territory" (Irons 1975, 47). Each *oba* had a "headman," Irons explains, and before the "establishment of effective government control" this was not a hereditary office but one filled by a representative of the local community. The *oba* appears as a sort of autochthonous tribal segment, a self-formed traditional body of nomads.

In fact, the *oba* was the administrative and tax unit used by both Russian and Iranian states to administer the Turkmen. In modern Turkish, the word means a large yurt or a group of nomads under the authority of a *bey* (lord), and it seems that this may well have been its original meaning among the Turkmen too. Vambery, who traveled through Turkmen territory in 1863, does not mention the term *oba* but does describe the *ova*, being the "house and court" of the local lords ("chiefs") with whom he stayed (Vambery 1970 [1864], 46). Given the interchangeability of "b" and "v" in this region, it may be that Irons's *oba* has its origins in Vambery's *ova*—the great house of a local noble.

The Turkmen, it would appear from Irons, did not traditionally have hereditary rulers, and any that they later acquired were forced on them by external administration. This was taken up as evidence—at last—of properly acephalous tribal nomadic society, so that Geiss uses this as his primary ethnographic material for his model of traditional acephalous tribal society in Central Asia. Among the Turkmen, "political authority was neither hereditary, nor could it be appropriated by military talent, wealth or religious reputation" (Geiss 2003, 97). Of course, this situation had been somewhat undermined by state interference. Irons notes that each of the larger divisions described as "tribes" (*il*) had historically been headed by a *thaqlau*, which Irons translates as "protector," who collected tribute from sedentary villages and organized defense against raids. Irons (1975, 68) writes that the post "was not hereditary, but rather fell to the man who was strong enough to hold it," itself a rather ambiguous description, since this might be a description of a choice restricted to one or two powerful families. The *thaqlau* had armed and mounted retainers paid for by the Persian government to "police their tribes," and they acted as an agent of indirect rule (Irons 1975, 68).

At first glance, nineteenth-century travelers' accounts of the Turkmen would seem to support the notion of an originally acephalous society. Vambery wrote, "what surprised me most during my sojourn amongst this people, was my inability to discover any single man among them desirous of commanding" (Vambery 1970 [1864], 309). He quotes a Turkmen saying "we are a people without a head" (Vambery 1970 [1864], 310). But as with Levchine, on careful reading it becomes clear that Vambery was concerned with the absence of overlords, not minor nobility.

Vambery describes the Youmut as divided into four major divisions called *taife*. This seems almost certainly to be the root of the term *taypa* in Iron's account. Interestingly, in modern Turkish this term means a body of people or the crew of a ship; it does not imply kinship connection. Vambery notes the four *taife* are divided into twenty-six subdivisions known as *tire*. This is the same term that Irons uses for small descent groups, and Vambery (1970, 302) notes that the word means "fragment" and is used to mean "lines or clans," although the literal meaning seems to be simply a "gathering," from the verb *tir-*, "to gather" (Wittfogel and Feng 1949, 433). The average size of these subdivisions was around 1,500 households, although Irons reported that in the 1960s the term was used for groups of ten to forty households. This would seem strange, until one considers the possibility that the "lines" mentioned by Vambery were the elite or politically dominant families of each subdivision.

For it seems almost certain that the Turkmen did, in fact, have a nobility. Vambery meets a Turkmen Khan, Khidr, whom he describes as a "chief" in the service of Russia and who clearly holds hereditary rank among the Turkmen. He goes on to become the guest of a man named Khandjan, who, he writes, was "the Aksakal (chief) of a mighty race, and even in the time of his father, no Dervish, Hadji, or other stranger ever dared to pass through [the region of] Gömüshtepe without having tasted his bread and drunk his water" (Vambery 1970 [1864], 38).

This Khandjan, it turned out, had the title of *bay* (Vambery 1970 [1864], 53), generally taken to mean "lord" in Turkic languages, and Vambery travels under his protection to the *ova* (house/court) of the neighboring Ana Khan, who was "chief of the Yarali tribe" (Vambery 1970 [1864], 52), a division of the Turkmen that he lists as including several thousand households. These local rulers clearly have men and resources at their disposal and appear to have a considerable amount of wealth, as the value of the jewelry of the women of their household indicates: "a Turkoman lady is not fashionably dressed, unless she carries about her person one or two pounds of silver ornaments" (Vambery 1970 [1864], 46). Another European traveler, O'Donovan (1882, 42), notes that the people he calls "Yamud Turkomans" had chiefs, and he meets one of these, named Il Geldi. He turns out to have the title of Khan and rules a number of villages (O'Donovan 1882, 197–198).

In fact, there are historical records of a series of Turkmen khans. Oraz Khan of the Teke Turkmen occupied the Merv oasis in the early 1830s. His successor was Kushid Khan, who defeated the Khivan army in 1855, and shortly after this Nur Vedi Khan united the Gökleng, Yomut, and Teke to defeat a military force under the governor of Bujnurd, Jafar Kuli Khan. Although Galkin apparently remarked that "anyone with a little extra wealth calls himself a khan" (Khazanov 1983, 175), some rulers must have been relatively wealthy and powerful. In the 1860s, Kushid Khan built a huge fort 2.5 miles long and 1.25 miles wide on the Murghab River (see Stewart 1977, 149–150).

But the khans were explained away as temporary leaders of "tribal coalitions" (see Geiss 2003, 100), and since they seemed *less* hierarchical than other pastoral polities, it seemed as if they should have no hierarchy at all. Geiss (2003, 100) writes:

In comparison to the Kazakh hordes, Turkmen understood and perceived khanship differently. This office was neither hereditary nor was it linked to Chingizid descent. It could not be appropriated, but relied upon the delegation of authority by the tribesmen. . . . In this way Turkmen also used other titles like *vekil*, *batyr* or *beg*, which indicated noble descent, rank and leadership positions among other Turkish tribesmen. Among Turkmen these titles, however, had no special or uniform meaning and could be held by representatives of *obas* as of whole tribes.

Geiss offers no evidence for this peculiar practice by which "leaders" of *obas* (itself probably a word meaning the house and court of a local ruler) and "tribes" should take noble titles but not actually think of themselves as nobility. Geiss (2003, 119) also dismisses the historical evidence for the appointment of khans by powerful local rulers, although his reason for doing so is far from convincing. "Recent Turkman historiographic scholarship holds the view that Turkmen 'nobles' received the title of 'khan' from Bukharan or Khivan rulers in recognition of performed services. . . . This is not very likely, as the Khan of Khiva would hardly gratify his followers by bestowing on them his own rank."[23]

Rather than reflecting a sort of tribal democracy, it seems more likely that nineteenth-century reports of Turkmen leaders as relatively weak and dependent upon the conditional support of their kin were descriptions of a dispersed nobility lacking a strong central ruler in the face of tsarist colonial expansion. Thus Colonel Stewart, who traveled to the region in 1880 with an eye to the military and political situation, wrote, "each clan is divided into many families, and these families have each a person called a khetkhoda who acts for the family in matters of policy, but he can only act according to the wishes of the clan" (Stewart 1977 [1881], 167). Stewart numbers the Turkmen *khetkhodas* in the Merv region at twenty-four, and he estimates the number of Turkmen households in the region at forty thousand, so this cannot possibly be a description of every ordinary family, since on average such a family would have over eight thousand members.[24] It seems more likely that the clans and families he describes are those with political power, since Stewart writes that in times of danger the *khetkhodas* elect a supreme khan. He also notes that they do not allow him to retain the position when the danger has past, and in this sense the office appears temporary, but careful reading shows that he is talking about the "supreme power" of an overlord (Stewart 1977 [1881], 167).[25]

But in any case, whether the Turkmen had hereditary political offices or not in the nineteenth century, there is little doubt that they had had an aristocracy before this time. The tribal model of the pastoral nomad allowed that peoples like the Turkmen might become hierarchical over time as a result of contact with states, but it would expect them to have been originally egalitarian.

However, the Turkmen have a long history of aristocratic, dynastic, and state power. The Turkmen Qara Qoyunlu and the Aq Qoyunlu dynasties ruled territories in modern-day Azerbaijan, Anatolia, western Iran, and northern Iraq from the late fourteenth to the early sixteenth centuries. The ruling lineages of these polities were the Barani and Bayundur respectively, the latter being an old Oghuz noble house and the name Barani being derived from the town of Bahar near Hamadan, which had been the capital of the thirteenth-century ruler Oghuz Sulayman-shah's domain (see Minorsky 1978, 13:391–395). These nobles are described as ruling hereditary fiefs (Minorsky 1978, 16:942). And before this time, the Oghuz polity, from which Turkman elites traced descent, was clearly stratified, with enormous inequality in the ownership of property, as noted by the tenth-century Muslim traveler Ibn Faḍlân, who recorded that while some Oghuz lived in poverty, others owned ten thousand horses and one hundred thousand sheep.[26]

Although Irons (1975, 172) notes that the written history of the Turkmen stretches back a millennium, he pays it almost no attention. The *Book of Dede Korkut*, for example, is a collection of stories of the Turkmen dating from the time of the Oghuz polity, written down in the early fifteenth century but thought to represent an even earlier body of oral traditions.[27] The society described in these stories is turbulent, but it is also thoroughly aristocratic. The heroes are princes, noble warriors, and ladies. Only two commoners have any substantial role in any of the eleven stories, and they are entirely loyal, attached to a named noblemen and described in terms of the service they render their lord. Khans have great wealth: one has ninety golden tents, at least one herd of ten thousand sheep, countless horses, and "heavy treasure" (Lewis 1974, 43). Perhaps most telling, however, is that there is no mention of descent groups at all, rather surprising if they constituted the building blocks of the social and political structure at that time. The lords and ladies are not described as leading named clans or descent groups but rather personal entourages, usually of a satisfyingly round number of retainers—generally forty but sometimes several hundred. In battle they command hundreds and sometimes thousands of warriors. Individuals do not bear clan or descent group names; instead, each noble is described as the son of an individual lord (some of whom come into the stories in their own right), just as one would expect, since high noble status was clearly hereditary. The "nobles of the teeming Oghuz" is a stock phrase for the Oghuz polity itself, and another much-repeated phrase describes khans giving out "lands and fortresses" to their followers (Lewis 1974, 57), which brings to mind a remark made by a Russian officer named Stebnitzky (1977 [1874], 67) who noted that in his day the Tekke Turkmen lived in the forty-three fortresses—altogether a rather different picture from the ideal typical "pure nomad."

By the time that the nineteenth-century accounts of the Turkmen were written, they occupied the border zone between the Persian and the Russian tsarist empires. As Akakca (forthcoming) suggests, their political decentralization and fragmentation was at least in large part due to the attempts of both powers to control and co-opt them as frontiersmen. It would seem, then, that the Turkmen became less—not more—hierarchical over time, since they are presented by Irons as having rather little hierarchy in the 1960s, other than that "imposed" by Iranian government. However, it turns out that among the Yomut there were ranked social strata at the time of Irons's study, although one has to study Irons's account quite carefully to discover this important fact.

Irons (1975, 51) reports that the nondominant descent groups in each *oba* are called *gonshi*, who would be "at a disadvantage" in a dispute with a member of the dominant lineage. This is all made to seem a rather unimportant consequence of the imperfect match between descent and residence, but elsewhere on the Turkic steppe the term had a rather wider social significance. In the Kyrghyz case, the historical meaning of the term *kongshu* is "the general name of all those who were in direct economic dependence on a rich person" (Yudakhin 1990, 404). In describing pre-Soviet Kirghiz society, Abramzon (1971, 160) notes, "a part of the poor people (kongshu) led a nomadic life together with the manaps and bais, and attended to their cattle." Khazanov (1983, 153) notes that among the Kazakhs *konsy/kongsy* "constituted a distinct social category" and describes them as "made up of poor individuals who had lost their links with their own auls."

Whether or not the term *gongshi/kongshu* also indicated economic and political dependence in the Yomut case, the society that Irons described was not at all egalitarian in terms of wealth distribution. The ten richest households in Aji Qui owned more wealth than the remaining forty-nine put together (Irons 1975, 160). As a result, some people hired themselves out to rich herd owners, and the wealthy could either employ herders and move with their livestock themselves or place a herd with a poorer household to pasture the livestock for them. This institution of "leasing out" herds was called *emanet* (Irons 1975, 157). Like the almost identical Mongolian *süreg tavikh* and the Kazakh *saun* (Khazanov 1983, 155), this practice seems to have all that is required for the accumulation of any amount of livestock wealth, since it entails ownership rights over animals herded by other households. Irons (1975, 168–169) conceded that "the institutions organizing economic production tend to create an unequal distribution of wealth." However, he mentions "leveling institutions" such as bridewealth, which he feels ought to reduce inequality to some extent, although for reasons that will become clear, bridewealth payments seem rather unconvincing candidates for this task. Irons (1975, 169) admits that "the various leveling institutions do not create anything approximating an equal distribution of wealth."

It is only in his treatment of marriage that Irons reveals that Yomut society actually does have formal stratification. He writes: "the descendants of slaves, either in the male or female lines, are defined as a distinct social category, designated 'qul,' in contrast to 'igh,' Yomut having no slave ancestry. . . . The status of qul is said to be inherited indefinitely" (Irons 1975, 122). Slavery had been a very significant institution in the region during the nineteenth century, and all contemporary reports describe the Turkmen's reputation for slave raiding and trading. The institution of slavery was played down in traditional treatments of the "pastoral nomadic society." Khazanov, for example, while admitting slavery is common, argues that it is "insufficient to make society stratified" since "when dependent groups and individuals are involved in the same pastoral production as other members of society, there must be relatively few of them for their dependent position to be preserved" (Khazanov 1983, 159). Social mobility, the standard argument went, would soon make the descendants of slaves into equal members of the tribe. But in the Yomut case, it seems that slave ancestry had important legal consequences. The *qul* were, quite literally, worth less than *igh* persons.[28] As in the Kazakh and Kyrgyz cases, the system for reckoning legal compensation for those killed in disputes made explicit the differences in status, as "two men of qul status must be killed to satisfy the blood debt created by killing one igh" (Irons 1975, 122). Tucked away, as it is, in the section on marriage, Geiss can be forgiven for missing what turns out to be rather an important detail when he wrote: "Unlike among the Kara-Kalpaks, Kyrgyz and Kazakhs, Turkmen had to pay the same khun [blood price] for each killed tribesmen. Thus the equal khuns reflected the egalitarianism among Turkmen tribesmen" (Geiss 2003, 99). It seems that in this respect they were not so egalitarian after all.

From Irons's description, one could be forgiven for thinking that the *qul* were a rather small group, not worthy of a mention in the account of the political system. But it turns out that the *qul* is actually a rather large and inclusive category. "Among the Yomut the categories of slave origin and non-Yomut origin are merged" (Irons 1975, 122). In fact, anyone who is not of "pure" bilateral Yomut ancestry is a *qul*. It turns out that the majority of Turkmen are *qul*. By Irons's own figures, 73 percent of the married people of Aji Qui were *qul*—a category he defines as "of Non-Yomut ancestry." *Igh* people, both men and women, should only marry other *igh* persons, and if members of the two strata did intermarry their children were of the lower *qul* status. Irons's figures show that in 97 percent of marriages both partners were members of the same social strata.[29]

So although Irons (1975, 163) thinks of bridewealth as a "leveling institution," it must have been quite ineffective—even in theory—at transferring wealth between the two social strata of *igh* and *qul*, since they were supposed to never marry each other and hardly ever did. Irons did not find out, or at least does not present in his text, the status of wealthy or poor households, but if the *igh* were originally richer than the *qul*, then strata endogamy would tend to reproduce the wealth differential.

In the end, it seems that only about a quarter (27 percent) of the Turkmen population that Irons studied were actually of Yomut descent. The majority of the population were social (and originally legal) inferiors, described as *qul*. This is a readily understandable term, since *qul / kul* in both ancient and modern Turkish and Kyrgyz means "slave" or "servant."[30] It seems that the (not terribly segmentary) genealogies that Irons gathered from a mixture of oral and written historical sources simply do not apply to the majority of the "Yomut" population, and that far from describing the basic kinship structure of the society as a whole they describe descent traced by an elite whose status and privileges depended upon their ancestry. This may not have been unique to the Turkmen: among the Kyrgyz there is a famous saying to the effect that those who do not know their *jeti ata* (seven forefathers) are slaves (Gullette 2006, 63). In the Yomut case we learn, in passing, of "large descent groups who are reported to be of slave origin, or their recent descendants, these descent groups have a precise position in the segmentary lineage system" (Irons 1975, 122). But Irons does not include any data on such *qul* groups in his genealogies, so we are left to imagine where these positions might be. Could it be, then, that this represents the solution of the mystery of the groups included in the Dath political grouping that were explicitly *not* of Dath descent? Perhaps the "precise position" of these groups was that of dependents attached to the "pure" *igh* families who *did* trace descent from Yomut ancestors?

In 1868, Gullibef de Blokwill (cited in Geiss 2003, 65n277) noted that Turkmen slaves became "commoners" in the second or third generation, although their slave ancestry was generally remembered. Slave raiding and trading had been outlawed since the end of the nineteenth century, so by the time of Irons's studies in the 1960s most of the *qul* families had presumably either attained something like the status of commoners or had always had it. If so, the *qul* strata had either merged with, or long been the same as, the Turkmen commoners. This suggests that the minority of Turkmen that had "pure Yomut descent" were either themselves the remnants of the nobility or had once contained such a strata, which had somehow disappeared by the time of Irons's study. In the time of de Blokwill, Turkmen society presumably consisted of either three strata: nobles / commoners / slaves, or two strata: nobles / commoners and slaves.

The *qul*/*igh* distinction not only dispels, once and for all, the mirage of the tribal society unified by common descent (since the *igh* elite certainly did *not* share descent with the *qul*); it also suggests that the term "Yomut," strictly speaking, referred to the elite of the society, not the majority of the people within it. This is not as strange as it may seem. The Bashkir historian Zeki Togan argued that the name "Kazakh" was originally reserved for the rulers and only later applied to their subjects (Paksoy 1992), and something similar occurred to the term "Mongol," as will be discussed in chapter 6. It is understandable, then, that Irons's informants could help him to collect Yomut genealogies and that these could be partially related to "dominant" families in the different *oba* districts. But these need have nothing to do with the genealogies of the majority of the Turkmen of the region, except insofar as those born *qul* might have been attached to various sets of *igh*.

Irons's treatment was a product of its era, very much in the mold of structural-functionalist accounts of idealized traditional social structures, but with a strong interest in adaptational evolutionism. Although Irons is concerned with reconstructing the social structure "before the estab-lishment of effective government control," he presents an almost entirely ahistorical account, concerned with a sort of self-contained social entity evolving and adapting in a sort of never-never time. He writes, for exam-ple, "social organization (as well as other aspects of culture) is a result of variation and selection similar in many ways to that underlying biological evolution" (Irons 1975, 172). He takes as axiomatic "the existence of distinct and in some way competing groups, such as the various tribal and lineage divisions of the Turkmen" and that "some of these groups introduce be-havioral innovations. . . . Advantageous variations tend to be retained and to spread" (Irons 1975, 172). This almost zoological approach leads Irons to the rather tautological conclusion that "Turkmen groups display differ-ences in social organization which it appears could effect their competitive success" (Irons 1975, 174).[31] The nomads still seem to be outside history in this account, just as Toynbee pictured them.

As Dyson-Hudson and Dyson-Hudson (1980, 15–16) remark, the influ-ence of the romantic stereotype[32] of nomads as

> brave, independent, fierce men, freely moving with their herds, and not hav-ing to deal with the constraints and frustrations we ourselves face in day-to-day "civilized" living . . . led anthropologists interested in pastoral societies to select as research subjects those "tribes" which apparently best fitted this stereotype. This, in conjunction with the dominance of British structural-functionalism among English anthropologists, with its assumptions about boundedness and stability of local systems, meant that too often anthropo-logical descriptions of nomadic pastoral societies attempted to reconstruct "traditional" social organisation and dismissed apparently anomalous be-haviours as resulting from contamination of the "pure pastoralists" by con-tacts with agricultural neighbours, with colonial administrations, or with other disruptive forces external to the pastoral society itself.

In retrospect, Irons's ethnography of the Yomut appears to be another example of this trend. Primed by descent theory and nineteenth-century accounts of the Turkmen as divided into political units described as clans and tribes, it is understandable that for an ethnographer to find any sort of patrilineal genealogy at all, particularly one that seemed to have a relation-ship to the political structure, would appear to be a confirmation of the model. After all, it was expected that the system would have decayed and been scrambled by recent state interference. But each piece of the apparent jigsaw was approached with the picture of segmentary kinship society already firmly in mind, and from a distance the resulting mosaic could be mistaken for the species of society the analysts were hunting for.

The perfect example of the ideal-typical pastoral nomadic society, composed of egalitarian clans of fierce and free tribesmen, organized by the principles of segmentary opposition, was like any good mythical beast: no one had actually seen it themselves, but everyone seemed to have it on excellent authority that someone else had. It is perhaps impossible to prove that a society resembling the model has never existed, but upon close inspection the evidence for each sighting seems to fade.

6

Creating Peoples
Nation-state History and the Notion of Identity

As Martin Thom points out in his paper "Tribes Within Nations: The Ancient Germans and the History of Modern France," the concept of the nation that emerged in the nineteenth century was powerfully influenced by debates about the Germanic tribes that invaded the Western Roman empire from the fifth and sixth centuries C.E. In his famous 1882 lecture "What Is a Nation?" Renan declared that "it was in fact the Germanic invasions which introduced into the world the principle which, later, was to serve as a basis for the existence of nationalities" (Renan 1990 [1882], 9).

In Renan's time, the conservative position of those such as the Comte de Montlosier, the eighteenth-century French publicist, was to identify the nation with the project of rulership, in particular with the noble houses that had emerged from the Germanic invasions. Inspired by the populist vision of the nation that emerged with the French Revolution, Romantic historians such as Thierry rejected this approach. "For Montlosier, as for other ultra-royalists, the French 'nation' had consisted of the free, warrior nobilities that had invaded Roman Gaul, for Thierry it was the original inhabitants, the Gallo-Romans" (Thom 1990, 28).

Renan's seminal theory of nationhood was part of a reaction by secular intellectuals determined to reject the claims of the monarchists and promote the populist vision of the nation, one constituted by its citizenry, not its rulers.[1] That tradition lived on in the work of Fustel de Coulanges and his pupil Emile Durkheim, and the notion of both nation and society that developed in the twentieth-century social sciences reflects the victory of this populist politics over the *"ancien régime."*[2] The desire to find a nonaristocratic tribal "other" was a central concern of the emerging social sciences. As noted in chapter 1 Thom (1990, 35) remarks:

> Within sociology itself, the special emphasis upon ethnology expressed a need, on the part of lay, republican intellectuals such as Durkheim and his pupils, to counter polemical celebrations of the martial and monarchical values of the ancient German tribes within France's national boundaries with the distant, purely human, universal values of tribes from without, from Australia, from Polynesia, and so on.

Durkheimian thought bears the imprint of Renan's nationalism, particularly his concern with solidarity and the collective conscience. One can almost see Durkheim's work as elaborating Renan's conception of the nation for use as a general theory of human aggregation. "A nation is a large-scale solidarity," writes Renan. "A large aggregate of men . . . creates a kind of moral conscience which we call a nation" (Renan 1990 [1882], 19–20). Similarly, Durkheim (1964 [1893], 79) writes: "The totality of beliefs and sentiments common to average citizens of the same society forms . . . the *collective* or *common* conscience." In his evolutionary scheme, primitive society, which he calls segmentary society, is held together by "mechanical" solidarity, caused by the mutual resemblance of unspecialized pasts and, he theorizes, "solidarity which comes from likeness is at its maximum when the collective conscience completely envelops our whole conscience and coincides in all points with it" (Durkheim 1964 [1893], 130). Advanced society, however, is bound together by "organic" solidarity generated by the reciprocal dependence caused by specialization, allowing the individual as well as the collective conscience to appear. This scheme helped to lay the foundations of social science.[3]

Like the nation, society stood for "the people" or *volk* as a whole, with its own generalized culture, traditions, and form. In this populist imagination, human aggregates were not simply the subjects of a ruler but must form social and cultural collectivities, and this was reflected in the emergence of various forms of folk studies. Sociology and particularly ethnology[4] took as their objects of study the cultural and the social as a mass or at least collective phenomena, conceived of in the populist mode, which was very different from the royalist historians of an earlier era. Had the Comte de Montlosier (1755–1838) studied the Turkmen, he would, I think, have been entirely at ease with the notion that "the Yomut" referred to elite families tracing descent from Oghuz Khan, not the numerical majority of *qul* households.

But, as Hobsbawm (1990) shows, in the age of populist national politics the notion of shared kinship was an important element in the new ideologies of mass mobilization. The idiom of familial and fraternal relations, projected onto the "family writ large" of the nation, became a dominant theme. Those engaged in the intellectual and political project of nation construction made claims of national unity based on the idea of common descent. In the socially heterogeneous and divided region that was to become Albania, for example, Albanian nationalists such as Naim Frasheri (1846–1900) claimed: "All of us are only a single tribe, a single family; we are of one blood and one language" (Hobsbawm 1990, 53–54). In this historical imagination, tribes were the protonational groups, the natural units or subunits of a given *volk*.

IMAGINING THE PROTONATION

The birth of Europe came to be envisaged as the *Völkerwanderung*—the "Wandering of Peoples." In this imagination, "peoples" appear as protonations, discrete populations in movement. This generated a sort of "billiard ball" model of history, in which prenational, tribal peoples moved as discrete integral units across Eurasia to collide with and displace each other. Davies (1997, 215), for example, describes the first few centuries C.E. in this way:

> Much of the population beyond the Roman frontier was on the move. Tribes and federations of tribes, large and small, conducted an unending search for better land. From time to time the pace of their wanderings would be quickened by dearth, or by the violent arrival of nomadic horsemen, in which case, having tarried for decades or even centuries in one location, they would suddenly move on to the next. . . . The critical cause of any particular displacement might lie far away on the steppes of central Asia; and a "shunting effect" is clearly observable. Changes at one end of the chain of peoples could set off ripples along all the links of the chain. Like

the last wagon of a train in the shunting yards, the last tribe on the western end of the chain could be propelled from its resting-place with great force. In this regard the Huns caused ripples in the West long before they themselves appeared.

This vision of history has survived the numerous studies showing that "tribes" such as the Franks or Saxons were political projects including a wide and usually heterogeneous assembly of large and small noble houses and their subjects (Yorke 1990). This has been shown so frequently that even Davies (1997, 217) comments on it: "Chroniclers and historians were tempted to write in terms of discrete, permanent, and self-conscious tribes where no such entities had necessarily existed. . . . All have suffered, too, from the attentions of nationalist historians in our own day, who think nothing of projecting modern identities into prehistory." But lacking a replacement for the old model, Davies feels bound to reproduce it. He continues: "In the absence of alternatives, it is difficult to know how one can describe the migrations except in terms of the traditional tribes." The key problem in describing "peoples" is that, as Wolfram (1988, 5) put it, "we have no way of devising a terminology that is not derived from the concept of nation created during the French Revolution."[5]

When these Germanic peoples migrated into or invaded parts of the Roman Empire, the historical record shows the process to have been very different from the vision of discrete population units displacing each other. The Germanic elites frequently negotiated an authorized position within the imperial apparatus, typically as allied local rulers, *foederati*, who received a subsidy in return for the obligation to provide military support to Rome.

Any neat boundaries between native inhabitants and invading tribes quickly disappears. The iconic "Alaric the Goth," for example, who sacked Rome in 410 C.E., was a Latin-speaking member of a Romanized Gothic aristocracy who commanded an army raised within the borders of the empire. It was well understood that the result of the Germanic invasions in Europe was not the replacement, *en masse*, of one human population with another, but the insertion of new aristocracies and their military followings into the existing order of the Roman provinces. Renan (1990 [1882], 9) writes of the invasions: "They effected little change in racial stock, but they imposed dynasties and a military aristocracy upon the more or less extensive parts of the old empire of the west, which assumed the names of their invaders."

But when considering the barbarian heartland of the east, beyond the parts of the empire that left written accounts of these processes of invasion and accommodation, the historical imagination had freer rein. The Romans had noted mass migrations of apparently entire populations among the Gauls in the first to the fourth century B.C.E., and movement seemed somehow characteristic of barbarism (Hornblower and Spawforth 2003, 625, 680). In the age of nationalism, the vision of the "wandering peoples" seeking their future national homelands became the powerful image that Renan wrote of.

Again, the influence of the tribal model is most clearly revealed in the translation of terms. At the time of the principal Roman sources on the Germanic and Gaulish peoples, such as Tacitus and Caesar, the term *tribu* ("tribe") indicated the administrative divisions of the Roman polity itself, a census and tax unit that was an integral part of the functioning of government. So when one encounters the term "tribe" in modern translations of classical texts it rarely refers to the Latin term *tribu*. The word that Roman authors generally used for the Gaulish and other European polities was *civitas*, which is generally translated as "state" when applied to nonbarbaric subjects but came to be conventionally translated as "tribe" when it referred to the Gauls or Germans (see Rives 1999, 153). As Rives (1999, 119) notes, most of the references to German "tribes" in Tacitus are actually translations of the term *natio*, a word that is variously translated as "nation," "race," or "people."[6] However, particularly in the case of the Germanic peoples, the term *gens* is also frequently used, a term generally translated as "clan" but in these cases often translated as "tribe," since it applies to political entities too large to fit the current notion of clan.[7] The meaning of the term *gens* at that time remains rather unclear.[8] However, there is no doubt that for Roman authors the most prominent *gentes* in their own society were the powerful aristocratic houses that formed the patrician class.[9] The term had none of the association with primitive society that the term "clan" came to acquire in nineteenth- and twentieth-century English.

Although the use of the term *gens* by classical sources reinforced the notion that Germanic "tribal" society was based on kinship, in fact it is clear that the *gentes* that the Roman sources describe do not share biological descent. As Wolfram (1988, 6) notes: "The sources attest to the polyethnic character of the *gentes*. These *gentes* . . . are . . . always mixed." Loyalty to the ruling family was the key criterion to membership, not descent, and the (retrospective) accounts of early Gothic history by those such as Cassiodorus describe groups formed by powerful leaders who recruit diverse followings and act more like "the kings of a migratory army" (Wolfram 1988, 12) than clan elders leading bounded communities of kin.

The Germanic "tribes" were not discrete bodies of kinsmen tracing common descent. They were the political entourages, and frequently the conquest projects, of noble families.[10] They displaced, or intermarried with, Roman elites, and the membership of their political formations was recruited from all sorts of sources, often from Roman subjects who preferred the new masters to their old ones. As Wolfram (1988, 8) notes: "From the first appearance of the Gothic hordes on Roman soil, they attracted people from the native lower classes. At the time of the migration this attraction was a great advantage because it alleviated a constant shortage of manpower. . . . Roman lower classes had been willing . . . since the third century: 'to become Goths.' "

The Germanic societies also had their aristocracy, although nineteenth-century scholarship tended to play this down, casting them as relatively egalitarian. Tacitus describes the Germanic *nobilis* (nobility) and contrasts them with the *plebs* (commoners) (see Rives 1999, 81, 170). Leading nobles administered cantons, units in which no common descent was implied, and they are described as leading a retinue (*comitatus*) of retainers (*comes*) rather than bodies of kinsmen (Rives 1999, 180).[11]

Neither did the other "tribal" societies of the Roman world resemble the nineteenth- and twentieth-century construction of kinship society. The Gaulish polities, usually referred to as "states" (*civitas*), were politically sophisticated and very clearly stratified into aristocracy, priesthood, and commoners. Caesar (6.14) notes:

> In the whole of Gaul two types of men are counted as being of worth and distinction. The ordinary people are considered almost as slaves: they dare do nothing on their own account and are not called to counsels. When the majority are oppressed by death or heavy tribute, or harmed by powerful men, they swear themselves away into slavery to the aristocracy, who have the same rights over them as masters do over their slaves. Of the two types

of men of distinction however, the first is made up of the druids, and the other of the knights.

(HAMMOND 1996, 126)

The early Germanic societies were a product of power relations between subjects and ruling families. They had a political rather than a cultural or "ethnic" definition. This contradicts the underlying logic of the tribal model since, as Erikson (2002, 10–11) notes, the notion of the tribe is intertwined with that of the ethnic group. In his later work, Sahlins (1983, 520–521) recognizes that there is a problem with the kin-based model of the tribe when he compares the Germans of Tacitus with the Fijians and Zulus, all of whom he characterizes in terms of "heroic society." Following Chadwick (1926), Sahlins contrasts the practices of elite history, which concerns itself with heroic rulers, with the recently more dominant notion of history as the study of the life of communities. Using the Scythian concept of divine kingship as a point of departure, Sahlins presents heroic history as a general cultural practice in which the main relationships of society are embodied in the persons of the rulers. In doing so he recognizes that—in the "heroic societies" of Polynesia, Nguni Africa, and premodern Europe at least—society is a "top-down" rather than a "bottom-up" product.

> We need a notion of "hierarchical solidarity" to go alongside Durkheim's mechanical and organic types. In the heroic societies, the coherence of the members of subgroups is not so much due to their similarity (mechanical solidarity) or their complementarity (organic solidarity) as to their common submission to the ruling power. The corollary of hierarchical solidarity is a devaluation of tribalism as we know it, since the collectivity is defined by its adherence to a given chief or king rather than by distinct cultural attributes—even as bonds of kinship and relations to ancestral lands are dissolved by such a process as heroic segmentation. Chadwick repeatedly remarks on the absence of "national" sentiment or interest in the European heroic age, by comparison to the prevailing concept of a state apparently "regarded as little more than the property of the individual" (1926: 336). And Benveniste observes that, apart from Western Europe, a term for society does not appear in the classical vocabulary of Indo-European institutions. Instead, the concept "is expressed in a different fashion. In particular one

recognizes it under the name of *realm* [*royaume*]: the limits of society coincide with a certain power, which is the power of the king" (1969 vol. 2: 9).

(SAHLINS 1983, 522)

But on reflection, the old Durkheimian notion of solidarity as a sort of social glue seems too entangled with populist visions of national cohesion for us to assume its universal presence. We do not know whether Chinggis Khan's Turkic-speaking Önggüd subjects felt solidarity with his Tatar ones, and we certainly need not assume that they did. Sociological terms developed in the age of popular nationalism are a poor guide to understanding what Anderson (1991, 19) calls the dynastic realm.

> These days it is perhaps difficult to put oneself emphatically into a world in which the dynastic realm appeared for most men as the only imaginable "political" system. For in fundamental ways "serious" monarchy lies transverse to all modern conceptions of political life. Kingship organises everything around a high centre. Its legitimacy derives from divinity, not from population, who, after all, are subjects, not citizens. In the modern conception, state sovereignty is fully, flatly, and evenly operated over each square centimetre of a legally demarcated territory. But in the older imagining, where states were defined by centres, borders were porous and indistinct, and sovereignties faded imperceptibly into one another. Hence, paradoxically enough, the ease with which premodern empires and kingdoms were able to sustain their rule over immensely heterogenous, and often not even contiguous, populations for long periods of time.

Societies are, as Leach (1982, 41) notes, political units in practice, and they are more clearly a product of common rulers than common cultures. As Gellner (1983b, 55) points out, the notion that people are bound to live in units defined by shared culture is a relatively recent one. "Culturally plural societies often worked well in the past: so well, in fact, that cultural plurality was sometimes invented where it was previously lacking." But in anthropology, the political construction of the social has often been backgrounded by the powerful heritage of classical ethnology, which assumed some more or less homogenous cultural and social entity as its object of study (the *ethnos*) and tended to regard "peoples" as cultural wholes.

The key process described as the *Völkerwanderung* was not a mass movement of populations—although this sometimes happened (Browning 1975, 36)—but the movement of the zones of control of the noble "barbarian" families that came to form political structures in the late Roman period. Similarly, in Inner Asia, ruling elites were frequently more mobile than their subjects. Historical accounts that might be interpreted as the migration of an entire "people" often refer to the movement of rulers and their entourages. In 105 C.E., for example, the northern Xiongnu were defeated and apparently "displaced" by the Xianbe, who "occupied all the old territories of the Hsiung-nu [Xiongnu]."[12] However, the Chinese sources make it clear that many of the inhabitants of the formerly Xiongnu territories took on the political identity of their new rulers. "The northern *Shan-yü* [*chanyu*, emperor] took flight and the Hsien-pi [Xianbei] moved in and occupied his land. The remainder of the Hsiung-nu [Xiongnu] who did not go with him still numbered over 100,000 tents and all styled themselves Hsien-pi [Xianbei]."[13] The Xianbei as a political entity had come to occupy all the old territories of the Xiongnu, but if there ever was anything like a Xiongnu *volk* it was not displaced by another such body.[14]

Like the Germanic invasions of the Western Roman Empire, the Mongol conquests also introduced a military aristocracy in the subject territories. The empire expanded as its armies advanced, but the numbers of "Mongols" (whoever is meant by that designation) involved were relatively small. Most Mongol armies numbered in the tens of thousands, the majority of whom were often drawn from subject allies such as Tatars, Kitans, and Türks. Although some troops were placed as garrisons (*tammachi*) in conquered territories, most were generally withdrawn after campaigns. After Batu's conquest of Russia and eastern Europe in 1238 through 1241, for example, the bulk of the Mongol army was withdrawn, and the Golden Horde rapidly acquired a Turkic character.[15] This was an imperial not a colonial process. The aristocracy installed in this way was not a homogenous ethnic strata of "Mongol tribesmen" superimposed upon the subject peoples, but noble Mongol families such as the Chinggisid "white bone" houses that continued to rule the Kazakhs until tsarist times. Far from becoming an imperial elite, the Mongol commoners often found themselves entirely impoverished by the process of conquest, so that some ended up having to sell their wives and children into slavery to meet the military and other obligations owed to their lords.[16]

It was common to find widely distributed aristocracies ruling culturally diverse subjects, often in different polities. In many cases, the power of these noble houses was more enduring than any of the states that they dominated. The Ashina, for example, seem to have been of Xiongnu origin (Atwood 2004, 553) and later formed an aristocracy that provided rulers for numerous steppe polities. They first came to prominence as the ruling dynasty of the Türk empire of the sixth to seventh centuries, the two main branches of the family ruling the eastern and western halves of the empire. In the west, the Ashina came to rule the Khazar state based in the northern Caucasian steppes from the seventh to the tenth centuries, and in the east seem to have given rise to the ruling house of the eighth-century Qarluq khanate of Turkestan (Golden 1990, 356). The Ashina rulers of the eastern Kök-Türk empire were overthrown by the Uighurs in the eighth century and fled to Tang Chinese territory to hold high military office there (Grousset 1971, 113–114).

Another example is the history of a Uighur noble house, the Shih-mo (Xiao), who after the overthrow of the Uighur state came to be one of the two ruling families of the ninth-century Kitan state, based in what is now Manchuria. The "native" Kitan aristocracy turned out to be no less mobile. Having founded the Liao dynasty that ruled northern China, they were eventually defeated around 1120 by a former vassal, the Jurchen lord Aguda. In 1124, a member of the Kitan imperial house, Yelü Dashi, fled west with fewer than ten thousand troops and conquered the Qarakhanid empire in Turkestan to found the "seminomadic" Qara-Kitan state, which included remnants of the Uighur khanate. The Buddhist Kitan royal house ruled a diverse set of largely Moslem subjects until the early thirteenth century. The last of the Yelü emperors was usurped by a treacherous Naiman prince, Güchülüg, who had been given refuge by the Qara-Kitan ruler when fleeing from Chinggis Khan. Güchülüg married the Kitan emperor's daughter and later seized his throne. In Manchuria and northern China, many Kitan nobles retained senior positions under the Jurchen emperors, and some members of the Kitan imperial family eventually sided with the Mongols, such as Yelü Chucai, who became the chief minister of the Chinggisid state. Another ancient house was the Jalayir, who were once rivals to the Mongol nobility but were defeated and forced to swear fealty to them in the mid-eleventh century. As dependent vassals or "slaves" (*ötögü bo'ol*) of Chinggis Khan's house, members of the Jalayir held high office in the Yuan dynasty, the Chagatay khanate and the Golden Horde, and a Jalayirid dynasty emerged to rule Iraq from 1358 to 1432 (Atwood 2004, 258).

Pareto may have remarked that "history is a graveyard of aristocracies," but in the Inner Asian case we find that history contains some noble lines that were remarkably long-lived and resilient. Chinggisid nobilities, for example, ruled Mongolia and much of Central Asia from the thirteenth until the twentieth centuries. The apparent ease with which steppe aristocracies replaced one another as rulers of often far-flung domains is less surprising when one considers the important links between them, particularly those of marriage. The use of diplomatic marriage to cement alliances and effect political incorporation was a routine aspect of statecraft, and within a generation or two this could intertwine previously distinct aristocracies. The royal house of the sixth-century Rouran empire of Mongolia and Manchuria, for example, intermarried with that of the Haital (Hephthalite) empire of Central Asia (Grousset 1971, 80). The Kitan and Uighur ruling families intermarried both with each other and with the royal house of the Tang dynasty. The Mongol Borjigin married members of the Merkit, Kereit, Tatar, and Onggirat nobility, and Chinggisid rulers formed marriage alliances with royal houses throughout Eurasia, from Korea to Byzantium.[17]

CONSTRUCTING THE MONGOL NATION

The nation-state as a political concept is conventionally contrasted to the empire. The nation-state is seen as a unitary political entity in which cultural forms have been made relatively uniform and largely correspond to the jurisdiction of the state (Gellner 1983b), whereas the empire is seen as a political assemblage with one or more subject societies under the rule of a central power.[18] But without the fiction of the tribe as a protonational ethnic unit, it becomes clearer that polities such as the Mongol Yekhe Ulus were in some senses imperial projects even in their earliest days. The Mongol "tribe" was microimperial even as it was formed by the various nobles who swore fealty to Chinggis Khan in 1206.[19] However, in the age of national populism, empires tended to be conceived of as made up of a number of *volk*, distinctive "peoples" pictured in the nationalist mould. So translations of the *Secret History of the Mongols* have generally translated the word *ulus* as "people" because it was used for political units that included populations.

But the description of collective identities in the *Secret History of the Mongols* does not match the ethnonational notion of "peoples" very well. The term *kitad*, for example, is used for the the people of northern China (*kitad irgen*), and its use includes in one category people who were culturally and linguistically diverse and would now be described as Kitan, Chinese, and Jürchen (De Rachewiltz 2004, 889). Since they were all subjects of the Jin dynasty that had replaced the Kitan *ulus*, they were all included in the term *kitad*. The term *monggol ulus* is used for a set of noble families and their subjects,[20] but there was no preexisting ethnonym for the people included in the new state, although it is clear that there was some notion of their distinctiveness, since it is also called "the *ulus* of the felt walled tents,"[21] indicating the common use of yurt (*ger*) dwellings.

The early uses of the term *monggol* only appear confusing if one is looking for a tribe in the traditional sense. The *Secret History* (§52) records that Ambagai Qan ruled over *qamug monggol*, which means "all the Mongols" (De Rachewiltz 2003, 296), and in this context the "Mongols" are clearly distinct from all their rival steppe powers, such as the Kereid, Tatar, Merkid, and Naiman. But after the establishment of Chinggis Khan's state, the ('great') *monggol ulus* included almost all of the subjugated steppe peoples, so if we think of this as the Mongol "tribe," then it must have somehow absorbed these other "peoples" in a few years. Some suggested that the term *"Qamug Monggol Ulus"* must have been the formal name of the earlier, smaller state ruled by Ambagai Qan, although there seems to be no evidence for this (De Rachewiltz 2003, 296). But the recognition of aristocracy allows us to see that since the term *monggol* indicated a set of ruling houses rather than a distinctive *volk*, their *ulus* could bear their name whether it was large or small, just as we might use the term "Norman" to designate both the great noble houses of medieval western Europe and the realms they ruled. Indeed, in the Chinggisid era the term *ulus* ("people," "nation") meant something very much like patrimony, domain, or appanage (De Rachewiltz 2003, 758). Jackson (2005, 367), for example, defines it a "complex of herds, grazing-grounds and peoples granted to a Mongol prince; used especially of the larger territorial units held by Chinggis Khan's sons and his descendants." A *monggol ulus*, then, was defined by the identity of its rulers, not by some form of ethnic or tribal identity among its subjects.

It has been argued that the meaning of the term *ulus* changed in the years of empire, from "people," when the Mongols were but simple nomads, to the appanages of princely rulers, when they became conquerors (De Rachewiltz 2003, 758). So when the *Secret History* records that To'oril Khan told Temujin, "I will reunite for you your divided *ulus*" (§104), it was translated as "people" (e.g., Cleaves 1982, 38; De Rachewiltz 2003, 34), because it was supposed to be in the prestate era, but when Ögödei Khan admits that one of his mistakes was to have had "the girls of my uncle's Odchigin's *ulus* brought to me" (§281), it is understood to mean a patrimonial domain.[22] But it seems more logical to assume that the authors and readers of the *Secret History* understood the term *ulus* in a consistent way throughout the text, and that it referred to a domain, including people, land, and property, defined by the rule of a lord.[23] Bodies of people required rulers, so Bodonchar, the ancestor of the Mongol nobility, was recorded as saying "it is right for a body to have a head, and for a coat to have a collar" (*Secret History* §33) when he encounters people who have no aristocracy—before promptly subjugating them. A key aspect of imperial or royal power was the right to reorder domains, to apportion peoples and territories to subordinates and descendants as appanages. This was done by the Türk Qahgans, by the Naiman Khan Inancha Bilge Khan in the late twelfth century (Atwood 2004, 397), by Qabul Khan when creating the Jurkin *obog*, and by many Chinggisid rulers. Far from being an unusual practice springing from the "distorting effects" of nomads conquering sedentary civilizations, this administrative constitution of units seems to have been an enduring feature of steppe life; indeed, the units created in this way were reproduced independent of effective imperial overlordship, as in the case of the Oirat and the largely independent Borjigin Mongol domains of the pre-Qing period.

As Atwood (2004, 19) puts it:

> After the fall of the Mongol Empire, appanage systems continued to divide the Mongols into districts ruled by hereditary noblemen. The units in such systems were called *tümen* and *otog* under the Northern Yuan dynasty (1368–1634), *ulus* or *anggi* under the Oirats and Züngars, and banners (*khoshuu*) under the Qing dynasty (1636–1912). While the systems varied, they all combined the idea of patrimonial rule and the union of pasture and people.

However, in the age of nationalism, polities defined by ruling aristocracies had to be reinvented as populist nation states. In the Mongolian case, it was not until the beginning of the twentieth century that we see the emergence of the discourse of nationality (Atwood 1994, 19). That is not to say that there was no pre-existing concept of distinctive *monggol* identity. From the time of the Chinggisid empire onward, the domains of Mongol rulers formed a meaningful political category, and there is mention of "all people of the Mongol tongue" (*qamug Monggoljin keleten*) in an early fourteenth-century text (De Rachewiltz 2003, 296). For administrative reasons, subjects of the chinggisid empire were placed in a series of political categories that distinguished "Mongols" from others. Under the Yuan, for example, there were four ranked administrative categories: first Mongols, then western and central Asians, then northern Chinese, and last southern Chinese. But these were political as much as ethnic categories, largely concerned with eligibility of appointment to government office and based on the polities absorbed into the Mongol empire. Although the Kitans probably spoke a Mongolic language, for example, they were placed in the northern Chinese category rather than in, or next to, that of the "Mongols." Over time, however, political, cultural, and linguistic distinctions generated collective identities that resembled the notion of "peoples" in some ways. As Christopher Atwood (1994, 8) notes, Mongol chronicles of the seventeenth century speak of *ulus* in the sense of a "realm," associating it with both people and territory, and Elverskog (2006a, 17) argues that *ulus* had come to be thought of as an identifiable community within a given state (*törö* [*törü*]).[24]

But the *ulus* was so clearly a political entity, regularly used to translate the Chinese *guo* (dynasty), for example, that another term was needed to express the notion of the Mongols as a *volk*. The term that was first taken up by early twentieth-century Mongolian nationalists was *monggol obogtan* [*obugtan*]—meaning those of the Mongol *obogs* (houses, families). This term appears in seventeenth-century texts such as the Altan Tobchi, where it is used to describe the original establishment of the Mongol line. "Börtechino . . . taking a girl called Goa Maral who had no husband, became the *Monggol obogtan*" (Munkh-Erdene 2006, 58). In the new discourse of Mongolian nationalism that emerged in the twentieth century, these historical references to common origins were used to build the notion of common "blood, race, descent, and the mysteries and mystifications of biological alikeness," the basic features that Geertz defines as central to the notion of nation or nationality (Geertz 2000, 231, cited in Munkh-Erdene 2006, 59).

But the term *obogtan*, although useful for establishing the notion of common Mongol identity, did not provide a very good match for the concept of *nationality* itself, and the Mongolian political elites of the early twentieth century had to fashion the new notion out of a number of terms such as *ugsaa* (origin, descent), *ijagur* (root, origin), and *ündüsü* (root, base). As Christopher Atwood (1994, 19–20) points out, up until this point these terms were used primarily to describe the legitimate ancestry of the Mongol nobility.[25] *Ijagurtan*, for example, was another term for the aristocracy, since having 'origins' indicated noble birth.

When casting back for records of common ethnic origin, then, the Mongolian nationalists could only find accounts of ruling lineages. As Munkh-Erdene (2006, 62) notes, "the Mongols' 'origin myths' were tied to the Chinggisid royal lineage that had established the Mongolian state and had been ruling the Mongols ever since." Historical Mongol texts included a great deal of genealogical information, but it almost all concerned the nobility, unsurprisingly perhaps, since for aristocrats descent was the basis for their position. When it came to the "original ancestor," the texts were concerned with the origins of the rulers, not the subjects. So the *Dai Yuwan Ulus-un bichig* (*Record of the Great Yuan* Ulus), for example, translated into Mongolian from Manchu around 1640–1644, states that "the ancestor of the Mongol people is Bodanchir"—that is, Bodonchar, the ancestor of the Borjigin aristocracy. Indeed, the very notion of *monggol* was in many ways defined by Borjigin rule. Mongol chronicles such as the *Altan Khürdün Minggan Khegesütü* written around 1739 describe the Oirat nobility's break with the Chinggisid rulers in the late fourteenth century as the separation of the Oirat's *ug ündüsün* (lineage/root) from the *monggol*. After this political act the Oirat are written of as distinct from the Mongols, although they continue to be included among those speaking Mongolian languages (*monggol kheleten*).[26] Being properly Mongol, then, meant to be properly ruled by Borjigid. The concepts of Borjigin and Mongol were so strongly connected that sometimes the terms are intertwined—as in the title of the 1732 chronicle written by the Kharachin nobleman Lomi, the *Monggol-Borjigid obog-un teükhe* (*History of the House of the Mongol-Borjigid*).[27] As Atwood (2004, 507) puts it: "[Chinggis Khan's] descendants, the *Taiji* class, were the only full members of the Mongolian community."

Mongol commoners did not share common descent with the Borjigid, nor could they even do so in theory, since descent from Bodonchar was the basis of aristocratic status. Grigorii Potanin, a Russian explorer who traveled through Mongolia in 1876 and 1877, recorded a number of origin myths of Mongol commoners, and these were nothing like those of the nobility (Munkh-Erdene 2006, 69) but involved mythical creatures who were generally not even human. But since the *monggol ulus* was defined by its rulers rather than its subjects, Bodonchar could be spoken of as the ancestor of all the Mongols, although it transpires that he was, more precisely, only the ancestor of the Borjigin nobility. Since the notion of the Mongols as a unity was inseparable from the project and personnel of rulership, this presented no contradiction. As Munkh-Erdene (2006, 74) shows, "the Mongolian nobility with its Chinggisid legitimacy was the symbol of Mongolian statehood . . . the elite tradition was a 'national' tradition." Like *yasu* ("bone"), the word *ündüsü* that was used to generate the term for "nationality" (*ündüsüten*) was another term indicating noble lineage. The "lineage of the Mongols," then, really only meant the aristocracy. Thus in 1912, for example, the ruling princes of Ulanchab wrote a letter protesting the new Chinese Republic's plan to incorporate Mongolian regions into China. They wrote, "if (we Mongols) become the citizens [*irgen*] of the Chinese Republic [*zhong hua irgen ulus*], and the five races [*töröl*] unite and Mongol can no longer be our distinct name, then the bone-lineage/nationality [*yasu ündüsü*] of the Mongols [*Monggol khümün-ü*], born from Heaven in ancient times, will probably be obliterated" (Munkh-Erdene 2006, 85–86).

But this aristocratic political discourse was fast being transformed by the new ideologies of ethnic nationalism. One of the principal architects of the Mongolian nationalist lexicon was Tsyben Zhamtsarano, a Buryat nationalist and ethnographer trained at St. Petersburg University, who became a powerful influence on the young Mongolian People's Republic after it was established. Zhamtsarano translated European notions of nationhood into a Mongolian context. He identified the different Mongol polities as "tribes," that is, as *"Mongolskie plemena"* in Russian. These were at a prenational stage but "spoke the various dialects of the Mongolian language and were dispersed throughout the vast land of Russia, China and Tibet, sometimes, called *Monggol kheleten* and *Monggol tuurgatan"* (Munkh-Erdene 2006, 90). He called for the establishment of a Mongol nation, arguing that all new states (*ulus törö*) were formed by a people sharing a common language (*khele*), ancestry (*ijagur*), religion (*shashin*), customs (*yosu*), teachings (*surtal*), and territory (*orun*) (Atwood 1994, 23).

The Mongolian independence movement constructed a new discourse of popular nationalism in which the shared descent of the Chinggisid lineage was used as the template for the concept of the Mongolian nationality. As Gellner (1983b, 57) notes, "nationalism is, essentially, the general imposition of a high culture on society," and in this case high culture included the tracing of descent back to Bodonchar. Munkh-Erdene (2006, 91) writes:

With the Chinggisid nobility and religious hierarchy's monopolization of the early national struggle, their ideology and conception shifted downward to the commoners, covering and embracing them just as "kingship organizes everything around a high center" (Anderson 1991, 19) . . . the terms and concepts of the Chinggisid lineage had became the lexical and conceptual underlying model and archetype of the Mongolian nationality lexicon. . . . The Mongol nobility presented at least a putative descent community that came down from time immemorial, a primordial community. While leading the Mongols toward independence the Chinggisid nobility and ecclesiastical lords spread their own ideology amongst the Mongols. . . . Consequently, "these ties were once imagined particularistically—as indefinitely stretchable nets of kinship and clientship" (Anderson 1991, 6) by the common Mongols. . . . Since the concepts of the Chinggisid lineage and the Mongols' traditional ethos were primordial in nature, they gave a rise to a primordial understanding and rhetoric of nation and nationality.

Kinship, then, was extended downward to embrace the commoners, and in the new discourse the subjects of the Borjigin lordly lineage became themselves members of a political category conceived of as a sort of lineage-nationality—not so much a new imagined community, since the aristocratic notion of the Mongol polity already existed, but a political community imagined in a new way, as a body with shared kin origins.

The notion of the polity, the *ulus*, was transformed during the Soviet period so that it resembled the Soviet version of the nation-state. Mongolian constitutions define the *ulus* in a way that is reminiscent of Stalin's notion of a nation. It had a territory and a *törö*—political leadership, or state proper. But a nation also required a national people, an equivalent for the Russian *narod*. The first Mongolian term used was *arad*, an old term that meant "commoner," which had rather too specific a position in the old political order. So the compound term *arad tümen* was devised, meaning something like "myriad commoners," to reflect the notion of the "whole people," the masses required by the new political order.

This was a new concept, since the aristocratic political discourse had not constructed the polity with reference to a single general "people." Subjects had appeared in discrete categories. There were the nobility (*taijinar* and *ijagurtan*), the *shar* (*shira*, members of the Buddhist monastic establishments), and the *khara* (secular commoners or *arad*). Political statements were constructed with respect to these categories rather than to a general and inclusive national people. As late as 1934, when a politically active senior lama sought to address the Mongolians of Inner Mongolia, he issued four separate pamphlets addressed to the *taijinar* (princes), the lamas, the youth, and the people (commoners) respectively.[28]

The reconceptualization of the Mongols did not stop at the national level. As Bulag (1998, 31–37) shows, the creation of ethnicity was another aspect of the socialist nation-building process. A set of Mongol terms were chosen to translate the key elements of Soviet theory on the historical stages of ethnic communities. The Russian *rod* (clan) was translated as *obog*, *plemya* (tribe) as *aimag*, *narodnost* (ethnic group / nationality) as *yastan* [*yasutan*], and *natsiya* (nation) as *ündesten*. These terms were organized according to the Marxist version of the nineteenth-century evolutionary scheme by which tribes were made up of clans.[29] In addition, however, following the USSR, in which the state citizenry was made up of peoples of many ethnic groups or "nationalities," Mongols were registered as members of ethnic or national minority groups—*yastan*.[30] This formed part of a wider vision by which "backward peoples would be upgraded, so as to merge with more progressive nationalities to become a Soviet nation" (Bulag 1998, 32). These became official identities, and the internal passports of citizens of the MPR recorded their *yastan*, such as Khalkha, Buryat, Barga, Dörvöd, Dariganga, Darkhat, Khoton, Khotgoid, Ööld, Torgut, or Zakhchin.

Like the tribe, the concept of ethnic group is rooted in the notion of kinship and common descent (Hobsbawm 1990, 63). But it is very clear that these "ethnic groups" were not autochthonous kinship communities but politically defined categories that had been historically formed by rulers. The Zakhchin ("Borderers"), for example, of southern Khovd province, originated as a Zünghar administrative division (*otog*) formed from a diverse set of subjects charged with the duty of acting as border wardens. After their lord surrendered to the Qing, they were formed into a banner (*khoshuu*) and assigned duties to support the Manchu *amban* at Khovd (Atwood 2004, 617). They remained administratively separate and in the Soviet area were judged to be sufficiently distinct to be labeled a *yastan*. Another example is provided by the Khoton (Khotong) of Uvs province, who originated as enslaved prisoners of war from Muslim areas of Central Asia, deported by the Zünghars. When their lord, the Dörböd prince Tseren Ubashi, surrendered to the Qing in 1753, they were allocated territory in what is now Uvs. We know that they were required to deliver forty sacks of wheat and send eleven laborers every summer to the prince's palace, and that by the early twentieth century they spoke a Dörböd dialect of Mongolian (Atwood 2004, 311). In these cases, the relatively late incorporation of former Zünghar subjects by the Qing has left us with historical records that make clear the administrative acts by which groups of people acquired distinctive political identities that were later used as grounds for their identification as "ethnic groups." But the conquest and relocation of populations date from the earliest historical times in Inner Asia. In any era, the political landscape would represent the cumulative product of countless comparable acts of designation and allocation, great and small. It is hard to imagine self-structuring autochthonous kinship groups surviving this process intact, even if they had ever existed.

The dislocation of population could be accomplished by marriage as well as by war. The steppe aristocracy had long practiced an institution known as *inje*: this was a sort of human dowry, a personal entourage of subjects and household servants that accompanied a noblewoman when she moved to live with her husband, and represented her share of her father's subjects. One of Chinggis Khan's wives, for instance, the Kereid lady Ibaqa Beki, had come to him with an *inje* of two hundred people.[31] And since this took place before the split between Temüjin and the Kereid khan, this indicates that the institution was not a peculiar product of conquest, but an established practice among the steppe aristocracy from before Chinggis Khan's time. Since exchanging marriage partners also led to an exchange of groups of subjects, and steppe rulers frequently had several wives from different regions, the encampments of steppe nobles must have been socially diverse, including people from many backgrounds. Large groups of people could also be moved in this way. The Khori division of the Tumad Mongols, for example, was designated as the *inje* of a noblewoman named Baljin Khatun, according to oral history (Rumyantsev 1962, 178), and must have numbered hundreds if not thousands of households. In the late sixteenth century, they had to move more than a thousand kilometers from their old territories in eastern Khövsgöl to lands near the Khinggan mountains when Baljin Khatun married a local lord there. Here again, the social landscape was formed by "top-down" processes of rulership; it is not just the state as a whole that is "regarded as little more than the property of an individual" (Sahlins 1983, 522), but also the subjects within the administrative divisions of the wider polity.

ETHNOS AND ETHNOGENESIS: CHARISMATIC LEADERSHIP
AND THE ETHNIC GROUP

The extent to which something resembling a nation existed before the advent of the recognizable "modern" form differs in the work of primordealist scholars (e.g., Shils 1957; Van den Berghe 1995) and constructivist ones (e.g., Hobsbawm and Ranger 1983; Anderson 1991; Gellner 1993). Gellner and Hobsbawm, for example, sought to counter dominant trends in history that projected modern national concepts onto past epochs and tried to show how nationalist ideology creates nations where they had not previously existed.[32] But the notion that nations are rooted in "ethnic" units of common descent has remained influential. Although Hobsbawm (1990, 64) points out that nations are not generally formed by preexisting ethnic groups, for example, he still considers the ethnic group to be a form of protonation. And Anthony Smith (2000, 12), who does not consider himself by any means primordealist, argues for the "vital role of ethnic ties and ethnic communities, or *ethnies*, in providing the basis for the emergence and persistence of nations. An *ethnie* [sic] may be defined as a named human population with a common myth of descent, shared historical memories, one or more elements of common culture, a link with an historic territory, and a measure of solidarity, at least among the elites." We might note in passing that by this definition we would have to see the Mongolian ethnos, as well as the nation, as being constructed in the twentieth century, since the Borjigin did not share a myth of common descent with most of their subjects before that time. Entangled as it clearly is with nineteenth-century theories of common descent as the universal basis of political units, the concept of *ethnies* seems of limited utility when it comes to rethinking these models.

Unsurprisingly perhaps, theories of *ethnies* as protonational entities became most elaborated in Soviet scholarship, firmly rooted as it was in nineteenth-century evolutionism. Ethnic studies in the USSR were based on the notion that ethnic groups were stable entities that transmitted their social structures from generation to generation (Khazanov 1990, 220). In the post-Soviet era, as Valery Tishkov (1994, 88) noted, *ethnos* and ethnogenesis remained powerful and almost sacred themes in anthropological and public discourse.

Lev Gumilev (1912–1992) was a historian and geographer whose theories of ethnogenesis became extraordinarily influential in late Soviet and post-Soviet Eurasia. Gumilev (1989, 481) argued that the ethnic unit—the *ethnos*—"naturally developed on the basis of an original stereotype of behaviour of a collective of people, existing as a power system (structure), opposing itself to all other similar collectives, proceeding from a sensation of complimentarity (*komplimentarnost*)." This *komplimentarnost* was close to patriotism and "is found in the competence of history, for it is impossible to love people, not respecting their ancestors" (Gumilev 1989, 225). The *ethnos* was born out of a desire for fundamental change—a concept that he terms *passionarnost'*—"passionarity"—by which he meant "the ability and aspiration towards changing the environment, or, translating this into the language of physics—breaking the inertia of a modular condition of environment." "Passionarity" was Gumilev's "factor x" in explaining social change. It represented a sort of group charisma or, perhaps more precisely, a form of revolutionary spirit. Shnirelman and Panarin (2001, 10) summarize Gumilev's view of ethnogenesis: "the birth of an *ethnos* [is formed] by [the] appearance of a small group of people, united by common sympathy and a great feeling of patriotism, who are prepared to sacrifice personal prosperity and even their lives for the achieving of their personal goal. In its name they are ready to break with the usual norms of behaviours, i.e. with the existing stereotype."

Gumilev's work was highly appealing to the emergent leadership of the newly independent states of post-Soviet Central Asia, perhaps because it seemed to celebrate successful political figures as catalysts of social and historical development. Politicians such as President Akaev of Kyrgyzstan made explicit use of Gumilev's theories in their own nation-building ideologies (Gullette 2006). In Kazakhstan, the new state named one of the country's largest universities after him, and official histories reproduce his theory of the distinctive *ethnos* (e.g., Ismagulov 1998).[33] In many ways, Gumilev and other theorists of ethnogenesis such as Bromley can be seen to have elaborated the well-established themes of national-populist social science.[34] Having pictured populations in terms of distinctive *volk* (Fichte) or large-scale solidarities (Renan, Durkheim), theorists had to explain how these collectivities came to obey rulers. Weber's solution was the notion of charismatic leadership, which could be subsequently routinized to become the self-sustaining traditional authority of the premodern state.[35] Gumilev's notion of passionarity reflects Weber's concept of charisma since, as Charles Lindholm (1997, 76) noted, Weber was influenced by Nietzsche, "whose superman was superior precisely because of the force of his passions."[36] Charisma solved the problem of how change could occur in otherwise changeless "traditional" societies, and it was therefore particularly influential in accounts of putative tribal nomadic society (e.g., Barfield 1989, 3; Sahlins 1968, 39). Bold (2001, 83), for example, writes, "the charisma of rulers was one of the main phenomena of Central Asian history." The formation of nomadic states and empires could be explained by the exceptional: the extraordinary personal leadership qualities of a Chinggis Khan or Attila. Through the power of personality, and perhaps the superstition of his followers, the exceptional leader unites the prenational tribe into a statelike structure. Traditions of statecraft and institutions of rulership need not be attributed to the societies of "simple nomads," since they are cast as having been swept up in the fervor of charismatic leadership. This was an old solution to the problem of reconciling the historical effects of steppe empires with the notion of a timeless, "arrested" society.

As Gellner pointed out, charisma removes the need for an explanation of leadership, since it is defined in terms of its effects. "It is recognition on the part of those subject to authority which is decisive for the validity of charisma" (Weber 1978, 242). Describing "great leaders" as being charismatic—that is, as being thought to have exceptional leadership attributes—does little more than restate their reputation in generalized sociological terms. But in the case of steppe rulers, it helped perpetuate the old notion of a timeless, simple society, occasionally rallied by some primitive Napoleon, as described by C. D. Forde (1934, 328), the anthropologist and human geographer:

> Central Asia is the traditional land of pastoral nomads who wander seasonally in search of pasture. . . . From time to time they have become the instrument of an organizing genius who has led them in rapid invasion over wide tracts of settled country and so given rise to the legend of the invincibility of the peoples of this nomad realm. Until the beginning of the nineteenth century this vast pastoral land had remained substantially unchanged since the times when the Scythians of its south-western marches became known to the Greeks or when Marco Polo journeyed among the tribes tributary to Chingiz Khan.

This tradition has tended to downplay the political institutions of steppe societies; the concentration on the occasional "organizing genius" helped obscure the powerful indigenous political heritage of Inner Asia. The historical record shows a rich diversity of political forms, all of which drew to some extent on techniques and institutions of governance that were parts of a distinctive steppe tradition. The decimal administrative structure was part of the tradition of statecraft on the steppe that dates back to the Xiongnu empire of the third century B.C.E. (Atwood 2004, 139; Di Cosmo 2002, 177; Sneath 2006). Other institutions are just as old—such as the "heavenly mandate" of the ruler,[37] the collective sovereignty of the ruling house, and, most fundamental of all, aristocracy as a political system. By rehistoricizing accounts of societies described in terms of tribal tradition, we can see them as elements in a history of political struggle, change, and innovation. The imperial polity of Chinggis Khan represents one of the more centralized of the political structures that steppe rulers and aristocracies were able to construct, and this centralization made it recognizably statelike, since it matched the Weberian ideal type to some extent. But the high tide of Chinggisid centralization passed relatively quickly, and the political order that emerged is just as revealing of the substrata of power upon which steppe government was based. As a political form, the nature of this underlying order offers a direct challenge to conventional notions of the centralized state.

7

The Headless State

Aristocratic Orders and the Substrata of Power

On September 20, 1640, a great assembly was held in Western Mongolia. It was attended by the most powerful lords of the eastern Eurasian
steppes—the Zasagtu and Tüshiyetü khans of the Khalkha (Outer Mongolia); the Oirat rulers Erdeni Baatur Khung-Taiji, Khoo-örlög Taishi, and
Güüshi Khan; along with some twenty other senior nobles. They were
meeting to form a new "state" (*törö*) and to draw up its code of laws. But
although it was described using the word for a state, the political formation they created would seem impossible in terms of the Weberian model
of the ideal-typical bureaucratic state. It had laws, rulers, and subjects, but
it was to have no capital, no center, and no sovereign. It was a distributed, headless state formed by independent nobles and their subjects and
sharing a common law code and aristocratic social order. We know more
about its internal structure than most nonimperial steppe polities because
its code of laws, the *Monggol-Oirad Chaaji*, has survived.

The standard historical narrative has represented both Oirat and Mongol society of the time as tribal (e.g., Soucek 2000, 170). This is understandable enough, since there was no identifiable imperial state ruling
their territories at that time. There had been little by way of real political
centralization among the Mongol princes since the collapse of the Yuan

dynasty at the end of the fourteenth century, (although Batmonkh Dayan Khan and his queen Mandukhai had briefly revived the dream of Mongol unity at the end of the fifteenth century). In the sixteenth century, even the Khalkha Mongol territory was divided between three dynasties, the Tüshiyetü khans, and Zasagtu khans in the west, and the Setsen khans in the east. At this time, the Oirat rulers controlled much of western Mongolia and what is now northern Xinjiang, and there had been a series of clashes between them and the Chinggisid Mongol princes since the end of the fifteenth century. But, perhaps spurred on by the growing power of the Manchus in the east, the leading Mongol and Oirat lords had decided that it was time to put aside old grievances and form a new political union. The confederation endured for forty-eight years before fracturing as war broke out between the Oirat Galdan Khan (1678–1697) and the Khalkha Tüshiyetü Khan Chakhundorji (1655–1699), which led to Galdan's 1688 invasion of Mongolia.

After swearing fealty to the Qing in 1691, the Borjigid Mongols of Khalkha replaced the Mongol-Oirat code with the a set of similar laws, the *Khalkha Jirum*, in 1709. But the 1640 law code continued to be used by the Oirats, and among the Volga Kalmyks it remained in force until the abolition of the nobility's authority by the tsarist colonial government in 1892 (Atwood 2003, 389). Riasanovsky (1965 [1937], 47) notes that it was the most widely applied of Mongol laws, apart perhaps from those of Chinggis Khan himself, for which we have only fragmentary records. The Mongol-Oirat laws of 1640 closely resemble an earlier code made by Altan Khan in the sixteenth century and are part of a tradition of state that stretches back to the Chinggisid era, if not earlier. It is the closest thing we have to what would be conventionally described as "tribal law."

But the political entity that was governed by this law was not an empire in the conventional sense, and it was certainly nothing like a centralized state. The territory of the union was not even contiguous. It included the domains of Khoo-örlög Taishi on the Volga, which later became the Kalmyk khanate, some three thousand kilometers to the west. It is hardly surprising that the *Monggol-Oirad Chaaji* has generally been treated as a treaty rather than as the charter of a new state, since it matched so few of the criteria of the state as it is usually conceived. But the union described itself unambiguously as *törö* [*törü*], which Humphrey and Hürelbaatar (2006) describe in this period as meaning "state," "sovereignty," or "government," indicating a concrete political formation as well as a principle of rulership.[1] The Mongol-Oirat union can be described as a confederation—not the "tribal" confederation of Morgan, but a joint project of rulership by powerful aristocrats.

Core features of the state as conceived of in nineteenth-century social science are present: codified law, a hierarchy of political offices, stratification, and property in the form of institutionalized rights over both resources and people.[2] The provisions of the law stipulate punishments for various offenses, usually livestock fines in units of nines and fives. But for the aristocracy, these fines included subject households, listed along with other possessions so that they are indistinguishable from property. For example, section 8 of the code reads:

> If a great noble (*yekhe noyan*) goes to battle and flees from the enemy, one hundred sets of armour, one hundred camels, fifty households of people and one thousand horses will be taken. If a *daiching* or *chüdger* level of noble goes to battle and flees from the enemy, fifty sets of armour, fifty camels, twenty five households of people and five hundred horses will be taken. From a lesser noble (*baga noyan*), ten sets of armour, ten camels, ten households of people and one hundred horses will be taken.
>
> (BUYANÖLJEI AND GE 2000, 34)

The code provides evidence of the entire apparatus of state other than a centralized authority. It mentions courts (*örgüge*), judges (*jarguchin*), military conscription, and a hierarchy of officials. There were distinctions within the nobility and a series of subaltern ranks, and this hierarchy and administrative structure was common to both Mongol (i.e., Chinggisid) and Oirat-ruled domains. The most senior figures were the "great lords" (*yekhe noyad*) holding the highest titles of rulership—Khans, Khung-Taijis, and Taishis. Next came those with marriage alliances with the rulers, the *tabunang* "sons-in-law," and grouped with them in this strata were the "officeholding" nobles, the *yamutu noyad*. The term *yamu* indicates a senior office of state and was later used for the ministries of government, but at this time it may be that the office concerned was membership in a senior council (Atwood 2006, 216) or may have simply been the rulership of the largest administrative divisions—the *ulus*, or *anggi* (noble appanages), which were themselves divided into units called *otogs*—the peoples and pastures allocated to a noble,[3] usually of a few thousand households in size and described by Atwood (2004, 430) as "the basic unit of Mongol socio-political life." They seem almost identical to the "banner" (*khoshuu*) unit, which is also mentioned at this time and later became the basic Mongol administrative unit under the Qing.[4] The rulers of these *otog*s may also have counted as officeholding nobles, or they may have been categorized in the next class down, the "lesser nobles" (*baga noyad*) and their sons-in-law (*tabunang*). All of these lords seem to have belonged to the ruling "bones"—Borjigin in the case of the Mongols and the Choros, Galwas, and other non-Chinggisid noble houses in the case of the Oirat. They raised taxes, levied military forces, and enforced the law in their own domains. Beneath them there were a series of ranked officials who administered the common subjects on their lord's behalf. The *otog* officials (*tüshimed, erkheten*) ruled subjects grouped into units of forty households (*döchin*), headed by an official named a *demchi*; these were divided into "twenties" (*khori*) headed by a *shigülengge*, and these were divided into groups of ten households, with a head.[5] Subjects were further classified into three ranks, the "good," "middle," and "base," and slaves (*bo'ol*) had a separate legal status.

The fines and punishments are routinely related to the status of the injured party, and sometimes commoners are not mentioned at all, suggesting that certain offences were not applicable to them. For example, section 17 reads:

> If [someone] attacks a great noble, confiscate all his properties. If [someone] verbally attacks an office-holding noble or son-in-law take one Nine, if they lay hands on them, take five Nines. If [someone] attacks a lesser noble or son-in-law, take a Five; if they lay hands on them and beat them heavily, take three Nines; lightly beat them, take two Nines. If [someone] attacks adjutants or *shigülengge* (tax collector or head of twenty households) verbally, take a horse and a sheep, if they beat them heavily, take a Nine, if they beat them lightly, take a Five.
>
> (BUYANÖLJEI AND GE 2000, 56–57)

On the other hand, the lower classes are assumed to have less property, so for some crimes the fines are smaller for lower-status offenders.[6]

The code also reveals an aspect of aristocratic power that is "pastoral" in the Foucauldian sense, concerned with the well being of subjects, and places a responsibility on rulers to provide for paupers. These "poor laws" appear in the additional clauses that were added to the 1640 document around 1677 by the Oirat ruler Galdan Khung-Taiji (1644–1697). The second of these articles reads "*Demchis* should look after the base [i.e., poor].

If they cannot look after them, they should tell their heads of *otogs*. Heads of *otogs* should look after them all without discriminating between their own and others'. If there is no way to look after them, report to one's superiors" (Buyanöljei and Ge 2000, 254).

This form of regulation penetrated every level of social life, including all manner of personal conduct.[7] Fines are stipulated for failure to report a theft, failing to pay a court fee, impersonating an official, insulting a social superior, and inappropriately placing wood in a domestic fire. The regulations extend to stipulating the size of dowries and wedding feasts for people of different ranks, the age of marriageable girls, and the number of marriages that should take place within the administrative units of forty households each year.

There is little doubt as to *whose* rule the code represents. This is the collective sovereignty exercised by a steppe aristocracy stretching from Manchuria to the Volga. Section 18 reads:

> If nobles holding offices and *tabunangs* (sons-in-law of a noble), junior nobles and *tabunangs*, *demchi* (head of forty households), *shigülengge* (head of twenty households) beat a person for the sake of the lords' (*ejed*) administration, law and order, they are not guilty, even if they beat someone to death. If these officials beat people in order to show off, fine them a Nine for heavy beating, take a Five for a middling beating and a horse for slight beating.
>
> (BUYANÖLJEI AND GE 2000, 59)

Here the plural form of *ejen* (lord) is used for the "the lords' administration"; the laws refer to the nobility's joint government of subjects. The code makes clear the mutual interests both aristocracies had in controlling their subjects and preventing commoners defecting to the jurisdictions of other nobles. "Those (people) who go to another *khoshuu* and those who move between them shall be gathered and seized. If they have no *otog* they shall belong to an *otog*, if they have no *aimag* [administrative division] they shall belong to an *aimag*." The regulations detail the punishments in the case of subjects leaving their allotted pastoral area (*nutug*) (Buyanöljei and Ge 2000, 258).[8]

THE STATE AS SOCIAL RELATION

Recalling Chandhoke's insight (1995, 49) that the "state is simply a social relation, in as much as it is the codified power of the social formation," we can see that in this sense the state is present in the power that any noble exercised over his subjects and in the wider political order that framed and empowered this rule—aristocracy. Indeed, we also find the key characteristics of the state according to classical social theory, since aristocracy entails both political office in the Weberian sense and class exploitation in the Marxian one. The use of descent to generate rulers and subjects permitted all the further political refinements represented both in the 1640 code and the more centralized political orders that could be established by imperial rulers. The "substrata of power" that underpinned each polity involved the construction of legal personhood in the form of rulers and subjects of various ranks, including slaves. The existence of slavery in most, if not all, steppe societies up until the nineteenth century has been generally recognized, but it has been downplayed (since it rather contradicted the egalitarian nomad model) on the grounds that slaves could never have been very numerous (e.g., Khazanov 1983, 159).[9] But it is the institution of slavery, rather than the absolute numbers of slaves, that is most revealing of the political order. The status of slaves was not an absolute one, but depended on that of their masters, at least in the Mongol case (Skrynnikova 2006), and they were not without some rights—the 1640 code stipulates fines for the killing of even one's own slaves. But even in the forms mentioned above, slavery is evidence of unmistakable relations of dominance, subordination, and stratification. That it could exist in such a wide range of different steppe polities suggests that it did not require the apparatus of a centralized state and that a distributed political order is perfectly capable of enforcing relations of lifelong dependency, as in the case of slavery among the "headless" nineteenth-century Turkmen.

By finally discarding the tribal model of an essentialized and timeless nomadic society, we can recognize innovation and political change as well as continuity. As Atwood (2006b, 237) points out, the strong centralized monarchy of Chinggis Khan's empire can be contrasted with the much more weakly centralized and relatively confederated Oirat polity. But by the seventeenth century, the Chinggisid domains were no more centralized than their Oirat counterparts, and the political union of 1640 represents another innovation in that it had no single overlord at all. It was, of course, a unique historical outcome, just as was the Chinggisid empire, but it was not entirely without precedent.

The Kimek polity that ruled the eastern Russian steppe in the tenth century was a monarchy—noted the tenth-century writer Hudud al-Alam.

"According to the *Hudûd* (our only source for this) the Kimek 'king' is called 'khâqân' and had eleven lieutenants who held hereditary fiefs" (Golden 2006, 29). However, by the twelfth century, the Kimek kingdom had given way to the Cuman or Qipchaq polity, which was clearly not a monarchy and seems to have been another headless aristocracy for much of its history.[10] Golden (1990, 280) notes, for example, that the late twelfth-century Jewish traveler Petahia of Ratisbon, who journeyed through Cumania, remarked that they "have no king, only princes and noble families."[11] Similarly, the Oguz seem to have had no overlord but many lords (*arbâb*), as the tenth-century Ibn Faḍlân reports (Golden 2006, 28). The history of Borjigid rule provides a spectrum of more and less centralized political formations within a single tradition, with effective overlordship in the times of Batmönkh Dayan Khan in the fifteenth century and Altan Khan in the sixteenth, but with the Chinggisid aristocracy jealously guarding its independence for much of the intervening time before finally swearing fealty to the Qing.

We also see political forms that might be notionally placed somewhere between autocratic and "headless" aristocratic orders, such as forms of elective monarchy. The khans of the Kazakh khanate were elected by senior nobles, and in the early Kitan polity the position of qagan appears to have been that of a "first among equals," elected by the eight senior lords for a three-year period of office, until Yelü Abaoji made himself a lifelong monarch in 907 and introduced imperial rule (Wittfogel and Feng 1949, 571; Atwood 2004, 315). When considering the histories of less exotic and more familiar political systems, it is very clear that socially stratified aristocracies need not exist *despite* a weak or absent center; they can actively promote one. The powerful patrician families of republican Rome, for example, famously resisted monarchy until the Augustinian period, and as Mosca (1939, 52) remarked, "what Aristotle called a democracy was simply an aristocracy of fairly broad membership."

A rather less distant historical parallel is provided by the elective monarchy of Poland, which stands as a striking exception to the political trends in the rest of Europe. "In the early modern period the continent witnessed the emergence of a new style of government based on centralization of political authority through bureaucratic techniques. . . . Poland, however, alone of all the great powers in Europe, failed to create the stable bureaucracy which could centralize political power within its sprawling domains" (Fedorowicz 1982, 2). Interestingly, the Polish case provides another example of the decentralization of power over time, whereby the originally strong monarchy of the Piast and Jagiellonian dynasties weakened before the growing power of the aristocracy in the sixteenth century, so that after the last of the Jagiellonian line died in 1572 an elective monarchy was introduced to rule the Polish-Lithuanian Commonwealth, in which all nobles could vote to elect the monarch. This excited a good deal of puzzled comment from other European observers, as Fedorowicz notes.[12] The system limited the powers of the Polish king to such an extent that Fedorowicz describes it as a republic of nobles that lasted until the commonwealth was partitioned between Russia, Prussia, and Austria around 1791–1795.

> The Commonwealth was a gentry republic unlike anything elsewhere in Europe. Something under 10 per cent of its population were acknowledged to be members of a ruling class . . . each of whom could feel that his *Rzecz-pospolita* [commonwealth] was a *respublica* in the literal sense, the common property of his social order: all other inhabitants of the Commonwealth were merely its subjects. A Polish noble enjoyed complete freedom from most forms of taxation. He had a voice in the local assemblies of his region, and he elected representatives to sit in the national Sejm [parliament]. As a noble, he was eligible for every military, civilian or ecclesiastical office in the state up to and including that of king . . . most other elective monarchies in Europe regularly restricted their choices to the members of one particular dynasty only. Perhaps most significantly . . . the nobility of the Commonwealth regarded itself as part of one indivisible "nation". . . . Their solidarity allowed them to dominate Polish life entirely in all its aspects.
>
> FEDOROWICZ (1982, 5–6)

Two aspects of this aristocratic order seem particularly relevant here. First, it emerged from a more centralized monarchy, and evolutionist treatments of the state would struggle to account for this development using the standard narrative of the increasingly centralized state. They might have to resort to describing it as a case of "devolution," as Service (1975, 82) did of European feudalism, which seems less than convincing. So a historical perspective on change provides a welcome replacement for the evolutionist narratives by which political forms develop unilineally, at a slower or more rapid rate, and timeless traditions either endure or decay. With the benefit of abundant written records, we can see political institutions as the products of particular historical developments, not as representatives of evolutionary stages such as "chiefdom" or "primitive state," and there seems no reason to return to evolutionism whenever historical records are scarce or the subject is exotic. Second, the power of this relatively decentralized state was very clearly not located in its center, but in the network of nobles and their local and regional political institutions across a huge realm that at its height contained most of central Eastern Europe. Indeed, this was the case to some degree in most preindustrial states, and Weber (1978, 1051) used the term "decentralized patrimonial domination" to describe polities in which dependent rulers were powerful relative to their notional overlord. However, Weber assumed this was a result of subordinate officeholders "appropriating" the powers of preexisting patrimonial rulers, and while this may describe the Polish case, I think we need not assume it for all.[13] Whatever their origins, then, powerful aristocracies have been far from rare.

POWER AND DESCENT

Central to the nature of aristocracy—the rule of an hereditary elite—are the processes and institutions of descent and the inheritance of status and political office. In the Chinese, Korean, and, I think, Mongol cases, we see that the patrilineage was not the original building block of a clan society but was introduced as a technique of the elite, as a means of ordering descent and inheritance. This returns us to the original insight offered by Engels in *The Origin of the Family, Private Property, and the State*, but from a new perspective. Forms of kinship and descent groups were indeed shaped by the requirements of inheritance, but this was not the transmission of the individual private property of a later age but rather the aristocratic inheritance of what Anderson called the dynastic realm—title, rank, and rulership. The presence of the state—the codified power required for the enterprise of governing subjects—generates a rationale for the tracing and ordering of descent as a mechanism for the reproduction of power relations.

In the age of national populism, distinct "peoples" were imagined as constituting themselves and could therefore give rise to national leaderships that represented each *volk* and their interests. It seemed natural that in prestate society people should also form popular political collectivities—groups of kin with leaders that represented *them*. But in the age of dynastic states, peoples were produced by rulers, and, in an analogous way, noble lines, lineages, and houses were generated by those with title, power, and wealth. An example of this process is provided by Meeker's study of the Ottoman legacy in Turkey, which not only reveals how the rule of hereditary elites constituted the substrata of state power but also provides another example of how easily representations of an unfamiliar society were distorted by anthropological notions of kinship society.

In his 2002 work *A Nation of Empire*, Meeker explains how, when he began his research in the Trabzon region in the 1960s, he was struck by the domination of public life by two ancient local families, the Selimoğlu and Muradoğlu. Primed by anthropological theory, he concluded that he was dealing with a "clan society" based on descent groups sharing patronymic names. But this analysis gave rise to nagging doubts. There were no assemblies of the clans by which members met, nor could he find common property, mutual obligations, or clear marriage prohibitions. The categories he had labeled "clans" were just amorphous groups of men claiming descent from the same patronymic ancestor, not corporate groups in any way. Meeker (2002, 23) writes:

> This meant that I had failed to discover how the Selimoğlu and Muradoğlu had dominated the public life of the district. Given this difficulty, I turned to a strategy of anthropological reconstruction. The patronymic groups in the present must be but a pale reflection of a more structured and institutionalized clan-society in the past. Once upon a time, when the authority of the central government was either weak or absent, there must have been a clan-society in the eastern coastal districts. Now its shadowy legacy continued to distort and subvert the institutions of the nation-state. As my theory of a social order divided from the state order was seriously mistaken, one might have expected that such a study of history would immediately reveal the flaws in my thinking. On the contrary, my errors were reinforced and compounded by the sources available to me.

However, Meeker eventually began to revise his views when he became more aware of the importance of the figures he had taken for clan leaders. These turned out to have been local "valley lords" holding the title of *agha*, who, until recently, kept large fortified mansions. He realized that the *aghas* were local elites claiming positions in the state system and who were able to establish family lines.

> To claim a patronym was therefore to claim descent from an individual who had some kind of standing in the imperial system. . . . It was always aghas who made large clans and never large clans that made aghas. Upon a re-

view of my field notes, I discovered that the ascendant of every large family grouping with which I was familiar was said to have held some kind of state position or appointment.

(MEEKER 2002, 31)

Rather than clan society standing in contrast to the state, Meeker was looking at something very different: a society that was thoroughly shaped by state power. He found that "the aghas, mansions, clans, and parties were not based on the elaboration of a local system of kinship. They were country extensions of the imperial military and administrative establishment. I therefore dropped the term 'clan' since it evoked the idea of a local social system complete in itself" (Meeker 2002, 32). The valley lords would also raise taxes, enforce laws, and sometimes defy central authority, and there was always a certain amount of rivalry between the *aghas*, which sometimes degenerated into military skirmishes and sieges. Meeker (2002, 38) notes that for the central ruler these local elites were "more dangerous than any kind of anti-state clan-society but also more useful, precisely because they represented social formations oriented toward the state system."

> My argument can be summarized as follows. Local elites backed by local coalitions had the ability to tax commerce, raise armies, requisition supplies, impose labor, apprehend fugitives, and exact punishment, that is, to do everything that higher state officials of the centralized government might be able to do. They could do so, even though the latter might sometimes attempt to prevent them, because they were able to do what the proper imperial system could do: to deploy the sovereign power of a family line through a following based on a discipline of interpersonal association. . . . The result was the decentralization of the state system, and, during periods of crisis, the vertical and horizontal fracturing of the structure of political authority.
>
> (MEEKER 2002, XX)

This posed a problem for standard theories of the state. The features of local order that Meeker had encountered, local hereditary elites wielding forms of sovereign power, were thought to be characteristic of a lack of state power, and yet Meeker shows that it was precisely these forms that constituted state power in the region. He notes (2002, 33) that this requires "a theory of a society within, rather than against, the state."

SOCIETY WITHIN THE STATE—
CULTURES OF ARISTOCRACY

We can, I think, entertain the idea that societies are made by the project of rulership without supposing that culture is entirely colonized by this project. However, when it comes to subjectification, the creation of political subjects, we are bound to regard the political order as the principal influence. Can we know anything about the subjectivities produced by the aristocratic orders of steppe polities? I think we can. This is not to say we should aim to understand the "inner selves" of those subject to these orders now or in the past. In representing others, as Rose (1996, 142) notes, "the human being is not an entity with a history, but the target of a multiplicity of types of work, more like a latitude or a longitude at which different vectors of different speeds intersect. The 'interiority' which so many feel compelled to diagnose is not that of a psychological system, but of a discontinuous surface, and kind of infolding of exteriority." So what kinds of work are done by an aristocratic ordering of society? In political terms, the central feature is the hereditary principle that designates some people as partners in the project of governing and others as the targets of that governance. This division by descent into the social categories of rulers and ruled must count as some of the most fundamental of what Rose (1996, 131) calls "the *practices* with which human beings have been located in particular 'regimes of the person.'" The subject constructed by an aristocratic order is different, to be sure, from the citizen-subject of the bureaucratic centralized state, but both share the central obligation of obedience to authority. If the state is a social relation, this would seem to be its most basic aspect.

As one would expect, narratives that explicitly represent the views of commoners as such are largely absent from the historical texts produced in the steppe aristocracies. Much of what we have in the Mongolian case dates from the time of revolution and was elicited as part of a process of vilification of the *ancien régime*. These include autobiographical accounts of grinding poverty and abuse at the hands of nobles and senior lamas. There is also a body of Mongolian folk tales published in the Communist period in both the Mongolian Peoples Republic and Inner Mongolia, and many of these tales include motifs of resistance in the face of overbearing nobles and lamas. In these narratives we find Robin Hood–like social bandits such as "Tiger Black" and trickster figures such as Balansengge who mock both respectability and officialdom (Bawden 2003, 327–556). But, published as they were in states that had recently waged revolutionary struggle and their own versions of class war, we must suspect claims that they represent a long tradition of explicit commoner resistance to aristo- cratic rule. Most of the narratives placed within this "folk" tradition reflect the values of aristocracy. *The Tale of the Two Dapple-Greys*, for example, is a poem thought to date from the fourteenth-century Chinggisid period and is a parable that teaches the importance of loyalty to one's ruler. It tells the story of two fine horses who rebel against their lord and escape to live in freedom, only to return when they realize the value of loyalty (Bawden 2003, 73–88). The great epics, such that of Geser Khan, are largely heroic tales of princes, lamas, monsters, and emperors inhabiting a magi- cal world filled with wonder and adventure.

The bulk of written historical sources, as one would expect, were writ- ten by or for the elite strata, and it is difficult to discern a distinctive com- moner voice before the twentieth century. Common subjects figure rather little in the *Secret History*, and when they do, they reinforce aristocratic values. There is the lament of Chilger, for example, who is wracked with guilt for living with a captured noblewoman (Temujin's wife). "I, Chilg- er . . . touched the Lady, the qatun. . . . Ignoble and bad Chilger, his own black (i.e., common) head will receive (a blow)."[14] Two commoner horse- herds who overhear a plot against Chinggis Khan and report it to him are rewarded by being elevated to the status of "freemen" (*darkhan*) (*Secret History of the Mongols* §187). Despite their many rewards (they are granted the right to wear quivers, which may have been forbidden to commoners, and were also given the whole of Ong Khan's palace tent and its rich con- tents), they are not made nobles (see Rachewiltz 2004, 108); freeman status seems to have been as high a rank as social mobility would allow.[15] There is also a strong tradition of Buddhist-inspired histories that date from the seventeenth century, works like the *Altan Tobchi* and *Erdeni-yin Tobchi*, and these are largely concerned with rulership—substantiating the ancient and sacred origins of the Mongol Borjigin khans in Buddhist terms, for example. In general, in both the oral and written traditions, aristocratic values are readily recognizable—a concern with military victory, wealth, position, title, marriage alliance, horseflesh, and hunting all figure promi- nently, and in the later work piety and the patronage of Buddhism appear as major themes. We also find a high value placed on justice and a fatherly concern for one's subordinates.

The prerevolutionary political discourse did not construct the polity with reference to a general "people." Persons came in discrete categories: nobles, subjects, and the members of the Buddhist monastic establishments. Political statements were constructed with respect to these different constituencies and it was usual to make separate statements or edicts for these different classes of subject.[16] Nobles were part of the political project of rulership, even if they held no administrative posts. They were free of the tax and corvée labor duties owed by common subjects to their lord and were entitled to a personal retinue of servants. The legal punishments for nobles were quite different from those for commoners and generally confined to fines of livestock; common subjects faced flogging, enslavement, or death should they break the law.

The ideology of government contained a strong strand of paternalism. One of the highest ranking Buddhist dignitaries to escape from Inner Mongolia before the communist victory was the Kanjurwa *Khutagt*. In his writings, he represents relations with subordinates in a characteristically paternalistic way, describing rulers as looking on their subjects as "our children and grandchildren," and stressing that superiors and subordinates "served each other in many ways" (Hyer and Jagchid 1983, 62). In his analysis of precommunist Chahar society, Aberle (1962, 53) notes similar attitudes: "The *amban* (ruling *khoshuu* official) was a 'father' to his people."

Notions of order and authority underpinned both household organization and the aristocratic order. Both the polity and the household required a "master": *ejen*. The Qing emperor was the Ejen Khan, the head of a household, the *ger-un ejen*. The proprietary authority of the *ejen* over his (or occasionally her) subjects was a central value, one that applied to a series of social scales—from the imperial to the domestic. The duties and obligations that subjects owed their lords and, ultimately, the emperor were metaphorically modeled on those of the household or, perhaps, vice versa.[17] In a Foucauldian sense, the relations of power contained in the notion of the *ejen* could be seen as "the concrete, changing soil in which the sovereign's power is grounded, the conditions that make it possible to function" (Foucault 1980, 187). Proprietary authority was so central to the notion of social order that to be "masterless" was to be wild or chaotic. The term *ejengui baidal* (literally, a situation without an *ejen*) means "anarchy."

This logic also applied to the spiritual world. The *gajar-un ejed*—(literally, "*ejens* of the land") are local deities that were, and still are, propitiated at the annual ceremonies held at ritual cairns called *oboo* [*ovoo, obug-a*]. These rites reflect the central role that notions of jurisdiction play in conceptualizing the environment. Something of the norms and values available to commoners can be deduced from the texts of such rites. Probably the earliest known Mongolian sutra describing an *oboo* ritual was written between 1649 and 1691.[18] This text (*obugan-u egüdkhu jang üile selte orusiba*—"customs and so on for the foundation of an *oboo*") describes three different types of *oboo* to be placed in different locations—the royal *oboo*s on the highest mountains, the noble *oboo*s to be placed on highland terraces, and the *oboo*s for commoners to be placed on mountain saddles. The list of benefits gained by worshippers include protection from illnesses and ghosts, the increase of children and grandchildren, and the multiplication of livestock and produce, understandable enough aspirations for commoners and aristocrats alike. The list ends with the following line: "By pleasing the stern authorities, great lords of the land, [one will] find rebirth in a great noble lineage." Written as it was in the age of noble patronage of Buddhism, one cannot read this as necessarily an expression of commoner aspiration to noble rebirth, but it does at least give some indication of the public transcript of ceremony at that time. Ritual sites were to be divided in the same way as political subjects, between royal, noble, and commoner.[19] Stratification appears as central once again. If we return to the notion of the state as a social relation, it seems that stratified society *is* society within the state; it exists in the space permitted by the power relations between rulers and ruled.

THE SUBSTRATA OF POWER: RETHINKING TRIBE AND STATE

Classical theories of kinship and tribal society dichotomized kin and class, tribe and state, tradition and modernity. But if we suspend our commitment to these distinctions, we see various continuities and similarities in power structures within a single analytical frame. The success of aristocratic houses or lineages over very long periods of time, in both centralized states and other political formations, reveals descent and kinship as enduring techniques of power and aspects of stratification rather than their antithesis.

There is good evidence of powerful indigenous aristocratic orders since the times of the Xiongnu, and they seem to form the basis of each steppe polity for which we have significant historical records.[20] The continuities are striking—the root metaphor for subject status in modern Mongolian, black or *khar* (*qara*), for example, stretches back at least as far as the Türk empire of the seventh century, in which *kara bodun* was the term for sub-

jects or vassals (Sinor 1990b, 310).[21] Another striking continuity is the use of forms of decimal civil-military administration, which appear over and over again in descriptions of steppe polities (Di Cosmo 2002, 177). There was clearly innovation and change in this administrative tradition. In Mongolia, the Chinggisid *minggan* fell out of use and the *khoshuu* was introduced by the end of the fifteenth century, although it appears to have originally meant a unit of a thousand horsemen (Bold 2001, 96). The Chinggisid-era *ja'un* hundred-unit disappears and in the Qing era we know subjects were administered in *sum*—administrative units from which a hundred and fifty troops could be mustered. The humble unit of ten (*arban*) seems to persist until the Bogd Khan state of the twentieth century. Having noted these adaptations and changes, though, the fundamental principle remained remarkably constant: nobles ruled subjects divided into nested series of administrative units from which a specified number of troops could be mustered.

Whenever there is evidence that describes them, it is clear that these aristocratic orders gave ruling nobles control of both production and co-ercion on the steppe, all the local powers needed for the grander imperial states. In the Mongol case, for example, since the twelfth century at the latest, groups of subjects could be sent as dowry (*inje*) with a noble bride to another aristocrat's domain, and in general, the position of common subjects resembled serfdom in a number of important ways. We know that in many polities subjects were bound to remain in their allotted areas of pasture and render the lord corvée labor or military service if required. In addition, they were liable for various levies of produce. We see this clearly in the Chinggisid state,[22] the Mongol-Oirat union of 1640,[23] and Qing-era Mongolia.[24] Something similar seems to have been usual for the Kitans,[25] Kazakhs, and Kyrgyz, at least at the time of engagement and in-corporation by the tsarist empire. The local power relations of aristocracy had all that was required to operate both the local political and economic formations in the *khoshuu* districts and the wider Manchu imperial state into which they fitted. When the Qing state collapsed in 1911, for example, the *khoshuu* of Inner Mongolia continued to operate, unless reorganized by Chinese warlord or Japanese administration, until the advent of com-munist control in 1947.

The standard narrative has been that both state and stratification were fragile in steppe societies and tended to be temporary. Without clear evidence of their existence, it was often assumed that "nomadic" society had collapsed back into its putatively basic tribal state. But on reflection, this seems implausible. The Mongols were largely expelled from China when the Yuan dynasty fell in 1368, for example, and were not incorporated into a powerfully centralized empire until they swore fealty to the Qing more than three centuries later. These would seem to be the perfect conditions for "retribalization." There was plenty of time for the imagined clan and tribal system to reassert itself, and since relations with the Ming were poor, there was as little influence of "proper state society" as in any other historical epoch. But the Borjigin aristocracy remained firmly in place and, judging from documents such as the 1640 Mongol-Oirat code, their powers over their subjects were at least as great as during the Qing. When the Manchu emperors became their overlords they had to prohibit the Mongol nobility's habit of selling and giving away *khamjilga* and *albatu* subjects, for example (Bold 2001, 123).[26] The principal threat they faced was not from autochthonous egalitarianism within their own domains but rather the encroachment of other steppe powers such as the Qing and Oirats. A variant of the standard narrative assumed, like Ratchnevsky (1991), that the original clan structure of steppe society was broken down beyond repair by the Chinggisid conquests, but in retrospect one wonders why anyone would suppose that such a structure had existed and been left intact by the many other empires of the steppes formed since Tumen's Xiongnu polity. Without the theory of an essentialized pastoral nomadic type toward which steppe society was bound to gravitate, we have no reason to disbelieve the evidence that suggests a long history of stratification.

The recognition that stratification and the state relation are not dependent upon a centralized bureaucratic structure makes it easier to discern the substrata of power, the aristocratic order that lay at the base. The extent to which hereditary local elites were integrated into larger imperial polities varied with the historical fortunes of the various Chinggisid, Manchu, and Oirat imperial projects of this period. The tendency, much remarked upon, for steppe polities to fragment has been commonly cast in terms of the struggle between "tribalism" and "the state," but on reflection, it is better seen as the result of processes that produced more or less centralized and imperial versions of an existing aristocratic order.

The long history of steppe polities and empires presents a picture of power structures interacting in various modes of articulation, competition, and superimposition as part of contingent historical processes. These various imperial projects resemble Tambiah's (1985, 261) "galactic polity" model of the state in Southeast Asia:

| 198 |

> What emerges is a galactic picture of a central planet surrounded by differentiated satellites, which are more or less "autonomous" entities held in orbit and within the sphere of influence of the centre. If we introduce at the margin other similar competing central principalities and their satellites, we shall be able to appreciate the logic of the system that as a hierarchy of central points is continually subject to the dynamics of pulsation and changing spheres of influence.

This fluidity is understandable because we can see that the relations between the centers and their satellites are personal relations between aristocrats. This was what Meeker called the "discipline of interpersonal association," by which an imperial system maintained the sovereign power of a family line over its vassals and local rulers deployed hereditary power over their subjects. Different empires, however, sometimes deployed very different strategies of power. In this respect, it is interesting to note the contrasting ways in which steppe societies were governed by the tsarist and Qing empires. In the case of the Qing, who made use of well-established methods of steppe statecraft (Di Cosmo 2006), the imperial authorities generally sought to support the Mongolian nobility (in part because the Manchu elite had intermarried with them). However, the tsarist empire pursued a more colonial strategy toward the Kazakh aristocrats, seeking to undermine and bypass them and introducing its own increasingly comprehensive forms of direct administration. Where the Qing viewed the Borjigin as a related aristocracy, the Russian court represented the Kazakhs as "savages" in need of more law and order (Levchine 1840, 305). In part this was because of the European tradition that found it exotic and faintly barbaric that people should live without fixed dwellings.

EXOTICIZING MOBILE SOCIETY

Such exotic images of nomadic tribalism continue to inform fashionable social theory. The work of Deleuze and Guattari follow the intellectual tradition in which mobile "nonstate" society is cast as an inverted image of the modernist nation-state but is homogenized and exaggerated. A brief examination of the misrepresentations this entailed provides fresh insight into the shortcomings of this theoretical tradition. Following Engels, Deleuze and Guattari locate their notion of "the nomad" in the evolutionary stage of "barbaric society" that emerged from "savagery."[27] In *Nomadology* (1986), they elaborate a theory of nomad society that they call "the war machine," reflecting the abiding vision of the warlike tribe:

> Primitive, segmentary societies have often been defined as societies without a State, meaning societies in which distinct organs of power do not appear. . . . Clastres goes further, identifying *war* in primitive societies as the surest mechanism directed against the formation of the State: war maintains the dispersal and segmentarity of groups . . . just as Hobbes saw clearly that *the State was against war, so war is against the State*, and makes it impossible. It should not be concluded that war is a state of nature, but rather that it is the mode of a social state that wards off and prevents the State . . . the war machine is realized more completely in the "barbaric" assemblages of nomadic warriors than in the "savage" assemblages of primitive societies. In any case it is out of the question that the State could be the result of war in which the conquerors imposed through their victory a new law on the vanquished, since the organization of the war-machine is directed against the State-form, actual or virtual.
>
> (DELEUZE AND GUATTARI 1986, 10–14)

A state may acquire military institutions, but these are anomalous and remain a potential threat to it.[28] "*The state has no war machine of its own*; it can only appropriate one in the form of a military institution, one that will always cause it problems" (Deleuze and Guattari 1986, 9).

There is no space here to discuss Deleuze and Guattari's general theory of war as the antithesis of the essentialized state, except to note that scholars such as Carneiro (1981) and Patterson (1991) argue convincingly that war is a fundamental ingredient in state formation and that it seems to have played a central role in all the steppe polities we have studied. The concept of the nomad war machine, however, reflects both the tendency to exoticize mobility as a characteristic of an entirely different mode of life and the association with war that has been such an important element of European representations of steppe "nomads" since Marlow's dramatic portrait of the Mongol warlord Timur—"Tamburlaine."

In this scheme, the notion of the nomad is made to stand for a sort of essentialized liberty, a fundamental antistate form. But Deleuze and Guattari also seek to identify general structural forms based on the actual histories of particular societies. They propose, for example, the numerical organization of society as one of three basic modes of social organization and an essential feature of the war machine, based on their reading of Chinggisid Mongol history and the Old Testament.

> Tens, hundreds, thousands, myriads: all armies retain these decimal groupings. . . . For so peculiar an idea—the numerical organization of people—came from the nomads. . . . Everywhere the war machine displays a curious process of arithmetic replication or doubling. . . . For the social body to be numerized, the number must form a special body. When Genghis [Chinggis] Khan undertook his great composition of the steppe, he numerically organized the lineages, and the fighters in each lineage, placing them under a cipher and a chief (groups of ten with decurians, groups of one hundred with centurions, groups of one thousand with chiliarchs). But he also extracted from each arithmetized lineage a small number of men who were to constitute his personal guard, in other words a dynamic formation comprising a staff, commissars, messengers and diplomats ("antrustions") . . . the war machine would be unable to function without this double series: it is necessary both that numerical composition replace lineal organization, and that it conjure away the territorial organization of the State. . . . Tensions or power struggles are also a result of this: between Moses' tribes and the Levites, between Genghis' "noyans" and "antrustions" . . . it is a tension inherent in the war machine, in its special power, and in the particular limitations placed on the power (puissance) of the "chief."
>
> (DELEUZE AND GUATTARI 1986, 63–71)

This part of Deleuze and Guattari's work is a reworked version of the familiar notion of tribal "kin" leaders in conflict with "state"-appointed ones, and it reveals several of the problems with the standard narrative of kinship society and the state. First, it draws upon the now largely discredited structural-functionalist account of "segmentary societies." Second, "the state" is treated in a highly ethnocentric way, in which the particularities of certain European centralized polities are taken as its necessary and eternal features. By accepting the "territorialization" notion of state formation and imagining that nomads have liberty of movement, Deleuze and Guattari immediately locate them outside the state and as opposed to it. The argument becomes circular: How do we know nomads do not have states? Because the state must be territorial in a properly sedentary way and nomads must a priori have a different sort of territoriality. Using this approach, Deleuze and Guattari are bound to reject the application of the same terms for political organization to both "nomad" and "sedentary" societies. Feudalism, for example, is a "properly sedentary category," so they are bound to seek other terms to describe nomadic society.[29]

But the historical record shows that many steppe polities had a series of features commonly used to characterize the state, including vassalage, taxation, and the granting of land by the sovereign. So Deleuze and Guattari (1986, 74) have to try to explain it away.

> There is no doubt that nomad organization and the war machine deal with these same problems [as sedentary states], both at the level of land and that of taxation. . . . But they invent a territoriality and a "movable" fiscal organization that testifies to the autonomy of a numerical principle: there can be a confusion or combination of the systems, but the specificity of the nomadic system remains the subordination of land to numbers that are displaced and deployed, and of taxation to relations internal to those numbers.

Having decided that the numeric principle is essentially nomadic, it is used to explain away the existence of taxation and land allocation, rather than used to describe the form that these practices take.[30] The fundamental characteristics of the state that they mention, *"territoriality, work or public works, taxation"* (Deleuze and Guattari 1986, 115), were all present in "nomadic" steppe polities in Mongolia and elsewhere. It would seem more reasonable to recognize that the practices we refer to when we use terms such as "taxation" and "land allocation" take different forms in different political economies and property regimes—be they pastoral or agricultural.

What Deleuze and Guattari offer us is a version of the common nineteenth-century myth of political evolution, but with the State cast in negative, monstrous terms. They project an idealized, timeless notion of nonstate society onto actual historical societies about which they know relatively little, fastening on a few exotic features such as mobility and a decimal system of military-civil administration. Although the civilized state is targeted and the nonstate "other" romanticized in the best Rousseauian tradition, the approach cannot but echo the orientalizing discourse of colonialism.[31] But as noted in chapter 5, recent ethnographic studies of "nomadic" societies show that rather than being defined by their mobility, pastoralists have a variety of ways in which they make use of movement as a technique, to a greater or lesser extent depending on circumstances. Deleuze and Guattari's work provides an example of what can go wrong when older thinking is uncritically absorbed and allowed to go unchallenged. If the study of mobile pastoral society is to usefully inform wider social theory, it must do so on a firmer basis.

ARISTOCRATIC ORDERS

It seemed to me that the revision of the dominant models of state and nonstate nomadic society entailed two sets of interrelated tasks. First, it required the critique of the colonial-era scheme of political evolution from tribal to state society and the associated concepts of kinship and pastoral-nomadic society as distinctive social types. Second, it involved the suspension of our commitment to national populist notions of culture and society as solidarities and wholes built by bottom-up processes.

This allows us to advance new conceptualizations of political order that are, I think, more faithful to the historical evidence than the kin-tribe model. In the cases examined in this book, and in the wider history of the Eurasian steppe, we can detect the importance of aristocratic orders. The term is used here as an inclusive category, rather than a particular model, to indicate societies that are shaped in fundamental ways by the power relations of hereditary rule. Here we see the deployment of descent and genealogy as technologies of power and forms of governance that administer political subjects in ways that can resemble those found in centralized state structures. In this conception, descent groups bear the imprint of the constraints and logics of power relations and their reproduction, just as we would expect them to in societies subject to "territorialized" states. In any given historical setting, the particular ideologies of descent, inheritance, and relatedness may vary from inclusive bilateral categories like the pre-Choson Korean *chok* to forms resembling the exclusive notion of the neo-Confucian patrilineage. But whatever their particularities in a given period, they are more likely to reflect contingent historical conditions and forms of government in the widest sense than the kinship structures supposed in the Morganian model of political evolution. The Lévi-Strauss-ian notion of "house society," in which marriage and descent reflect the requirements of transmission of tangible and intangible properties, provides a useful shorthand term for this perspective and accommodates critiques of classical kinship theory by Schneider (1984) and Bourdieu (1977 [1972]).

As with forms of descent, the incidence and nature of steppe aristocracy has clearly varied enormously in different social and historical settings, just as in "sedentary" polities. The Chinggisid nobility, for example, seem to have maintained strong administrative powers over their subjects in both the centralized imperial and Qing periods and in the "headless" Mongol-Oirat state. To be sure, the Turkmen nobility of the nineteenth century appears to have been weak, divided, and less secure in its power than the Kazakh aristocracy of that time, which also had some difficulty controlling its subjects in the face of the expanding power of the tsarist state. But these various political conditions reflected particular contingent historical circumstances, not the presumed limitations of pastoral nomadism as an ideal type. In this sense, we can compare weak or absent monarchies found in periods of Mongol history with those of "sedentary" polities such as the Polish-Lithuanian Commonwealth, although the political economies concerned were undoubtedly very different.

Since the "headless state" seems able to reproduce aristocracy without the centralized, bureaucratized state required for class stratification in Marxist and other nineteenth-century social theory, we are bound to rethink the classical models of the state. Current interest in the distributed nature of state power allows us to reconceptualize what was once thought of as a distinct structure. Instead, we can picture the state as a process, a way of exercising codified power, or, in Chandhoke's handy phrase, as a social relation. On these grounds, the institutionalization of the relations between rulers and their political subjects found in aristocracies appear as statelike as those of the grander imperial polities.

Aristocratic order, then, spans the divide between centralized and decentralized states—often providing a common mode and language of power that could allow rapid incorporation. It appears as a term within a wider perspective in which, rather than imagining distinct tribal peoples generating their own social forms and leaderships, we are free to consider societies as the products of historical projects of rulership and government. Of course, the concept of aristocracy as an analytical and comparative term deserves to be developed more fully than I have been able to in this work. But it seems to me that it offers far better prospects of genuine insight into the political orders of "tribal" societies than the reproduction of nineteenth-century evolutionary schemes and the dubious analytic terms they generated.

| Notes |

1. INTRODUCTION

1. Abrams (1988) viewed the state as an "allegorical contrivance through which self-interest and sectional power are masked as independent moral entities." He writes: "The state comes into being as structuration within political practice; it starts life as an implicit construct; it is then reified—as the *res publica*, the public reification, no less—and acquires an overt symbolic identity progressively divorced from practice as an illusory account of practice." Similarly, Mitchell (1991, 77) considers one of the distinctive features of modern states to be the illusory nature of the separation of the state that stands apart from society as a "fair arbiter." He writes, "state-society boundaries are shown to be distinctions erected internally, as an aspect of more complex power relations."

2. This was by no means novel. Malinowski (1944, 166) had seen the "tribe-state" as the "executive committee" of the society, with political organization, a military class, and arms as instruments of power. For Malinowski, monopoly of force gave unity to the tribe, transforming it into a state whose hegemony extended over a determined territory.

3. With reference to elite theory, it might, perhaps, be useful to note the distinction between what Pareto called governing and nongoverning aristocracies (and what C. Wright Mills [1956, 162] termed the power elite) and the upper classes—law codes such as the 1640 Mongol-Oirat regulations and the Khalkha Jirum distinguish office-holding nobility from the rest.

4. In general, when rendering Mongolian names and terms, I have tried to use the most commonly found forms of words such as Khan (*Qan, obog,* and *Khoshuu (Khoshigu),* so that readers may more easily identify them. Otherwise I give transliterations of words as they appear in classical Mongolian script since the seventeenth century generally following Atwood (2004), in some cases alongside the more phonetic current transliteration from the Cyrillic script and placing the most appropriate version (classical or Cyrillic) first. For thirteenth-century Mongolian I have, as far as possible, followed De Rachewiltz (2004). In quotations I retain the original forms as far as possible.

5. A typical arrangement was for the herding family to retain all the wool and milk of the herd while the owner gained all the offspring. Other agreements were less generous, with the owner taking all the wool and giving the herding family a few livestock in payment.

6. The prerevolutionary monasteries, for example, could own more than 60 percent of the total livestock in a district (Lattimore 1940, 97n50).

7. This strata appears to have been quite small, but both nobles and commoners might own slaves, provided they had the wealth to support them. Legal documents from the eighteenth century bear testimony to both the suffering of slaves and a certain, if very limited, concern for them by the Qing authorities. In 1789, for example, a thirty-two-year-old slave woman named Dashjid tried to kill herself and her children, one of whom was killed before help arrived. She was the daughter of a *khamjilga* named Nomon who was so poor that he had sold her as a child to a *taiji* before himself dying of starvation. Unhappy with each of a succession of masters, the girl repeatedly ran home to her mother only to be sold to someone else. Eventually, in despair and pregnant for a fourth time, she had tried to kill herself and her children. The Qing authorities punished almost everyone connected with the case except Dashjid (Bawden 1968, 139–140).

8. In fact, they often became liable for such obligations in practice (see Bawden 1968, 150).

9. Legal documents from 1822, for example, describe a case in which a *taiji* punished a son of one of his *khamjilga*s for being slow to learn his lessons by leaving him tied up, naked, outside on a winter night. Of course the boy froze to death. The noble was fined "two nines"—eighteen head of cattle (Bawden 1968, 141).

10. This status is not to be confused with the Darkhad ethnic group of northern Mongolia. See Jagchid and Hyer (1979, 287–288) for a discussion of the rights and status of the Darkhad.

11. See Simukov (1936, 49–55) and Bawden (1968, 181). For discussion, see Sneath (1999).

12. For example, the emperor had the right to give land to groups such as the Barga in what is now Hulun Buir, Inner Mongolia. See Lattimore (1935, 158–160) and Tubshinnima (1985, 90–95). Sanjdorj (1980, 1) takes a Marxist line and states that in the sixteenth and seventeenth centuries "the land . . . was the property of the feudal classes."

13. This is reflected in the records of legal petitions made to the Bogd Khan, the ruler of Outer Mongolia after the collapse of the Qing in 1911. For example, in one document banner officials insisted that several commoners move with their animals south of a river, but by giving the officials over

160 sheep and twenty rubles the plaintiffs obtained permission to stay on the better northern side until the weather became warm (Rasidondug and Veit 1975, 142, 124). What was being acquired in this way was in no sense the ownership of the land, but rights to use territory at a certain time in the annual cycle.

14. For a detailed reconstruction of the pastoral system of Lamyn Gegen *khoshuu* (as Simukov called it) see Sneath (1999, 223–226).

15. See, for example, Simukov (1936, 55–56) and Bawden (1968, 109).

16. Such a review could not hope to be comprehensive in a work of this length. The studies examined in the rest of this book are by necessity a tiny selection from a large field, but my aim is polemical—to critically examine the common model applied to each—and I hope that the selection is sufficient for this purpose.

17. I use polity to mean a political unit, following Colson (1986, 5): "By polity I simply mean a unit that is self-governing, no matter what the nature of its political organisation or its size."

18. After their defeat, remnants of the Cimmerians fled into Asia Minor—gaining footholds in Phrygia, Cappadocia, and Cilicia, finally establishing themselves in Pontis. The Scythians sent armies in pursuit of their ousted rivals and clashed with the Assyrian empire; in 678, the Scythian king Ishkapai mounted an unsuccessful invasion. Another Scythian king, Bartatua, formed an alliance with the Assyrians and gained their approval to advance into Pontis to destroy the final power of the Cimmerians.

19. It seems that the Ashina had originally been Xiongnu nobles who had fled persecution in northern China with just five hundred subject families in 439 (Atwood 2004, 553).

20. The Haital had also been subjects of the Rouran (Grousset 1970, 67) and seem to have originally been one of the ruling families of the Kushan empire. The Kushan empire stretched across the region of Bactria and the Hindu Kush in the first to the third centuries. It was formed by the Guishuang, one of five aristocratic families of the Yuezhi polity that ruled the northern Xinjiang and Gansu area before being ousted by the Xiongnu in the second century B.C.E. It seems that the Haital may have been another of these five families (Enoki 1970).

21. It is thought that one of the effects of the Mongol rule of Persia was to stimulate the development of mobile pastoralism in areas such as the Zagros mountains, later associated with the Bakhtiari pastoralists of that region.

22. This reveals a number of continuities in traditions of state and techniques of rulership, such as the recurrent use of decimal administrative units. Another continuity is the ideology of the "heavenly mandate" justifying

imperial rule. The *chanyu* was "born of heaven and earth and ordained by the sun and moon" just as the Türk qaghans were "heaven-conceived" (Golden 2006, 12). Chinggis Khan ruled "by the power of eternal heaven" and his ancestors were described as "sons of heaven." Nurhaci claimed heavenly approval in his dealings with the Chinggisid nobility (Di Cosmo 2006, 245). The notion of the heavenly mandate to rule was part of what Di Cosmo (1999, 20) calls the "ideology in reserve" by which local ruling families could legitimate their imperial claims when the opportunity arose (see Sneath 2006).

2. THE MYTH OF THE KINSHIP SOCIETY: EVOLUTIONISM AND THE ANTHROPOLOGICAL IMAGINATION

1. *Tribu* appears in Middle English in the mid-thirteenth century and had itself replaced the Greek *phylon* in Biblical texts. The "tribes of Israel" were thought of as descendants of a common ancestor, although neither *tribus*, *phylon*, nor the Hebrew terms they indicated (*matteh*, *shebet*, or *shevet*) were necessarily groups essentially defined by descent. The *phylon* in classical Athens was an administrative division whose origins are a matter of speculation, and *tribus* itself was used to describe the constituents of the trifold division of the people of Rome into Latins, Sabines, and Etruscans, political categories which may or may not have been defined by descent (Fried 1975, 3–5).

2. Similarly, Ehrenberg (1960, 13) notes: "It is doubtful whether in early times we should think of the clan (*genos*, *patra*); there is much to be said for regarding it as a product only of settled conditions."

3. Starr (1961, 125) notes: "The *demos* (people) was organized in subdivisions, tribes and phratries above all, for military purposes, for the preservation of law and order." There is not much data on what the *phylon* ("tribe") was like before it became an administrative unit of the state, but the idea that these were self-formed units of common descent is implausible, since they appear after the Doric migrations, in which an incoming elite was superimposed on local populations with whom they could not have shared descent. So Starr (1961, 135) writes: "If the tribes were institutions of the invaders, the natives must somehow have been absorbed; in historic times no one seems to have stood outside these units."

4. For the Soviet view, see Kozlov (1974, 77–78).

5. Sahlins (1968, 5–6) was at pains to retain this theory despite the abundant evidence to the contrary. "The state differentiates civilisation from tribal society.... A contrast with tribalism is not usefully made by reference to one or a few simple features. It has proved futile to search for some

decisive invention standing at the evolutionary divide . . . 'kinship to territory'—supposing primitive society to be 'based on' kinship, civilisation on territory—better expresses the evolutionary transformation. But it is overly compressed, and thereby vulnerable to naïve criticism. The rankest anthropological novice can point out that many primitive peoples occupy and defend discrete territories. . . . The critical development was not the establishment of territoriality in society, but the establishment of society *as* a territory."

6. The title "chief" was adopted by British colonial authorities for local-level rulers of medium-scale "tribal" units, and those below them were generally termed "headmen." This often meant overriding indigenous classifications if they already existed. Before these matters were regularized, a wide variety of titles, both indigenous and foreign, were used in the literature and by early administrators (including the Germans in East Africa). However, the British did retain grander (and sometimes indigenous) titles for some more important rulers, for example, the king or *kabaka* of Buganda. In some countries, for example, socialist Tanzania, "chief" became very unfashionable after independence, and the chiefs were stripped of their administrative powers. Elsewhere, for example Kenya, chief and subchief have been retained as administrative titles, though these are government appointments, not inherited offices, and are no longer linked to any idea of tribal representation or authority over tribal territory.

7. The publication in 1969 of *Elementary Structures of Kinship* by Levi-Strauss helped shift anthropological interest away from descent theory and toward processes of alliance and exchange, and the failure to find classic unilineal descent in other parts of Africa and the world undermined the theory (see Kuper 2004). Another factor was the major shift in African anthropology led by the Rhodes-Livingstone Institute and the Manchester School under Max Gluckman. This led to a greater emphasis on historical studies, the analysis of social change, urban ethnographies, treating ethnicity as situational, introducing agency as an analytic category, and more of a focus on economic relations.

8. Nonetheless, in Africa the classic model lingered longer than it did elsewhere. One development, similar to Kirchoff's conical clan, was Aidan Southall's concept of the "segmentary state" composed of a hierarchical pyramid of chiefdoms. This appears in his *Alur Society* (in Uganda) (1956). This was applied, for example, by Aylward Shorter, in his *Chiefship in Western Tanzania: A Political History of the Kimbu* (1972). Another development and later survival was the "lineage-based mode of production" models proposed by various French Marxist anthropologists such as Meillassoux and Terray.

9. There is not space here to properly review the anthropological discussion surrounding the definition of the state, but it is worth noting that on close inspection most of the rationales advanced by the structural-functionalists for the distinction between state and nonstate societies are, to say the least, highly debatable. Meyer and Koppers (1954), for example, argued that the state was universal to all societies, and Lowie (1962 [1927]) accepted this up to a point but placed it in an evolutionary scheme of increasingly stable and permanent government. The compound definition of the state that emerged was rather vague and circular, depending a good deal on it not being tribal.

10. Tapper (1990, 55–56) admits: "The nature of indigenous concepts of tribe . . . has too often been obscured by the apparent desire of investigators (anthropologists, historians, and administrators) to establish a consistent and stable terminology for political groups. . . . Middle Eastern indigenous categories (of which perhaps the commonest to have been translated as tribe are *qabila, ta'ifa, quam,* and *il*) are no more specific than are English terms such as 'family' or 'group.' Even in the most apparently consistent segmentary terminology, individual terms are ambiguous, not merely about level, but also in their connotations of functions or facets of identity—economic, political, kinship, and cultural. As with equivalents in English practice, the ambiguity of the terms and the flexibility of the system are of the essence in everyday negotiations of meaning and significance. Most of the terms that have been translated as 'tribe' contain such ambiguities, and attempts to give them—or tribe—precision as to either level, function, or essence are misdirected. Tribe, I suggest, is rather a state of mind, a construction of reality, a model for organisation and action." Lacking level, function, or essence, Tapper's notion of tribe as a state of mind rather begs the question of *whose* minds we are concerned with, scholars or "tribespeople."

11. There was a good deal of criticism of this approach at the time. Asad (1979) had rejected the notion of the pastoral nomadism as an ideal type and Beck (1983) follows Asad in pointing out that as all "pastoral nomadic" societies interact with "state-organized" societies, the "internal dynamics" of the former cannot be seen apart from relations with the latter.

12. Hager (1983, 94) describes Pashtun tribal structure in segmentary terms as one of "progressively more inclusive groupings of lineage and faction." But Glatzer (1983, 221) writes, "Pashtun nomads . . . are organised socially not on the basis of a segmentary lineage or clan system, but on other bases." It is not descent but locality, interest, and political and economic structures that are the bases for social organization in Pashtun areas.

13. Hager (1983, 107), for example, writes, "with the gradual growth of government and the urban classes, and with the penetration into rural areas of modernising technology, from roads and radios to tractors, tribes and tribal organisation have undoubtedly weakened."

14. Elsewhere Krader writes: "The nomadic village as a corporate body has the same structure as a clan in miniature," and he also generalizes that "the village of the ordinary nomads contains about ten families" (Krader 1963, 335–337). He is quite wrong in both respects. Mongolian pastoral encampments are fluid and changing residential forms, they very frequently include nonagnates and non-kin, and they rarely include more than eight households—see Sneath (2000, 212–215; Humphrey and Sneath 1999, 139–178).

15. Thoroughly indoctrinated by the writings of Krader and company, when I began fieldwork in Inner Mongolia in the late 1980s I was at first perplexed to find nothing that corresponded to his picture of kinship organization, but I assumed it must have been based on Outer Mongolian research. However, fieldwork in Outer Mongolia in the 1990s convinced me of what the more detailed historical studies already clearly indicated: Krader's model really was simply wrong.

16. Digard (1983, 332) writes: "Garthwaite seems to me to be on quite the wrong track . . . we must abandon the myth, which has been decidedly tenacious since *The Nuer*, that segmentary systems are necessarily acephalous. . . . Moreover, how can it be maintained that a segmentary structure is *inherently* contradictory with a class structure, when, as a matter of *fact*, these two forms of organisation coexist and 'function' simultaneously in several societies, including the Bakhtiari?"

17. A written source dating from 1725 that lists the ranks and honors given to Persian *amirs* (emirs) notes the governor of Bakhtiari as a top position (Garthwaite 1983, 322).

18. The northern Chahar Lang region was within the administrative control of Luristan in the nineteenth century (Brooke 1983, 351).

19. Garthwaite (1983, 323–324) himself describes an administrative system staffed by aristocrats. "Official Zand documents . . . clearly indicate that the Haft Lang was treated as an administrative unit. In the [documents] awarding . . . governorships, exemptions, and admonitions to eighteenth-century Duraki notables, they possessed the titles of *sardar, beg, aqa, rish-safid, zabit,* and *hakim*. These documents suggest only the relationship between the Haft Lang leaders and their taifehs, and add little to our knowledge about Bakhtiari commoners, except their organisation into small groups headed by kadkhudas and kalantars."

20. There simply was no ranking of collateral lines according to genealogical relationship to the ancestor and no consistent norm of primogeniture. As Khazanov (1983, 174) notes: "Krader's view that the conical clan exists amongst Turkic and Mongolian nomads is the result of a misunderstanding, the reasons for which still remain a mystery to me. . . . Krader (1963, 370) does note that the Mongols of Ordos . . . the Kalmucks, Kazakhs, and Kirghiz began to move away from the principle of the conical clan. But the fact remains that there *was* no such principle."

21. This document has been read as a sort of "mythic charter" of a simple tribal people. So, for example, it is often translated as showing Chinggis Khan's original ancestors to have been two fantastical animals—a blue-grey wolf and a fallow doe—whereas one of our major sources for the period, Rashid-ad-Din, makes it explicit that these were the names of people—Börtä china (*Börte Chinua*, "Blue Wolf") was "an important commander" and Qo'ai Mara (*Gooa Maral*, "White Doe") was "his chief wife" (Thackston 1998, 114).

22. Most of the named groups that are mentioned were thought to be descended from a number of brothers, thus providing little of the classical structure of segmentary kinship (see Onon 1990, 174–176).

23. For example, to battle with the forces of a relative (Jamuqa) whose army included forces led by a named group closely related to him (the Tayyichi'ut), Chinggis Khan allied himself with the khan of the Kereyid who, like most of the other important named polities of the region (the Tatar, Merkit, and Naiman), had no genealogical connection with the Borjigid at all. A generation earlier, the khan of the Kereyid had recruited the military support of Chinggis Khan's father against his own family (see Onon 1990, 65). In both cases, the politically expedient relationship of *anda* (alliance, sworn "brotherhood") was used without reference to genealogical distance.

24. These strata were clearly separated—there is recorded the lament and wretched confession of a subject who cohabited with a captured noble-woman and was filled with guilt at his own presumption. "I, Chilger . . . touched the Lady, the qatun . . . Ignoble and bad Chilger, his own black [i.e., common] head will receive [a blow]" (Onon 1990, 40).

25. Onon (1990, 56); Cleaves (1982, 66 67).

26. See the *Secret History*: "Then Chinggis Qahan plundered the Tayichi'ut. The people of Tayichi'ut bones (lineages/houses)—A'uchu-ba'atur, Qoton-örcheng, Qudu'udar and others of the Tayichi'ut, from their seed to their seed—he killed. . . . The people of their *ulus* (realm) he brought (with him)." Clearly the people of the Tayichi'ut *ulus* were not members of the Tayichi'ut bones (Onon 1990, 63; Cleaves 1982, 76).

27. Two military units of ten thousand were raised from the Kereyid. For example, see Pelliot (1949, 26).

28. Carpini writes of a dux by the name of Correnza (Beazley 1903, 94), for example, but Rockhill's (1900, 6) translation calls him a "chief," while Carpini's Dux Wasilco (Beazley 1903, 92) is translated (along with all the other European nobles) as "duke" (Rockhill 1900, 3).

29. Specialists have also questioned the interpretation of historical materials through the prism of kin-society theory in the Middle East. One example is the exchange between the historians Helfgott and Reid in the journal *Iranian Studies*. Tapper (1983, 7–8) writes that Helfgott "characterises Iranian tribes as pastoral nomadic kinship-based chiefdoms [but] unfortunately he produces little evidence for his argument, overstresses the role of pastoral nomadism, kinship and chiefship . . . he is accused of theoretism by Reid." Reid argues that "tribes" of Iran were actually products of the complex and centralized administrative divisions known as *oymaqs*, which flourished under the Safavids and were neither simply pastoral nor based on kinship. The word *oymaq* is a rendering of the Mongolian word *aimag*, introduced by the Chinggisids during the Ilkhanate period. These were clearly administrative divisions and not based on kinship in the Safavid period (1501–1722), but scholars have been loath to conclude that this may have been the case in the original Mongolian setting and have assumed again that the term was transformed as a result of contact with sedentary states.

30. He notes that the term "tribe" is commonly understood to mean "a group descended from a common ancestor, divided into clans, possessing a territory, common language, culture and shared identity and often economic pursuits" (Golden 2001a, 20).

31. See Golden (2001a, 21n87).

3. THE IMAGINARY TRIBE: COLONIAL AND IMPERIAL ORDERS AND THE PERIPHERAL POLITY

1. Similarly, Gongor (1991 [1970], 46), faithful to Marxist theory, places the earliest occurrence of the term *aimag* in the period of the breakdown of kinship society and the transition to class society, so as to conform to the concept of tribe/*plemya* as a group of people of common descent sharing a territory (*nutug*). However, in the feudal period, which he dates from the twelfth century, he describes the *aimag* as a lord's share (*khubi / khuv'*) of a kingly polity (*khanglig ulus / khanlig uls*).

2. Similarly, as discussed in chapter 4, the term *obogton* [*ovogton*], which means "family" or "line" in modern Mongolian, has been taken to mean "clan" or "tribe" in the older texts.

3. There were four grades of *taiji*, the first being for those governing *khoshuus* and the second to fourth for those without *khoshuus*.

4. See Jagchid (1999, 36–43).

5. See Atwood (2002, 949).

6. There was a tradition by which the youngest son inherited the core possessions of the parental couple while older siblings received a portion upon marriage, and this seems to have applied to appanages in the Mongol imperial period (Lattimore 1940, 292; see also Khazanov 1983, 174).

7. The Buryats may have had genealogies for commoners and descent groups that predated Russian administration (see Humphrey 1983, 51).

8. Geiss has his own version of the Morgan-Engels model of evolution. Society starts with stage (a), which he calls "acephalous tribalism," then moves on to (b) "cephalous tribalism," and so on to (c) "tribal confederacies," (d) "agricultural states," (e) "mercantile states," (f) "industrial states," and finally, (g) the "constitutional state." He cites Barfield in justifying the view that "nomadic empires are more similar to tribal confederacies than states" (Geiss 2003, 11).

9. The terms "Kazakh" and "Kirghiz" were used rather interchangeably in early accounts. Levchine, writing in the 1830s, for example, describes the Kirghiz-Kazakh khanate. Later the term "Kirghiz" was used to describe the subjects of Kokhand khanate, and "Kazakh" those who had been subject to the "Kirghiz-Kazakh khanate" before tsarist control of the region.

10. The celebrated Täuka Khan ruled ten or eleven towns or forts (*gorodki*) before his defeat by Gandan Khan in 1681 (Burton 1997, 337).

11. Misunderstandings of Mongol social forms were used as evidence to support the vision of the clan system. Olcott (1995, 6) writes of the Kazakhs: "the clan structure was modified to resemble the Mongol *ulu* (clan) system." By *ulu*, Olcott presumably means *ulus*, the Mongol appanage or domain of a ruler, which was certainly not a clan.

12. In the Kazakh case, the category had been expanded to include *qojas*—those tracing descent from the Prophet (see Privratsky 2001, 35).

13. Privy Councilor Alex Levchine was the tsarist envoy to the Kazakh steppes and originally published his book on the Kirghiz-Kazakh in 1832.

14. Since this sort of anarchy does not fit with the social equilibrium of the tribal model, Geiss (2003, 2) applies the usual conceptual apartheid between state and tribal societies. Levchine must have been mistaken in describing such anarchy. "Political order of tribal and non-tribal societies might be of a different kind. What seems to be chaos and anarchy from

the perspective of centralised state power, might have referred to quite ordered patterns of tribal authority relations."

15. I have left the term *chef* in the French, since it has a wider application (as meaning a "boss" of some kind) than the English term chief, which is primarily associated with tribal society. At the time, *chef*—chief—was often used for non-European aristocrats. A contemporary of Levchine, Victor Fontanier, a French consular official in Ottoman Turkey from 1821 to 1833, for example, wrote of Trabzon: "chiefs [*chefs*] have the title of aghas, and were formerly called derebey. . . . This institution is precisely the feudal system of thirteenth-century Europe; the aghas reside in fortified mansions, sometimes equipped with cannons, where they preserve their families and treasures; they go about surrounded by servants and armed partisans, impose laws, raise taxes, and take refuge in their retreats, from where they defy the authority of the pasha, even the fermans [decrees] of the sultan" (Meeker 2002, 40). In his theory of elites, Pareto used the term *chef* to mean leader.

16. The smallest administrative unit, the *aul* had fifty to seventy households with an *aksakal* theoretically elected; the *volost* included ten to twelve *auls*, ruled by a *bii* and a sultan (this office remained hereditary) confirmed in office by the governor-general of Omsk. The *okrug* contained twenty to forty *volosti* ruled by a senior sultan elected by the *volost* sultans and confirmed by the governor (Geiss 2003, 179).

17. Levchine (1840, 395) writes: "The power of the Kirghiz *chef* is not that absolute, even that of the khans, a title that no longer exists, but for the Middle and Small Hordes." In the French edition, a footnote adds: "This was written in 1822. Since this time the Russian government has completely suppressed the title of khan in the Kirghiz hordes."

18. Some remarks of Levchine suggest that only the Aq Süyek or "white bone" (in Russian, *kost*) were nobility. "The white kost is only composed of khans and their descendents who have the title of sultans. The Mohamedans classify also in the same class the khodjas or descendents of saints in Mohamedan legend. We call the black kost not only the base people but also the former elders and *chefs* who don't have hereditary title" (Levchine 1840, 304–305). But it seems to me that Levchine, who himself was a senior member of the Russian court, meant senior hereditary titles, not simple membership of the local gentry strata. Schuyler describes the "white bone" as "blue blood"—that is, royalty—and this suggests a higher status than the wider nobility. Khazanov (1983, 177) thinks the "black bone" elite could not pass on hereditary power because the Russian administration insisted on elected local office, but this leaves open the question as to whether they formed a nobility before tsarist con-

trol. Martin (2001, 27) notes, citing Valikhanov, that the position of "black bone" *biy* could be inherited and "black bone" nobles were found among the neighboring Kyrgyz.

19. The French version of the text reads *"Toute homme en état de porter les armes doit payer chaque année au khan at aux chefs de la nation un tribut de un vingtieme de ses biens"* (Levchine 1840, 401). Martin (2001, 175) notes the existence of two other institutions: the *sibagha* was the portion of meat given in spring to the sultans and *biis* and the *soghim* was livestock slaughtered in winter and given by each family to the sultan. But in line with the kinship-society model, she describes these as "tokens of respect for kinship group leaders" (Martin 2001, 24).

20. The Kazakh law codes are almost certainly derived from the Chinggisid Mongol laws, and Riasanovsky (1965, 311–312) notes the similarities between the law attributed to the Täuka Khan, the Mongol-Oirat code of 1640, and the Khalkha Jirum (see chapter 7).

21. Similarly, in his description of the Kyrgyz, Radloff (1863, 318) mentions the "tribe" of the Bougou, writing, "among this tribe one can name the following families" and listing seventeen names. However, it turns out that the Bougou comprise some ten thousand households (Radloff 1863, 320), which gives an average of around three thousand persons per "family." This would be an impossibly large corporate descent group, but is readily understandable if the "families of the tribe" were the local nobility.

22. Martin (2001, 22) also remarks, however, that "Kazakh kinship organization was highly complex, and identification of a strict structure is impossible."

23. Khazanov (1983, 132) writes: "One early observer (Levshin, 1832, Pt III: 24) wrote 'The Kirghiz [i.e. Kazakhs—A.K.] rarely roam in great numbers in one place, for then their herds are crowded; but associations consist of several families which are connected by kinship or mutual need . . . this mobile village they call an *aul*; the number of *kibitkas* [households] in an *aul* depends on individual circumstances.' . . . Sometimes . . . nomadic communities, coincide with primary kin groups. But this is not always the case. Frequently they consist not only of agnates and their families but also of affines, cognates and individuals connected only by distant kinship, and sometimes not even that (see, for example, Zimanov, 1958: 77 on the Kazakhs). . . . "

24. For example, Levchine (1840, 300–301) writes: "The Little Horde was originally composed of the powerful Altchine race and seven little tribes which, during the civil wars and the reprisals (baranta) were not strong enough to resist the Altchine race which was superior in number, [they] were united by the celebrated Tiavka, khan of the Kazakhs, into one race

which is known today as the race of the seven tribes (Sémirodsk). The ancient name of Altchine was found again in the correspondence of the khan Aboulkhair with the Russian government, in the first half of the last century. This race was composed of two parts named Alimouly, which means sons of Alim, and Baiouly, that is to say the rich sons. And after the new subdivisions that took place in the horde the generic name was forgotten, but the name of the two original parts to which the race belonged remained." Similarly, Martin (2001, 21) remarks that the "loose territorial affiliation" of the Kazakh "can be traced back to the *ulus* system of inherited patrimony developed under the Mongol empire" and notes that "there was no affiliation of a particular clan with a particular *ulus*, indeed they were very mixed" (Martin 2001, 174).

25. Privratsky (2001, 116–117) notes that when Hudson traveled to Almaty in the 1930s, he found no one who could remember the names of the forefathers back to the seventh generation, as they were supposed to, and the locals had "variable understandings of kinship." He concluded that the kinship system must have been in decline and that various disruptions prevented "cultural content" from being transmitted.

26. Martin (2001, 22) notes: "The clan was not a fixed group, but a flexible affiliation that combined genealogy with ties formed by allocation of land and grazing rights."

27. In 1822, four *okrugs* and eighty-seven *volosti* were formed; four more *okrugs* were added in 1844 as Russian control rolled eastward. Later, in 1867 and 1868, new statutes were introduced that abolished the *okrug* as an administrative unit and replaced it with the *uezd*, headed by tsarist commanders rather than sultans; the *volosti* remained about the same but the number of households per *aul* doubled on average (Levchine 1840, 467–474; Geiss 2003, 179–182).

28. Bacon (1966, 99). She also notes the term *upravitel* ("chief") was used for native officials.

29. In theory, one of every five households was selected to vote for the *volost* judge.

30. As Khazanov (1983, 177) notes: "The influence of such ['black bone'] leaders . . . increased as the influence of the 'white bone' waned (Viatkin 1941: 114). However the top echelon of the 'black bone' did not become a closed estate and could not turn its influence and authority into hereditary power, partly because of opposition from the Russian administration. According to the 'Law of the Siberian Kirghiz' of 1822 the posts of *biis* were announced for election and the results of the election were approved by state power (Zimanov, 1958: 196–197)."

31. The region that has become Kazakhstan was originally constituted as the Kyrgyz ASSR in 1920 but was renamed the Kazakh ASSR in 1925 (Olcott 1995, 302).

32. Published Kyrgyz "tribal" genealogies all appear to be of noble houses (see Attokurov 1995).

33. On commenting on the Chinese source quoted by Khazanov, for example, Geiss (2003, 110) writes, "it clearly emphasises that leadership passed from father to son and that other tribesmen were not able to become leaders. The source does not say, however, that this was so due to the hereditary character of leadership. Tribesmen usually elected rich and influential persons as their leaders."

34. This is rather strange, since as Khazanov (1983, 175) notes, at the end of the nineteenth century the genealogies of the Kirghiz *Manaps* numbered fourteen to eighteen generations (Petrov 1961, 122).

35. Semenov's (1998, 144) account is one of lordly power threatened by hostile nobles. He writes: "Burambai's joy at the arrival of Russian assistance was explained by his absolutely critical situation, as the whole of the eastern half of the basin of Lake Issyk-kul', which was in his domain, was virtually already lost to him. He had evacuated it along both the northern and southern shores of the lake (along Kungei and Terskei) since his defeat in the autumn of 1854 and moved to winter quarters by the Santash Pass, leaving behind only a few auly in the valleys of the rivers Tiup and Dzhargalan, the eastern tributaries of the lake. It was to these auly that the Sarybagish tirelessly directed their baranty [raids]. . . . "

36. For example, Manas becomes good friends with an Oirat prince named Almambet. At one point, the prince declares, "the commoners would not heed me" (Hatto 1990, 27).

4. THE STATE CONSTRUCTION OF THE CLAN: THE UNILINEAL DESCENT GROUP AND THE ORDERING OF STATE SUBJECTS

1. *The Seattle Times*, Sunday, October 24, 2004. Available online at http://seattletimes.nwsource.com/html/nationworld/2002071306_mongolia24.html.

2. An earlier article by John Pomfret of the *Washington Post*, for example, took a similar line: " 'Mongolia's Communist rulers attacked the hereditary aristocracy in 1921, killing tens of thousands of princes and princesses. Four years later, as the revolution intensified, the Communists banned last names. The intention was for people to forget which class they belonged to, forget that the state killed their relatives, forget Mongolia's past. People didn't even know 1921 happened. They didn't even know

they had lost their names,' said Serjee Zhambaldorjiin, director of the State Central Library and an expert on modern Mongolian history, who like many other Mongolians—and Russians—uses a second name based on his father's given name. 'It was a way to eliminate the influence of the nobles and princes. This was a wiping out of nobility in Mongolia'" (*Washington Post*, July 11, 2000, A1).

3. A fourth category of names are thought to be those of groups of people moved from one administrative division to another and are then known by the name of their original division.

4. The six *sums* and forty-four *otogs* of Borjigin Janjin Beiliin Khoshuu are listed by Badamkhatan (1972, 10–11).

5. The Mergen Gegeen (1717–1766) was a leading ecclesiastical figure, author of the great Mongolian-language history of Buddhism, the *Altan Tobchi* (*Golden Summary*).

6. Vreeland (1962, 155) notes, for example, that among the Chahar of Inner Mongolia at that time, "the *törel* [*töröl*] (kindred) was not a residential group, and persons who were of the same *törel* might be widely scattered."

7. A nominal unit of twenty households also existed, although it seems to have had less administrative importance.

8. Mostaert (1957, 246–248), for example, makes it clear when he describes the Mongol clans (*omok* in this case) that this largely concerned the nobles, and gives almost no information at all regarding kinship structures of the commoners, although he notes that exogamy is not strictly observed by commoners but is obligatory for the nobility. He assumes, like his contemporaries, that kinship structures must have declined, but more among the commoners than the aristocracy.

9. Interestingly, when Manchus did take a Chinese-style "clan name" (*xing*), they did not use their *hala* or *mukun* but would take the first character of the personal name of their father or grandfather. This was an old practice, used by urbanized Jurchen since long before the Qing period (Crossley 1990, 38), and it would seem a strange choice in a society already organized into exogamous patrilineages.

10. Humphrey (personal communication 1990).

11. Shirokogoroff seems to have recognized that both *obog* (*omog*) and *hala* were administrative units and not clans. In describing the Tungus, he notes that they would say that the old *omok* (*obog*) and *kala* (*hala*) organization was declining, and that ethnographers "believed in the decline of the clan system, whereas in fact they have been dealing with the decline of the former fixed administrative and territorial units" (Ssorin-Chaikov 2003, 35).

12. On this point, Ebrey (1986, 40) quotes Watson in pointing out that "it is difficult for many anthropologists, given their frog-in-the-well view of Chinese society, to accept that lineage and related social forms . . . emerged as a consequence of an ideological transformation among the national elite."

13. The result was a system that gave a nobleman not one but eight ancestral lines, known as the *p'alcho*.

14. Commoner clans are said to be found in Hinggan, Jirem, and Juu Ud leagues, among the Mongoljin and Tümed Mongolians of Liaoning, the Chahar, and the more western Mongol groups—the Tümed, Ordos, Bayan Nuur, and Alasha Mongolians. However, most Shilingol Mongolians, including the Sünid, Üjümchin, and Abaga, also lack clans other than the Borjigin. See Sneath (2000, 197).

15. In the *Altan Tobchi* (chap. 32, p. 53), for example, he wrote: "It is unbearable when, even under the excuse of observing rules of ceremony, people bow their heads to officials who lower the meaning of the state and religion. . . . There is no need for a genealogy book for those people who give less value to the gold and silver of the *törül* [*töröl*] *udum* (relatives of the male line) and raise up the value of the iron and copper of the *urug sadun* (relatives through marriage)."

16. In fact, the standard translation of the term *obog* as "clan" does not accord with anthropological kinship terminology very well. In anthropological usage, a clan is a group of people who consider themselves descendants of a common ancestor but cannot trace all the genealogical connections to him or her. But many of the *obogs* mentioned in the early sources are described in terms of their precise lines of descent from ancestors, and for this reason would be described as lineages in classical anthropological terminology.

17. Cleaves (1982, 3) translated this as: "What [manner of] person art thou?" For the reconstructed Mongol texts, see Pelliot (1949, 6).

18. Indeed, in the seventeenth and eighteenth centuries the term *monggol obogtan* ("those of the Mongol *obogs*") starts to appear in texts to describe the Mongol polities as a whole. See Munkh-Erdene (2006, 57).

19. The text actually reads that they were *jörkimes*, an unglossed word that De Rachewiltz translates as "inflexible" (see De Rachewiltz 2004, 511).

20. The great wrestler, Büri Bökö, was the nephew of Ökin Barqaq, not his son or grandson. He is written of as a member of the Jürkin (§131), and later (§140) we are told that he decided to join them (see Cleaves 1982, 61, 68).

21. The Tayichi'ud, for example, are described as an *obog* in §47, but in §148, when the *Secret History* describes the extermination of the nobility, it de-

scribes the Tayichi'ud "bone," presumably indicative of the Tayichi'ud lineal descent. See Cleaves (1982, 10, 76). It is conceivable that other terms indicate more and less inclusive categories of this sort. The term *omog*, for example, seems to be a synonym for *obog*, although it is interesting to note that when describing the *irgen* (subjects) of the Jürkin, the *Secret History* uses the term *omog*, while the rulers themselves are associated with the term *obog*. See §139.

22. The *inje* were a set of personal subjects sent with a noblewoman when she married. This institution dates from pre-Chinggisid times and is discussed further in chapter 6.

23. Sorqan-shira, who helped Temüjin escape from the Tayichi'ud, uses the phrase when warning him that they are approaching, although the Tayichi'ud are only distantly related to Temüjin (see *Secret History of the Mongols* §82; Cleaves 1982, 27).

24. There are ambiguous passages. The entry for *urug* (affines/kin/dynasty) reads *aliba khuda obug-un khamiya-tu khuumün-i chöm urug khememüi* (*Khorin Nigetü* 1979, 146), and this could be read two ways. It could mean "all people related to the affinal *obog* are called *urug*," but it could be read to mean "any people who are related by *huda* [*khuda*] and *obog* together are *urug*," as Munkh-Erdene (2006, 65) does. This second reading would suggest the *obog* was not exogamous.

25. Something of this ambiguity appears to be reflected in the work of Mongolian historians such as Gongor (1991 [1970], 7, 280). Although he largely reproduces the standard Marxist evolutionary succession from kinship society/organization (*urag töröliin baiguulal*) to feudalism, he often describes the *obog* in terms of both *yas* (bone) and *tsus* (blood), and this latter term could be taken to indicate matrilateral rather than patrilineal kinship.

26. She goes on to note: "In both societies primogeniture was unknown, and no common ritual or economic actions are discernable" (Deuchler 1992, 291).

27. Bourdieu writes, for example, that "far from obeying a norm which would designate an obligatory spouse from among the whole set of official kin, the arrangement of marriage depends directly on the state of the practical kinship relations" (Bourdieu 1977, 52). He goes on: "the matrimonial game is similar to a card game, in which the outcome depends partly on the deal, the cards held . . . and partly on the player's skill: that is to say, firstly on the material and symbolic capital possessed by the families concerned . . . and secondly on the competence which enables the strategists to make the best use of this capital" (Bourdieu 1977, 58).

28. For Bourdieu, the term "symbolic capital" stands for power, influence, and respect within a social network; he likens it to the "capital of authority" (Bourdieu 1977, 40).

29. Ibn Khaldûn (1967, 273–276), for example, uses the term "house" (*bayt*) in a comparable way, and notes " 'house' and nobility come to clients and followers only through their masters and not through their own descent."

30. The text reads *"ulus bayi'ululchan yabulduqsat—ta minqan minqalaju minqas-un noyat tuushijü soyurqal üga ügülasü"* (see Pelliot 1949, 77).

31. The *stong sde* "thousand-districts" were also fundamental administrative units of Song Tsen Gampo's seventh-century Tibetan state (Uray and Uebach 1994, 913).

32. Watson describes the lower-order leaders as "chiefs," in line with the tribal model. However, in the original text Sima Qian (1982, 110) uses the same term (*zhang*) for both the senior lords of ten thousand and their subordinates.

33. As Di Cosmo (2002, 177) notes: "Key characteristics of the government—the appanage system, the division of official posts into two halves ("left" and "right," corresponding to east and west), the decimal military structure (e.g., units divided into tens, hundreds, thousands, etc.), and the limited number of top-ranking commanders and ministers gathered in council—are all traits that can also be found in later Inner Asian States."

34. Chinese texts record that except for the two ruling houses, the Kitans had no *xing* (clan names/clans) and "did not marry according to the Chinese code of proper behavior" (Wittfogel and Feng 1949, 17). Wittfogel and Feng (1949, 204) note: "A survey of the social history of Inner Asia shows that many pastoral tribes counted their kin for a limited number of generations only." The Chinese texts speak of *bu* ("tribes") and *zu* ("lineages" or "houses"), and Wittfogel and Feng were puzzled to find that newly formed Kitan *bu* did not have *zu*. They write, "the *tsu[zu]*-less organizations referred to are the two tribes composed of former camp bondsmen . . . probably prisoners of war . . . but it is difficult to understand why, if they ever had *tsu* [*zu*], these *tsu* were so quickly forgotten, even when a restored tribal status would naturally have suggested the restoration of their traditional kinship organization" (Wittfogel and Feng 1949, 202). This suggests there was no such traditional kinship organization, and that where they are mentioned the *zu* may have been prominent or noble houses, who would be absent in units newly formed from prisoners.

35. It also appears that the Kitans may have also used the decimal administrative units. At the small scale, Wittfogel and Feng (1949, 84) note that Abao-ji's Kitan subjects were organized into "divisions" (*yüan*) that "originally contained 'one hundred families.'" At the larger scale, Song ambassadors

to the Liao mention that the eight major divisions of the Kitans (they describe these as "military prefectures" but they are often described as "tribes") are governed by two kings (*wang*), each of whom commanded ten thousand troops (Wright 1998, 43).

36. Indeed, in the Chinese texts the original eight "tribes" of the Kitans were described as the eight *bu* of the legendary Kitan ruler Qishou (Wittfogel and Feng 1949, 85), each ruled by one of his sons.

5. THE ESSENTIALIZED NOMAD:
NEOCOLONIAL AND SOVIET MODELS

1. As Grousset remarks (2002, 10): "It is possible that the Scythians of southern Russia were never more than an aristocracy superimposed on a Cimmerian—that is a Thraco-Phrygian—substratum."

2. See Phillips (1965, 74). As Phillips notes (1965, 83), Herodotus's credibility was further enhanced by the discovery that his description of the embalming process of the Scythian kings was confirmed by archaeological studies of royal burials.

3. (*Obshchestvennyi Stroi Mongolov. Mongolskii Kochevoi Feodalizm*)

4. A debate as to how to define the essence of the "patriarchal-feudal conditions of nomadic peoples" emerged in 1955 in the journal *Voprosy Istorii* (*Questions of History*) and drew in Potapov, Tolybekov, and Zlatkin (Bold 2001, 22).

5. Gellner (1983, xxii) summarizes Tolybekov's characterization of Kazakh society and of pastoral nomads in general like this: "Its culture is widely and evenly diffused and encapsulated in its members, its stratification is ephemeral and weak, its political formations are fragile and elusive, and even if on occasion they grow into something bigger, this leads to no permanent, irreversible, structural changes in society." He goes on to note: "The two men who continued Tolybekov's argument against the feudalizing thesis, and the recognition of the basically stagnant or oscillating nature of pastoral nomadic society, are G. E. Markov and A. M. Khazanov."

6. Since independence, official histories of Kazakhstan, while retaining the notion of a "semifeudal" prerevolutionary structure, are critical of Stalinist policies on the grounds that they were based on a "misunderstanding of the specific character of the pre-capitalist structures" of the nomadic *aul* (Abylkhozhin, Aldazhumanov, and Romanov 1998, 148). In this narrative, the policies of "class war" and "new revolution" launched by the local party leader Goloschyokin in 1928 led to the expropriation of the lands of the *bais* (semifeudal lords), but the failure to understand the specific character of the productive relations of the nomadic *aul* led to a collapse in the

standard of living of Kazakhs and destroyed the "age old traditions of the *aul*." (Abylkhozhin, Aldazhumanov, and Romanov 1998, 50).

7. Bloch (1961, 446) characterizes feudalism thus: "A subject peasantry; widespread use of the service tenement (i.e. the fief) instead of salary . . . the supremacy of a class of specialised warriors; ties of obedience and protection which bind man to man and, within the warrior class assume the distinctive form called vassalage; fragmentation of authority . . . and . . . the survival of other forms of association, family and State." However, Bloch terms this *European* feudalism, and actually supports the flexible application of the term "feudalism" to other societies, such as Japan. He writes: "Just as the matrilineal or agnatic clan or even certain types of economic enterprise are found in much the same form in very different societies, it is by no means impossible that societies different from our own should have passed through a phase . . . [that can be termed] . . . feudal."

8. Indeed, Gledhill (1994, 55) suggests that a Weberian understanding of feudalism need not necessarily include rights over land at all. The key criteria he identifies are that "rights to exercise authority are delegated from higher to lower-ranking power holders in return for services of a military or administrative character through a contractual relationship between lord and vassal." This certainly resembles the Chinggisid political order, in which nobles who swore fealty to Chinggis Khan made elaborate pledges of military support (see Onon 1990, 46). Indeed, the right and obligation to raise troops for an overlord seems likely to have been the basis of the relationship between the ruler and nobility of the ancient Xiongnu polity, since the titles held by the nobility indicated the nominal number of horsemen they could muster in time of war. This raises the question as to whether the power of the khan over the aristocrats was absolute (as in "oriental despotism"), or entailed obligations on both sides (as in feudalism). Certainly the relationship between at least one vassal and the Kereid khan seems to have been contractual: *The Secret History of the Mongols* records what the khan says he will do in return for Temujin's fealty and tribute. The Chinggisid period seems to have led to a marked centralization of power in the hands of the emperor, but the historical sources give ample evidence for the autonomous impulses of the Mongolian aristocracy, who traditionally tended to consider their fiefs to be their own domains and resented interference by the emperor. See Mote (1994, 662) and Hsiao (1978, 521).

9. As Gledhill (1994, 55) points out, the fief need not even be rights over land, but could be other sorts of authority in Weber's formulation.

10. It is perhaps worth noting that when it comes to his original specialty—ancient Scythian society—Khazanov is much more aware of stratifica-

tion. He describes the ruling aristocracy as "an estate, the members of which led separate subdivisions of nomads" (Khazanov 1983, 178).

11. Although in his early work Lattimore (1940, 381) was still sufficiently convinced of the tribal model to write that "steppe tribalism—the society of pastoral nomadism—cannot properly be described as feudal even in its origins," in his later work he became convinced of the opposite view. Mongolian historians are also divided.

12. He writes, for example: "In very ancient times the Mongols lived in primitive communes (*khui nigedul*). People with common ancestors lived together and jointly struggled with nature. They made slow social progress. At that time the common ancestral group was the *obog*. . . . Because the forces of production were weak in ancient times the *obog* institutions could not support a large population. . . . With the break down of primitive communist society, the appearance of private property and class stratification, *obog* institutions also lost their blood descent (*chisun udum*) character, and gradually became a unit of territorial relationships (*gajar nutug-un kharichagan-u nigech*)" Rinchin (2001, 57–58).

13. He writes, for example, that before the thirteenth century Mongolian society saw the gradual disappearance of "clan communism" (*zhi zu gong she*) and the emergence of feudal elements (Zhou Qingshu 2001, 7).

14. A major inspiration to this model was E. Bacon's 1958 work *Obok* [*obog*], in which she argues that the segmentary lineage is found throughout the livestock-keeping areas of Asia and ancient Europe as well as widely in northern and eastern Africa (see Goldschmidt 1979, 21).

15. Under the subheading "attitudes," for example, we can read "self-determination and independence," but under "specifics," another bizarre mixture of items: "explicit self-interestedness; high status concern, low affect, empathy; objectification of persons, acting out of hostile impulses" (Goldschmidt 1979, 19).

16. Irons (1979, 363) also seems influenced by Barthian transactionalism. His theory supposes that "individuals will behave in such a way as to maximise the advantages and minimize the disadvantages of their behaviour."

17. Asad (1979, 422) writes: "Nomads use various objects of consumption (especially tools and weaponry) which are only produced in settled communities, whereas the latter are able to do without the animal products of pastoralists, and it may be thought that this very condition constitutes an important universal feature of 'nomadic society.' Yet it is equally plain that townspeople need food and raw materials which are only available in the countryside, and that peasants can do without the luxuries produced in urban centres. The crucial question to ask in each case is how, theo-

retically, a determinate historical pattern of the social division of labour comes to acquire *class* characteristics—or more precisely, how the systems of production and circulation in which different groups are involved create and confirm the social imbalances of need and power to satisfy need."

18. Galaty is, however, loath to give up the typology entirely, on the grounds that notions of nomadism and pastoralism remain important for identification.

19. Irons (1975, 30) notes, for example, that he took the situation he described as characteristic of "earlier social conditions."

20. Irons (1975, 60) records that his informants told him that such retrospective modifications of genealogy to fit residence did not occur. If they were right, then the expression of political relations in the idiom of kinship would have been virtually unviable.

21. The "forefather group"—a descent group who shared common patrilineal ancestors up to the seventh generation before their own, is a standard feature in the kinship society model of Turkic "nomads." The ethnographic evidence for this is rather slight. Geiss (2003, 52) notes, for example, that "Irons is one of the few anthropologists who systematically researched forefather groups."

22. Irons (1975, 15) notes the difficulty he had collecting genealogical information, in particular for the fifth and sixth ascending generations. He explains this by the fact that he only slowly learned to speak their language, had poor relations with locals, and for a long time dealt with them almost exclusively through a single "servant and interpreter" who told the locals that Irons was politically suspect and that he must be the sole point for their contact with the foreigner. In the end, his principal informants were three educated men, two being religious teachers.

23. This does not seem as unlikely to me as it does to Geiss. From her study of Persian sources, Tulibaeva (2001, 152) notes that many Kazakh sultans were raised to the throne in Khiva.

24. This impression is reinforced by other parts of Stewart's account. When he writes (1977, 167) "in some of the clans one family has rendered itself more powerful than the others," he is describing the Beg clan that Kushid Khan united to build the huge fort on the Murghab and his son Baba Khan who succeeded him, not everyday Turkmen families. Indeed, his account is very much concerned with the various Turkmen khans, such as Noor Verdi Khan of the Wakil, for example. One of his sons, Mahomad Yusuf Khan, succeeded him in leading the Wakil; his other son Mukdum Kuli Khan ruled the Akhal Tekke.

25. The same tendency to refer to influential families appears in Russian accounts of the time. Stebnitzky, a Russian colonel, made a survey of the region in 1872 and estimated there were 77,500 Yomuts and 150,000 Tekke at the time (Stebnitzky 1977, 67–68). He describes the Yomut as divided into halves, one of which was "subdivided into several smaller tribes and families under their respective chieftains" (Stebnitzky 1977, 65–67). The "several families" cannot mean the forty thousand or so Yomut of this division, but, like "tribe," must refer to a reasonably large political segment. Stebnitzky (1977, 67) also notes the Tekke lived in forty-three fortresses—rather odd for a traditionally acephalous society.

26. See Khazanov (1983, 179); Stone (1979, 2).

27. Something of this had clearly remained important to Irons's informants. Irons (1975, 40) writes of "the descent of all Turkmen from a single mythological character, Oghuz Khan."

28. I could not identify a word similar to *igh* in modern Turkish, but it is interesting, perhaps, to note that the Yomut seem to have used at least one local term that was originally Mongolian. Irons (1975, 68n13) notes: "Darugheh is a local synonym for sarkardeh [an official appointed by the Persian governor during the Kajar period]." This is almost certainly a version of the ancient Mongolian word *darga* (*daruga*), meaning the "head" or "boss." In Mongolian there is a word like *igh*—the term *ikh* (*yekhe*) means "great" or "grand."

29. Describing first marriages in Aji Qui, Irons (1975, 130) notes that in 107 out of 150 marriages, both partners were *qul*, and in five of the remaining forty-three, one partner was also of "non-Yomut" origin.

30. The term *qul* for slave appears in eighth-century Turkish inscriptions (see Golden 2001b, 28).

31. Irons (1975, 173–174) goes on to argue: "Thus intertribal warfare in the Turkmen region is probably best thought of as only one aspect of a broader selective process that favored not only forms of social organization which contributed to military strength, but also ones which contributed to such things as effective organization of economic activities, the maintenance of a healthy balance between population and resources, or any of a number of other things affecting a particular population's chances of survival" (Irons 1975, 173–174).

32. Dyson-Hudson and Dyson-Hudson (1980, 15) give as an example Walter Goldschmidt's description of "pastoralists as people having 'a pride, a hauteur, a strong sense of individual worth and a strong sense of pastoralism as a calling,' and specifically acknowledges that 'it is this generalization that initially attracted me to the study of pastoralism.'"

6. CREATING PEOPLES: NATION-STATE HISTORY AND
THE NOTION OF IDENTITY

1. Although Renan attempted to denaturalize the nation, and show, as Gellner (1987, 8) put it, that "nations are made by human will," he still reproduced the standard nineteenth-century evolutionary scheme that cast tribes as ancient kinship societies. "The tribe and the city were then [in antiquity] merely extensions of the family. At Sparta and at Athens all the citizens were kin to a greater or lesser degree . . . this is still the case with the Arab tribes" (Renan 1990 [1882], 13).

2. As Hobsbawm (1990, 18–19) notes, the concept of the nation is historically very young, emerging during the Age of Revolution, in which new political elites, particularly in France and America, began to articulate a new political vocabulary to express the common interest of members of the state in opposition to monarchical identification of the state with the monarch of the *ancien régime*. "The 'nation' so considered, was a body of citizens whose collective sovereignty constituted them as a state which was their political expression" (Hobsbawm 1990, 18–19).

3. Durkheim's scheme generated several of the key concepts of the tribal model. He wrote, for example, "an absolutely homogenous mass whose parts are not distinguished from one another. . . . We proposed to call the aggregate thus characterised, *horde*. . . . We give the name *clan* to the horde which has ceased to be independent by becoming an element in a more extensive group, and that of *segmentary societies with a clan base* to peoples who are constituted through an association of clans . . . a clan . . . this word . . . expresses its mixed nature, at once familial and political. It is a family in the sense that all the members who compose it are considered as kin to one another" (Durkheim 1964 [1983], 174–175).

4. Assuming some more or less homogenous cultural and social entity as its object of study (an *ethnos*), classical ethnology reflected ethnonational historical thought, concerned with internal cohesion and "peoples" as cultural wholes.

5. Hobsbawm (1990, 48–49) also notes the suspect nature of claims to have discovered popular protonationalism in the past. He notes, for example, that terms like the eighteenth-century Estonian term *saks*, which has been read to mean a member of "the German volk," at the time probably just meant "lord" or "master."

6. Rives (1999, 119) writes that Tacitus "often uses *gens* to mean the Germans as a whole, whereas he normally uses *natio* of individual tribes."

7. Classical authors such as Cassiodorus used words such as *gens*, *genus*, *genealogia*, and *natio* for early Gothic polities. However, such work was

concerned with the history of the royal families of the Gothic kingdoms that emerged from the invasion period, and it is understandable that they were concerned with descent. These accounts were later elevated to become "national" histories (see Wolfram 1988, 5).

8. Wolfram (1988, 5) notes: "Even during the Early Middle Ages, the meaning of the term *gens* changed to such an extent that it came to embrace a wide spectrum of meanings, sometimes even contradictory ones."

9. See Gelzer (1975).

10. As Wolfram (1988, 6) notes, these leading families formed the "nuclei of tradition" of rulership, about which "tribes" took shape.

11. The customary translation of Tacitus has tended to render the term *principes* as "leading men," which gives the impression of egalitarianism. But the term indicated a senior aristocratic position in Roman society, and Gelzer (1975, 44) does not hesitate to translate it as "prince." Some German *principes* were selected to rule cantons, and as Rives (1999, 169) notes, nineteenth-century scholars saw this as evidence of the formal election of leaders, whereas a closer study of the text suggests that some from among the *principes* were selected by an aristocratic assembly. Rives (1999, 152) also notes that mention in Tacitus of "family connections" as motivating the army had once been taken to mean that the army was organized in clans, but he shows the passage does not indicate this at all.

12. *Hou han-shu*, chapter 90, cited in Jagchid and Symons (1989, 35).

13. *Hou han-shu*, chapter 90, cited in Barfield (1989, 87).

14. Such an account sits uneasily with the tribal model: what of the solidarity of common descent? Had all these supposed "kinsmen" of the Xiongnu emperor suddenly invented corresponding genealogical links to the Xianbe ruler? The usual interpretation was to take this as a feature of the "tribal federation." The Xiongnu tribe proper ruled, as first among equals, many other tribes. With the defeat of the Xiongnu "core," these other tribes could join the Xianbe confederation. But as Khazanov (1983, 152) notes, the notion of nomadic "confederation" is inappropriate, since the polities concerned are generally formed by conquest.

15. The Mongol component was probably not more than a few thousand. Rashid ad-Din records that Batu had no more than four thousand Mongols allocated to him to rule the whole of the southern Russian steppe (Grousset 1970, 393); however, the *Secret History* suggests eight units of a thousand were allocated to Jochi's *ulus* (see Atwood 2004, 202).

16. This had become such a large problem that by the late thirteenth century both Qubilai Khan and Ghazan Khan in Iran had taken measures to try and relieve the situation (see Atwood 2004, 506; Khazanov 1983, 247).

17. Hulugu's successors, for example, married Kitan, Kereyid, Seljuk, and Byzantine princesses, to name but a few, and the Yuan emperors intermarried with Naiman, Tangut, Qarluq, Qipchak, and Korean nobility (see Atwood 2006a, 170).

18. Doyle, for example, defines the term in this way: "Empire . . . is a relationship, formal or informal, in which one state controls the effective political sovereignty of another political society" (Doyle 1986, 45).

19. This included the nobles Jelme and Sübodei from the Uriangqai, who were not considered "native Mongols" by Rashid-ad-din but who quickly became members of the ruling circle (see Skrynnikova 2006, 88).

20. The *Secret History* (§202) records the names of the lords of the ninety-five *minggan* thousand units of the Mongol *ulus* that Chinggis Khan established in 1206. It is clear that the Barulas, Onggirad, Ilkires, and the probably Turkic Önggüd are included in this *monggol ulus* category, and the numerous Borjigin nobles mentioned in the list must have been ruling many former subjects of the Tatar, Kereid, Merkid Tayi'chud, and Naiman nobles.

21. The term is *sisgei to'urqatu ulus*, the literal meaning being something like "the felt-skirted *ulus*" (*Secret History* §202).

22. De Rachewiltz (2003, 217).

23. The other term translated as "people" was *irgen*, which also had the meaning of subject (De Rachewiltz 2003, 303), and like *ulus* was clearly a term that implied political relations with a lord.

24. Perhaps as a result of the impact of Buddhist cosmological notions (Elverskog 2006, 112), in particular the concepts of the great continents, these sources describe the world as divided geographically into realms or countries described as *ulus*. The *Erdeni tunumal neretü sudur oroshiba*, the 1607 biography of Altan Khan, for example, speaks of how he pacified the "great realms of Mongolia and China" (*Monggol khitad khoyar yekhe ulus*). See Atwood (1994, 9).

25. As Atwood (1994, 21) puts it: "*Ugsaa* derived ultimately from the word *ug* (stump, base, origin, or beginning, and, as an adjective, original, basic, or initial). It was primarily used in the Qing period to mean a lineage, as in *khaan-u ugsaa* (royal lineage). *Ündüsü* had a similar primary meaning (root, beginning, origin, base, or, as an adjective, original, basic, fundamental, or principal). It was often used as a term to describe the legitimate ancestry of the Mongol nobility, as in phrases such as *khad-un ündüsü*, 'the origin/lineage of the sovereigns.' Along with *ijagur*, another term primarily meaning 'root' and later applied to royal lineages in particular, these three terms, combining and recombining in a variety of binomes, formed the main lexical resource out of which the post-1911 ter-

minology of nationalities (as distinct from countries) would be formed." During the twentieth century, the favored term for "nationality" became *ündüsüten* rather than *obogtan*, probably because of the influence of Jamsarano, the prominent Buryat-Mongol nationalist who perhaps sought a more open and inclusive term; see Munkh-Erdene (2006, 61).

26. This term is used to denote all the Mongols including the Oirads in the "*Rab hbyams-pa Zaya-Pandit-iyn saran-yin gerel khemekhü tuguji*," an early *Todo* ("clear" or "lucid") script chronicle written by Zaya-Pandit Namkhaijamtsu's disciple Radnabadra in 1691 (see Munkh-Erdene 2006, 58).

27. Lomi's history explicitly equates Borjigin rule with the Mongol *ulus* (see Bawden 1968, 5).

28. This was the Janggiy-a Khutugtu, active in the Ordos region. The term used in this document for "people" (*khümün arad*—"person commoner") was an unfamiliar one—a direct translation of the Chinese term *ren min*. This suggests that no Mongolian term came readily to the Khutugtu's mind, despite the fact that the Mongolian People's Republic had been using their own term—*arad tümen*—for some time (see Yang and Bulag 2003, 88–89). Neither did Buddhist prayers utilize the notion of a general "people" in the political sense; instead, they used a yet broader category: *khamug amitan* (all living creatures), which included both humans and animals.

29. As noted in chapter 5, the standard historical treatments in both Mongolia and Inner Mongolia followed the Marxist evolutionary scheme, with a kinship system/society (*urag töröliin baiguulal*) giving way to class relations and private property (see Gongor 1991; Rinchin 2001).

30. There are seventeen notionally Mongol *yastan* and four groups considered Turkic, the Kazakh, Urianghai, Uzbek, and Tuvans. See Hirsch (1997, 267) for the evolutionist scheme of *narodnost'* and *natsional'nost'*.

31. This is noted in the *Secret History of the Mongols* (§208). There is no reason to think this figure of two hundred servants is unusual. Ibaqa Beki was not one of Chinggis Khan's most important wives, and her father was not a khan. The number of her *inje* are only mentioned incidentally, when Chinggis gives Ibaqa Beki away to one of his more deserving generals and retains half of her servants for himself.

32. As Gellner (1983b, 55) puts it, for example: "Nations can be defined only in terms of the age of nationalism, rather than, as you might expect, the other way round." Hobsbawm (1990, 10) notes: "Nations do not make states and nationalism but the other way round."

33. Ismagulov (1998) writes, for example, that the "peculiar cultural-historical community, typical of the Kazaks" developed over thousands of years.

34. Bromley, for example, defines the term *ethnos* (Russian *etnos*) in the mould of Stalin's formulation of the dominant notion of nationality. Thus Stalin

(1970, 60) wrote: "A nation is a historically constituted, stable community of people, formed on the basis of a common language, territory, economic life and psychological make-up manifested in a common culture." Bromley's *ethnos* is "an historically formed aggregate of people who share relatively stable specific features of culture and psychology, an awareness of their unity and their differences from other similar groups, and an ethnonym which they have given themselves" (Bromley 1980, 155). Much of the Soviet-era work on ethnogenesis concentrated on identifying a core *ethnos* with recognizable elements of Stalin's notion of nationality (see Shanin 1989, 10).

35. By "charisma," Weber meant "a certain quality of an individual personality by virtue of which he is considered extraordinary and treated as endowed with supernatural, superhuman, or at least specifically exceptional powers or qualities . . . and on the basis of them the individual concerned is treated as 'leader'" (Weber 1978, 241).

36. See Gullette (2006) on Gumilev and his relationship to Weber and Nietzsche.

37. The "heavenly mandate" is the doctrine that imperial rulers are favored by heaven (*tngri*) and, in the ancient Türk, Xiongnu, and Mongol cases, that emperors are of heavenly descent. This notion of heavenly favor is extremely old and remained important in the Qing period (see Di Cosmo 2006; Sneath 2006).

7. THE HEADLESS STATE: ARISTOCRATIC ORDERS AND THE SUBSTRATA OF POWER

1. They write: "It denoted not only *the idea of* 'the state' or 'sovereignty', but was also used to refer to *actual* political arrangements. One example is the lengthy speech of regret, attributed to Chinggis Khan by several seventeenth century chroniclers, where he admits his fault in failing in his duty to his *törü* in Mongolia while he was enjoying himself campaigning in Korea (Bawden 1955; Choji 1983, 404–415) . . . *törü* here (a) is already conceptualised as one idea and (b) that it also refers to the concrete political set-up in Mongolia (Bawden 1955, §44) . . . In some seventeenth century contexts, *törü* has been translated as 'government'. For example, Bawden's translation of *Altan Tobci*" (Humphrey and Hürelbaatar 2006, 267).

2. Service (1975, 15), for example, declares that "civil law and formal government" are the elements that characterize the state.

3. Dylykova (1981, 117) translates the term *otog* as "pasture and livestock keepers belonging to a nobleman," and Atwood (2004, 431) notes there

is evidence that in the sixteenth century *otogs* were formed for leading nobles such as the grandsons of Batu-Möngke Dayan Khan.

4. The *otog* seems to have also been called a *khoshuu* in some documents (Bold 2001, 96), and it seems they were similar if not identical administrative units from the references in the code. See Buyanöljei and Ge (2000, 258).

5. These are mentioned in §3 of the laws added by Galdan Khung Taiji (Buyanöljei and Ge 2000, 256).

6. For example, section 8 details fines for fleeing on the battlefield. For the most senior commanders, the fine is a hundred sets of armor, a hundred camels, fifty households of subjects, and a thousand horses. But lower ranks have proportionately smaller fines, so that for elite troops the fine is just four riding horses, and from the most junior commoner, one quiver and one horse. A slave was just humiliated (see Buyanöljei and Ge 2000, 34).

7. As Durkheim (1964 [1893], 159) remarked: "The state exercised its tyranny over the smallest things."

8. See also Altangerel (1998, 70). For alternative wordings in Russian and English, see Dylykova (1981, 53, 117) and Bold (2001, 117).

9. In the case of the Xiongnu, for example, Golden (2001, 35) uses Kychanov's 1997 estimate of 180,000 to 190,000 slaves out of a total population of 1.5 to two million—about 10 to 12 percent.

10. Horvath (1989, 45) notes the failure of one lord, Könchek Khan, to establish a monarchy in the late twelfth century. The Pecheneg or Kangar polity of the eighth to tenth centuries also appears to have had very weak central authority, but was composed of eight principalities, each with five subdivisions, ruled by a hereditary aristocracy. However, the Byzantine source Constantine Porphyrogentius notes names and titles of Pecheneg lords that suggest offices of court, an indication, perhaps, of another headless state form (Horvath 1989, 15). In the usual way, Horvath describes the ninth-century political subdivisions of the Pechenegs as clans while noting they were not actually kinship units at all. He writes: "These clans were no longer social units based on ties of kinship but the nuclei of territorial organization directed by a clan aristocracy. Power lay in the hands of noble clans which were separate from the common people" (Horvath 1989, 14).

11. Similarly, social organization in post-Chinggisid "Qipchak" polities such as the Nogai horde are described by contemporary observers in terms of lordly or kingly domains. The sixteenth-century English traveler Anthony Jenkinson, for example, noted that "every horde had a ruler whom they

obeyed as their king," and Al-Hasan the Arab also describes the "kings and nobles" of the region (Haidar 2002, 55).

12. The English envoy who witnessed the election of Wladyslaw IV in 1632 related that the gathered nobles "sat in the open field under the blue canopy of heaven without even tents to keep them from the rain." When it was over he wrote: "The Parliament knelt down and sang Te Deum Laudamus, which, being ended, they proclaimed the king among the people. It is said that there were 150,000 horsemen in the field that day. . . . I am sure I never saw the like in my life before, neither do I think that I shall ever see the like again" (Fedorowicz 1982, 3).

13. See Weber (1947, 347–351). At first glance, Weber's characterization of the patrimonial state may seem appropriate for the sorts of dynastic realms formed by steppe rulers. But Weber stresses the importance of a single ruler in his ideal type of the patrimonial state and the formation of a personal staff standing outside "traditional" structures. These assumptions seem ill-suited for universal application, and on reflection the model of patrimonialism seems too deeply entangled with Weber's notion of traditional authority and a particular theory of the evolution of political forms. This is pictured in terms that rather reproduce nineteenth-century social theory, as an evolution from equality to hierarchy, so that a figure with authority that was purely exemplary "as in the case of the Arabian Sheik" (Weber 1949, 346) comes to control military force. Hence "traditional authority tends to develop into 'patrimonialism' where absolute authority is maximized it may be called 'Sultanism'. The 'members' are now treated as 'subjects'. An authority of the chief which was previously treated principally as exercised on behalf of the members, now becomes his personal authority which he appropriates in the same way as he would any ordinary object of possession" (Weber 1949, 346–347).

14. Onon (1990, 40); Cleaves (1982, 46). Chilger appears to have actually been of the Merkid nobility himself, but the idiom of common status was used to indicate lord-subject relations, so in the wake of Chinggis Khan's defeat and subjugation of the Merkit polity Chilger's humble lament indicates that with respect to the new royal family he is but a lowly "commoner," that is, of subject or vassal status.

15. As the work of Skrynnikova (2006) and Atwood (2006a) shows, in the Chinggisid state the term *qarachu*/*kharachu* cannot be simply understood as "commoner" in the usual sense of the term. It could be applied to aristocrats who were not members of the ruling houses. The term "vassal," while undoubtedly a poor match for a complex and incompletely understood political term, might be closer to the sense of *qarachu* than "commoner." Skrynnikova shows that the term *bo'ol*, generally translated

as "slave" (which approximated to its later meaning), was applied to very senior servants of Chinggis Khan and his successors and indicated different forms of relative political dependency rather than absolute status. While the *bo'ol* of an ordinary subject might be a drudge, the *bosoqa-yin bo'ol* (threshold or doorkeeper *bo'ol*) was a very senior position. Instead of a nested series of kinship relations, then, this vocabulary suggests homologous political relations applied at different scales, so that relations between local lords and their subjects might be described in the same idioms as those between the imperial house and its noble vassals.

16. As late as 1934, when a politically active senior lama sought to address the Mongolians of Inner Mongolia, he issued four separate pamphlets addressed to the *taijinar*, the lamas, the youth, and the commoners respectively (see Yang and Bulag 2003, 88–89).

17. The norms associated with the position of *ejen* entail some obligations as well as rights; indeed, in a number of contexts the meaning of the term resembles that of the English word "patron." It can also be taken to mean "host," and this indicates that the householder has an obligation to act in an appropriate way. The position of *ejen* entails a responsibility for one's subordinates—the phrase *ejen bolokh* (to become an *ejen*) means to vouch for something or someone or to take responsibility for them. This is the usage in which it most resembles our term patron—as someone who supports a junior. The Mongolian term *ejengüi khükhed* (a child without an *ejen*) means an illegitimate child.

18. For a translation and discussion of this text, see Sneath (forthcoming).

19. Later, with the increasing influence of the Buddhist monastic establishment, *oboo* ritual became more inclusive and better embodied the administrative hierarchy of the Qing state. Officials responsible for the political divisions of administrative districts oversaw the *oboo* ceremonies for their own unit and attended those for the larger districts as representatives. The administrative architecture of the state was reproduced in rituals of this sort (Sneath 2000, 235–250).

20. To name but a few of these: Sima Qian describes the aristocracy of the Xiongnu of the third century B.C.E. through first century C.E., the Orkhon inscriptions refer to nobility in the early Türk empire of the sixth to eighth centuries C.E. (Sinor 1990, 297), the *Liao-shih* describes the Khitan aristocracy of the ninth to twelfth centuries (Franke 1990, 405), and the *Secret History of the Mongols* details the aristocratic political landscape of the twelfth century.

21. The Türk inscriptions of around 726 C.E. give us some idea as to the political ideology of the Türk rulers who wrote of their ancestors as already being Qaghans "when the blue sky above and the dark earth below were

created" (Sinor 1990, 297). These became masters of men and established an empire. When praising the victories of a Qaghan (emperor), an inscription reads, "by the grace of Heaven he deprived of their state those who had a state, he deprived of their qaghan those who had a qaghan, he subjugated his enemies" (Sinor 1990, 265–266). In the light of other aristocratic orders, it seems likely that those who were being deprived of their state were the rival nobility who were joint members of the project of rulership.

22. William of Rubruck, the observant Franciscan who traveled to the Mongolian capital in the 1250s, wrote: "Every captain (*capitaneus*), according to whether he has more or fewer men under him, knows the bounds of his pasturage and where he ought to feed his flocks in winter, summer, spring and autumn" (Beazley 1903, 147, 188; Dawson 1955, 94). Ch'i Ch'ing Hsiao (1978, 10), using Yüan dynasty sources, also notes: "Each unit was assigned grazing land (*nutug*) and water sources (*usun*) for the purposes of production and self-sufficiency."

23. Section 10 of Galdan's regulations notes that anyone changing their designated *otog* and *nutug* will be fined along with the unit head, and stipulates rewards for those that bring back runaways (Buyanöljei and Ge 2000, 270).

24. Riasanovsky (1965, 113) notes that Mongol subjects were required to stay in their *khoton* units.

25. Wittfogel and Feng (1949, 84, 193) note, for example, the Kitan commoners' obligation to do labor service and their allocation to units, ruled by nobles, in which "several families . . . lived together on a definite tract of pasture-land allocated to them."

26. Nobles often gave commoners to senior Buddhist figures in the seventeenth century (see Bawden 1968, 106).

27. They reproduce the segmentary kinship model for nonstate society in their own highly functionalist account of social form, which they describe in terms of machine systems. This leads them to adopt the standard narrative in which segmentary opposition prevents the stratification required for state formation. "The segmentary territorial machine makes use of scission to exorcise fusion, and impedes the concentration of power by maintaining the organs of chieftainry in a relationship of impotence with the group: as though the savages themselves sensed the rise of the imperial Barbarian, who will come nonetheless from without and will overcode their codes" (Deleuze and Guattari 1986, 167).

28. "We are compelled to say that there has always been a State, quite perfect, quite complete . . . the State itself has always been in relation with an outside. . . . The law of the State is not the law of All or Nothing (State-

societies *or* counter-State societies), but that of interior and exterior. The State is sovereignty. But sovereignty only reigns over what it is capable of internalizing, of appropriating locally" (Deleuze and Guattari 1986, 15–16).

29. They write: "Attempts have been made to apply a properly military category to the war machine (that of 'military democracy'), and a properly sedentary category to nomadism (that of 'feudalism'). But these two hypotheses presuppose a territorial principle: either that an imperial State appropriates the war machine, distributing land to warriors as a benefit of their position (*cleroi* and false fiefs) or that property, once it has become private, in itself posits relations of dependence among the property owners constituting the army (true fiefs and vassalage). In both cases, the number is subordinated to an 'immobile' fiscal organization, in order to establish which land can be or has been ceded as well as to fix the taxes owed by the beneficiaries themselves" (Deleuze and Guattari 1986, 73–74).

30. I might add that the division of the population into numerically defined administrative groups appears to be as old in "sedentary" polities as steppe ones. The Chinese *jun-xian* system in which "county" districts (*xian*) are defined as having a notional five hundred hearths is at least as old as the Qin dynasty (third century B.C.E.) and dates from the same period in which we have the first evidence of a steppe empire using a decimal system of administrative units based on notional numbers of subjects.

31. In their account, the imperial "barbarian" state is created when the despot (described as the "great paranoiac") harnesses the existing "autochthonous rural communities" with their "primitive" regime, just as in the Marxist account of the Asiatic Mode of Production (Deleuze and Guattari 2004, 213). Elsewhere they remark, "in the Orient, the components [of the State] are much more disconnected, disjointed [than in the West], necessitating a great immutable Form to hold them together: 'despotic formations,' Asian or African, are rocked by incessant revolts" (Deleuze and Guattari 1986, 58).

| References |

Aberle, D. F. 1962. *Chahar and Dagor Mongol bureaucratic administration: 1912–1945.* New Haven, Conn.: Human Relations Area Files, Inc. (HRAF Press).

Abizadeh, A. 2005. Was Fichte an ethnic nationalist? On cultural nationalism and its double. *History of Political Thought* 26, no. 2: 334–359.

Abrams, P. 1988. Notes on the difficulty of studying the state. *Journal of Historical Sociology* 1, no. 1: 58–89.

Abramzon, S. 1971. *Kirgizy I ikh etnogeneticheskie I istoriko-kul'turnye svyazi.* Leningrad: Nauka.

Abylkhozhin, Zh., K. Aldazhumanov, and Yu. Romanov. 1998. Kazakstan in the system of the kazarmennyi socialism. In *History of Kazakhstan*, ed. A. K. Akhmetov and M. K. Kozybaev, 142–159. Almaty: Ministry of Science, Academy of Sciences of the Republic of Kazakstan.

Agamben, G. 1998. *Homo sacer: Sovereign power and bare life.* Stanford, Calif.: Stanford University Press.

Akakca, F. Forthcoming. Political order and disorder among the Turkmen: An historical examination.

Akiner, S. 1995. *The formation of Kazakh identity: From tribe to nation-state.* London: Royal Institute of International Affairs.

Allard, F., and D. Erdenebaatar. 2005. Khirigsuurs, ritual, and mobility in the Bronze Age of Mongolia. *Antiquity* 79: 547–563.

Allsen, T. 1987. Mongol imperialism: The policies of the Grand Qan Möngke in China, Russia, and the Islamic lands, 1251–1259. Berkeley: University of California Press.

Altangerel, T. 1998. *Mongol Oiradyn Ikh Tsaaz.* Ulaanbaatar: Tuüünii Sudalgaa.

Anderson, B. 1991. *Imagined communities: Reflections on the origins and spread of nationalism.* London: Verso.

Anderson, D. 2002. *Identity and ecology in arctic Siberia: The number one reindeer brigade.* Oxford: Oxford University Press.

Asad, T. 1970. *The Kababish Arabs: Power, authority, and consent in a nomadic tribe.* New York: Praeger.

―――. 1979. Equality in nomadic social systems? Notes towards the dissolution of an anthropological category. In *Pastoral production and society: Production pastorale et société*, ed. L' Equipe Ecologie et Anthropologie des Sociétés Pastorales. Cambridge: Cambridge University Press.

Attokurov, C. 1995. *Kyrgyz sanjyrasy* [*Kyrgyz genealogies*]. Bishkek: Muras.

Atwood, C. 1994. National questions and national answers in the Chinese revolution; or, How do you say Minzu in Mongolian? Available online at http://www.indiana.edu/~easc/resources/working_paper/noframe_5b.htm.

―――. 2002. *Young Mongols and vigilantes in Inner Mongolia's interregnum decades, 1911–1931*. Leiden: Brill.

―――. 2004. *Encyclopedia of Mongolia and the Mongol empire*. New York: Facts on File.

―――. 2006a. *Ulus* emirs, *Keshig* elders, signatures, and marriage partners: The evolution of a classic Mongol institution. In *Imperial statecraft: Political forms and techniques of governance in Inner Asia, 6th–20th centuries*, ed. D. Sneath. Bellingham, Wash.: Western Washington University, Center for East Asian Studies.

―――. 2006b. Titles, appanages, marriages, and officials: A comparison of political forms in the Zünghar and thirteenth-century Mongol empires. In *Imperial statecraft: Political forms and techniques of governance in Inner Asia, 6th–20th centuries*, ed. D. Sneath. Bellingham, Wash.: Western Washington University, Center for East Asian Studies.

Bacon, E. 1958. *Obok: A study of social structure in Eurasia*. New York: Wenner-Gren Foundation for Anthropological Research.

―――. 1966. *Central Asians under Russian rule: A study in culture change*. Ithaca, N.Y.: Cornell University Press.

Badamkhatan, S. 1972. Borjgin-Khalkh. In *Etnografiin Sudlal* 4: 7–9 devter. Ulaanbaatar: Institute of History of the Academy of Sciences of the MPR.

Baker, R. 1975. "Development" and the pastoral people of Karamoja, northeastern Uganda. An example of the treating of symptoms. In *Pastoralism in tropical Africa*, ed. T. Monod, 187–205. Oxford: Oxford University Press.

Barfield, T. J. 1981. The Hsiung-nu imperial confederacy: Organisation and foreign policy. *The Journal of Asian Studies* 41: 45–61.

―――. 1989. *The perilous frontier: Nomadic empires and China*. Cambridge, Mass.: Basil Blackwell.

Barnes, J. 1962. African models in the New Guinea highlands. *Man* 62, no. 2: 5–9.

Bawden, C. 1968. *The modern history of Mongolia*. London: Weidenfeld and Nicolson.

————. 1997. *Mongolian-English dictionary*. London: Kegan Paul.

————. 2002. *An Anthology of Mongolian Traditional Literature*. London: Kegan Paul.

Beazley, C. R., ed. 1903. *The texts and versions of John De Plano Carpini and William De Rubruquis as printed for the first time by Hakluyt in 1598, together with some shorter pieces*. London: London Hakluyt Society, Cambridge University Press, J & C. F. Clay.

Beck, L. 1983, Iran and the Qashqai tribal confederacy. In *The conflict of tribe and state in Iran and Afghanistan*, ed. R. Tapper, 284–313. London: Croom Helm.

Beidelman, T. 1971. Nuer priests and prophets: Charisma, authority, and power among the Nuer. In *The translation of culture: Essays to E. E. Evans-Pritchard*, ed. T. Beidelman. London: Tavistock.

Biran, M. 2006. Between China and Islam: The administration of the Qara Khitai (Western Liao), 1124–1218. In *Imperial statecraft: Political forms and techniques of governance in Inner Asia, 6th–20th centuries*, ed. D. Sneath. Bellingham, Wash.: Western Washington University, Center for East Asian Studies.

Bloch, M. 1961. *Feudal society*. 2 vols. London: Routledge & Kegan. Reprinted in 1989, with a forward by T. S. Brown.

Bodger, A. 1988. *The Kazakhs and the Pugachev uprising in Russia, 1773–1775*. Bloomington: Indiana University, Research Institute for Inner Asian Studies.

Bold, B. 2001. *Mongolian nomadic society: A reconstruction of the "medieval" history of Mongolia*. Richmond: Curzon.

Boldbaatar, J., and D. Sneath. 2006. Ordering subjects: Mongolian civil and military administration (17th–20th centuries). In *Imperial statecraft: Political forms and techniques of governance in Inner Asia, 6th–20th centuries*, ed. D. Sneath. Bellingham, Wash.: Western Washington University, Center for East Asian Studies.

Bourdieu, P. 1977 [1972]. *Outline of a theory of practice*. Cambridge: Cambridge University Press.

Bromley, Yu. 1980. The object and the subject-matter of ethnography. In *Soviet and Western anthropology*, ed. E. Gellner. London: Duckworth.

Brooks, D. 1983. The enemy within: Limitations on leadership in the Bakhtiari. In *The conflict of tribe and state in Iran and Afghanistan*, ed. R. Tapper, 337–363. London: Croom Helm.

Browning, R. 1975. *Byzantium and Bulgaria: A comparative study across the early medieval frontier*. London: Temple Smith.

Bulag, U. E. 1998. *Nationalism and hybridity in Mongolia*. Oxford: Clarendon Press.

Burnham, P. 1979. Spatial mobility and political centralisation in pastoral societies. In *Pastoral production and society: Production pastorale et société*, ed. L' Equipe Ecologie et Anthropologie des Sociétés Pastorales. Cambridge: Cambridge University Press.

Burton, A. 1997. *The Bukharans: A dynastic, diplomatic, and commercial history, 1550–1702*. Richmond: Curzon.

Buyanöljei, E., and B. Ge, trans. 2000. *Monggol—Oirat-un Chaaji-yin Bichig*. Hohhot: Inner Mongolian People's Press.

Cable, M., and F. French. 1950 [1942]. *The Gobi desert*. London: Readers Union / Hodder and Stoughton.

Cannadine, D. 2002. *Ornamentalism: How the British saw their empire*. London: Penguin.

Carneiro, R. 1981. The chiefdom: precursor of the state. In *The transition to statehood in the New World*, ed. G. D. Jones and P. R. Krautz. Cambridge: Cambridge University Press.

Carrère d'Encausse, Hélène. 1967. Organizing and colonizing the conquered territories. In *Central Asia: One hundred and twenty years of Russian rule*, ed. E. Allworth, 132–168. New York: Columbia University Press.

Carsten, J., and S. Hugh-Jones. 1995. Introduction to *About the house: Lévi-Strauss and beyond*, eds. J. Carsten and S. Hugh-Jones, 1–46. Cambridge: Cambridge University Press, 1995.

Cavalli-Sforza, L. 1996. The spread of agriculture and nomadic pastoralism: Insights from genetics, linguistics, and archaeology. In *The origins and spread of agriculture and pastoralism in Eurasia*, ed. D. Harris, 51–69. London: UCL Press.

Chadwick, H. 1926. *The heroic age*. Cambridge: Cambridge University Press.

Chan, Wing-tsit. 1982. Chu His and Yüan neo-Confucianism. In *Yüan thought: Chinese thought under the Mongols*, ed. Hok-lam Chan and Theodore de Bary. New York: Columbia University Press.

Chandhoke, N. 1995. *State and civil society: Explorations in political theory*. London: Sage.

Chatty, D. 1996. *Mobile pastoralists: Development planning and social change in Oman*. New York: Columbia University Press.

Chimhundu, H. 1992. Early missionaries and the ethnolinguistic factor during the "invention of tribalism" in Zimbabwe. *Journal of African History* 33, no. 1: 87–109.

Clastres, P. 1977. *Society against the state*. Oxford: Blackwell.

Cleaves, F. W. 1951. The Sino-Mongolian inscription of 1338 in memory of Jigüntei. *Harvard Journal of Asiatic Studies* 14, nos. 1–2.

———, ed. and trans. 1982. *The secret history of the Mongols*. Cambridge, Mass.: Harvard University Press.

Cole, D. 1975. *Nomads of the nomads: The al-Murrah Bedouin of the Empty Quarter*. Chicago: Aldine.

Colson, E. 1986. Political organization in tribal societies: A cross-cultural comparison. *American Indian Quarterly* 10, no. 1: 5–19.

Cornell, T. 1995. *The beginnings of Rome: Italy and Rome from the Bronze Age to the Punic Wars (1000–246 B.C.)*. London: Routledge.

Crossley, P. 1990. *Orphan warriors: Three Manchu generations and the end of the Qing world*. Princeton, N.J.: Princeton University Press.

———. 1997. *The Manchus*. Oxford: Blackwell.

Dahl, G. 1979. Ecology and equality: The Boran case. In *Pastoral production and society: Production pastorale et société*, ed. L' Equipe Ecologie et Anthropologie des Sociétés Pastorales. Cambridge: Cambridge University Press.

Dardess, J. W. 1996. *A Ming society: T'ai-ho county, Kiangsi, fourteenth to seventeenth centuries*. Berkeley: University of California Press.

Davies, N. 1997. *Europe: A history*. London: Random House.

Dawson, C. 1955. *The Mongol mission: Narratives and letters of the Franciscan missionaries in Mongolia and China in the thirteenth and fourteenth centuries*. London: Sheed & Ward.

Deleuze, G., and F. Guattari. 1986. *Nomadology: The war machine*. New York: Semiotext(e).

———. 2004 [1972]. *Anti-Oedipus: Capitalism and schizophrenia*. London: Continuum.

Deuchler, M. 1992. *The Confucian transformation of Korea: A study of society and ideology*. Cambridge, Mass.: Harvard University Press.

De Rachewiltz, I., ed. and trans. 2004. *The secret history of the Mongols*. 2 vols. Leiden: Brill.

Diamond, S. 1974. *In search of the primitive: A critique of civilization*. New Brunswick, N.J.: Transaction Books.

Di Cosmo, N. 1999. State formation and periodization in Inner Asian history. *Journal of World History* 10, no. 1: 1–40.

———. 2002. *Ancient China and its enemies: The rise of nomadic power in East Asian history*. Cambridge: Cambridge University Press, 2002.

———. 2006. Competing strategies of Great Khan legitimacy in the context of the Chaqar-Manchu wars (c. 1620–1634). In *Imperial statecraft: Political forms and techniques of governance in Inner Asia, 6th–20th centuries*, ed. D. Sneath. Bellingham, Wash.: Western Washington University, Center for East Asian Studies.

Diemberger, H., and C. Rambal. Forthcoming. Rethinking the demise of kinship in Tibet: A case study from the village of Kardum, western Tibet.

Digard, J-P. 1983. On the Bakhtiari: comments on "tribes, confederation, and the state." In *The conflict of tribe and state in Iran and Afghanistan*, ed. R. Tapper, 331–336. London: Croom Helm.

Dobrova-Iadrintseva, L. 1925. *Tuzemtsy Turukhanskogo kraiia* [*Natives of the Turukhansk region*]. Novonikolayevsk: Izdaniye Sibrevkoma.

Doyle, M. 1986. *Empires*. Ithaca, N.Y.: Cornell University Press.

Dresch, P. 1988. Segmentation: Its roots in Arabia and its flowering elsewhere. *Cultural Anthropology* 3, no. 1: 50–67.

Durkheim, E. 1964 [1893]. *The division of labor in society*. New York: MacMillan.

Dylykova, S. D, ed. 1981. *Ikh Tsaaz "Velikoe Ulojenie"* [*The great code*], *Pamyatnik Mongoliskogo Feodalinogo Prava XVII v*. Moscow: Nauka.

Dyson-Hudson, R., and N. Dyson-Hudson. 1980. Nomadic pastoralism. *Annual Review of Anthropology* 9: 15–61.

Earle, T. 1994. Political domination and social evolution. In *Companion encyclopaedia of anthropology*, ed. T. Ingold, 940–961. London: Routledge.

Ebrey, P. B. 1986. The early stages in the development of descent group organization. In *Kinship organization in late imperial China, 1000–1940*, ed. P. B. Ebrey and J. L. Watson. Berkeley: University of California Press.

Edgar, A. 2004. *Tribal nation: The making of Soviet Turkmenistan*. Princeton, N.J.: Princeton University Press.

Ehrenberg, V. 1960. *The Greek state*. Oxford: Basil Blackwell.

Ellen, R. 1994. Modes of subsistence: Hunting and gathering to agriculture and pastoralism. In *Companion encyclopedia of anthropology*, ed. T. Ingold, 197–225. London: Routledge.

Elliot, M. 2001. *The Manchu way: The eight banners and ethnic identity in late imperial China*. Stanford, Calif.: Stanford University Press.

Elverskog, J. 2006a. *Our great Qing: The Mongols, Buddhism, and the state in late imperial China*. Honolulu: University of Hawaii Press.

———. 2006b. The legend of Muna mountain. *Inner Asia* 8, no. 1: 99–122.

Engels, F. 1959 [1886]. Ludwig Feuerbach and the end of classical German philosophy. In *Basic writings on politics and philosophy [by] Karl Marx and Friedrich Engels*, ed. L. S. Feuer. Garden City, N.Y.: Doubleday.

———. 1986 [1884]. *The origin of the family, private property, and the state*. Harmondsworth: Penguin.

Enoki, K. 1970. The Liang shih-kung-t'u on the origin and migration of the Hua or Ephthalites. *Journal of the Oriental Society of Australia* 7, nos. 1–2: 37–45.

Eriksen, T. 2002. *Ethnicity and nationalism: Anthropological perspectives*. London: Pluto Press.

Evans-Pritchard, E. 1933–1935. The Nuer: tribe and clan. *Sudan Notes and Records* 16: 1–53; 17: 51–57; 18: 37–87.

———. 1938. Review of G. W. Murray's *Sons of Ishmael. Africa* 11, no. 1: 123.

———. 1940. *The Nuer: A description of the modes of livelihood and political institutions of a Niliotic people.* Oxford: Clarendon Press.

Fedorowicz, J., ed. and trans. 1982. *A republic of nobles: Studies in Polish history to 1864.* Cambridge: Cambridge University Press.

Ferguson, R. B. 1997. Tribes. In *The dictionary of anthropology*, ed. T. J. Barfield, 475–476. Oxford: Blackwell.

Fiskesjö, M. 1999. On the "raw" and the "cooked" barbarians of imperial China. *Inner Asia* 1, no. 2: 139–168.

Fletcher, R. 1991, The summer encampment of Batu Khan in AD 1253: An initial enquiry into its plan and size. *Journal of the Anglo-Mongolian Society* 13, nos. 1–2.

Forde, C. D. 1934. *Habitat, economy, and society: A geographical introduction to ethnology.* London: Methuen.

Fortes, M. 1949. *The web of kinship among the Tallensi.* Oxford: Oxford University Press.

Fortes, M., and E. Evans-Pritchard, eds. 1940. *African political systems.* Oxford: Oxford University Press.

Foucault, M. 1986. *The Foucault reader.* Ed. P. Rabinow. Harmondsworth: Penguin.

Franke, H. 1990. The forest peoples of Manchuria: Kitans and Jurchens. In *Cambridge history of early Inner Asia*, ed. D. Sinor, 400–423. Cambridge: Cambridge University Press.

Fried, M. 1975. *The notion of tribe.* Menlo Park, Calif.: Cummings.

Gailey, C. 1987. *Kinship to kingship: Gender hierarchy and state formation in the Tongan islands.* Austin: University of Texas Press.

Galaty, J. G. 1981. Introduction to *Change and development in nomadic and pastoral societies*, ed. J. G. Galaty and P. C. Salzman. Leiden: Brill.

Garthwaite, G. 1983. Tribes, confederation, and the state: An historical overview of the Bakhtiari and Iran. In *The conflict of tribe and state in Iran and Afghanistan*, ed. R. Tapper, 314–330. London: Croom Helm.

Geertz, C. 2000. *Available light: Anthropological reflections on philosophical topics.* Princeton, N.J.: Princeton University Press.

Geiss, P. 2003. *Pre-tsarist and tsarist Central Asia: Communal commitment and political order in change.* London: RoutledgeCurzon.

Gellner, E. 1983a. Foreword to *Nomads and the outside world*, by A. M. Khazanov. Cambridge: Cambridge University Press.

———. 1983b. *Nations and nationalism.* Oxford: Blackwell.

———. 1983c. The tribal society and its enemies. In *The conflict of tribe and state in Iran and Afghanistan*, ed. R. Tapper, 436–448. London: Croom Helm.

———. 1987. *Culture, identity, and politics*. Cambridge: Cambridge University Press.

———. 1988. *State and society in Soviet thought*. Oxford: Blackwell.

———. 1994. *Conditions of liberty: Civil society and its rivals*. London: Hamish Hamilton.

Gelzer, M. 1975. *The Roman nobility*. Oxford: Basil Blackwell.

Giddens, A. 1985. *A contemporary critique of historical materialism*. Vol. 2, *The nation-state and violence*. Cambridge: Polity Press.

Gifford, E. W. 1929. *Tongan society*. Bulletin 61, Bernice P. Bishop Museum.

Glatzer, B. 1983. Political organisation of Pashtun nomads and the state. In *The conflict of tribe and state in Iran and Afghanistan*, ed. R. Tapper, 212–232. London: Croom Helm.

Gledhill, J. 1994. *Power and its disguises: Anthropological perspectives on politics*. London: Pluto Press.

Godelier, M. 1977. *Perspectives in Marxist anthropology*. Cambridge: Cambridge University Press.

Godley, A., trans. 2000 [1921]. *Herodotus: The Persian wars*. Loeb Classical Library. Cambridge Mass.: Harvard University Press.

Golden, P. 1990. The peoples of the south Russian steppes. In *The Cambridge history of early Inner Asia*, ed. D. Senor, 256–284. Cambridge: Cambridge University Press.

———. 2001a. Ethnicity and state formation in pre-Chinggisid Turkic Eurasia. *Central Eurasian Studies Lectures* 1. Bloomington: Department of Central Eurasian Studies, Indiana University.

———. 2001b. The terminology of slavery and servitude in medieval Turkic. In *Studies on Central Asian history in honor of Yuri Bregel*, ed. D. DeWeese. Bloomington: Indiana University Research Institute for Inner Asian Studies.

———. 2006. The Türk imperial tradition in the pre-Chinggisid era. In *Imperial statecraft: Political forms and techniques of governance in Inner Asia, 6th–20th centuries*, ed. D. Sneath. Bellingham, Wash.: Western Washington University, Center for East Asian Studies.

Goldschmidt, W. 1979. A general model for pastoral social systems. In *Pastoral production and society: Production pastorale et société*, ed. L' Equipe Ecologie et Anthropologie des Sociétés Pastorales, 15–28. Cambridge: Cambridge University Press.

Gongor, D. 1991 [1970, 1978]. *Khalkha Tobchiyan [Khalka Tovshoon] (I, II) [History of Khalkha, I, II]*. Beijing: Nationalities' Publishing House.

Goody, J. 2000. *The European family: An historico-anthropological essay.* Oxford: Blackwell.

Gordon, T. 1992. Review of *Kinship to kingship: Gender hierarchy and state formation in the Tongan islands. American Ethnologist* 19, no. 3: 601–604.

Gottlieb, A. 1992. *Under the Kapok tree: Identity and difference in Beng thought.* Bloomington: Indiana University Press.

Gough, K. 1971. Nuer kinship: A reexamination. In *The translation of culture: Essays to E. E. Evans-Pritchard,* ed. T. Beidelman. London: Tavistock.

Grodekov, N. I. 1889. *Kirgizy i karakirgizy—Syr-Dar'inskoi oblasti* [*The Kirghiz and Karakirghiz of the Syr-Dar'insk oblast*]. Tashkent: S. I. Lakhtin.

Grousset, R. 1970. *Empire of the steppes: A history of Central Asia.* Trans. N. Walford. New Brunswick, N.J.: Rutgers University Press.

Gullette, D. 2006. *Kinship, state, and "tribalism": The genealogical construction of the Kyrgyz republic.* PhD thesis, Department of Social Anthropology, University of Cambridge.

Gumilev, L. N. 1989. *Etnogenez i biosfera Zemli.* Leningrad: Izdatel'stvo Leningradskogo universiteta.

Hager, R. 1983. State, tribe, and empire in Afghan inter-polity relations. In *The conflict of tribe and state in Iran and Afghanistan,* ed. R. Tapper, 83–118. London: Croom Helm.

Haidar, M. 2002. *Central Asia in the sixteenth century.* New Delhi: Manohar.

Hammond, C. 1996. *Julius Caesar: Seven commentaries on the Gallic War with an eighth commentary by Aulus Hirus.* Oxford: Oxford University Press.

Hansen, T., and F. Stepputat. 2001. Introduction: States of imagination. In *States of imagination: Ethnographic explorations of the postcolonial state,* ed. T. Hansen and F. Stepputat. Durham, N.C.: Duke University Press.

Hatto, A. 1990. *The manas of Wilhelm Radloff.* Wiesbaden: Otto Harrassowitz.

Hirsch, F. 1997. The Soviet Union as a work-in-progress: Ethnographers and the category of nationality in the 1926, 1937, and 1939 censuses. *Slavic Review* 56, no. 2: 251–278.

Hobbes, T. 1996 [1651]. *Leviathan.* Oxford: Oxford University Press.

Hobsbawm, E., and T. Ranger, eds. 1983. *The invention of tradition.* Cambridge: Cambridge University Press.

Honey, D. 1990. The rise of the medieval Hsiung-Nu: The biography of Liu-Yüan. *Papers on Inner Asia* 15. Bloomington: Indiana University Research Institute for Inner Asian Studies.

Hornblower, S., and A. Spawforth, eds. 2003. *The Oxford classical dictionary,* 3rd ed. Oxford: Oxford University Press.

Horvath, A. 1989. *Pechenegs, Cumans, Iasiams: Steppe peoples in medieval Hungary.* Gyomaendrod: Kner.

Hostetler, L. 2001. *Qing colonial enterprise: Ethnography and cartography in early modern China*. Chicago: University of Chicago Press.

Hourani, A. 1990. Conclusion: Tribes and states in Islamic history. In *Tribes and state formation in the Middle East*, ed. P. Khoury and J. Kostiner, 303–312. Berkeley: University of California Press.

Hsiao, Ch'i-ch'ing. 1978. *The military establishment of the Yuan dynasty*. Harvard East Asian Monographs 77. Cambridge, Mass.: Harvard University Press.

Hucker, C. 1985. *A dictionary of official titles in imperial China*. Stanford, Calif.: Stanford University Press.

Humphrey, C. 1983. *Karl Marx Collective: Economy, society, and religion in a Siberian collective farm*. Cambridge: Cambridge University Press.

Humphrey C., and D. Sneath. 1999. *The end of nomadism? Society, state, and the environment in Inner Asia*. Durham, N.C.: Duke University Press.

Humphrey, C., and A. Hürelbaatar. 2006. The term *Törü* in Mongolian history. In *Imperial statecraft: Political forms and techniques of governance in Inner Asia, 6th–20th centuries*, ed. D. Sneath. Bellingham, Wash.: Western Washington University, Center for East Asian Studies.

Hutchinson, S. 1996. *Nuer dilemmas: Coping with money, war, and the state*. Berkeley: University of California Press.

Hyer, P., and S. Jagchid. 1983. *A Mongolian living Buddha: Biography of the Kanjurwa Khutughtu*. Albany: State University of New York Press.

Ibn Khaldûn. 1967. *The Muqaddimah: An introduction to history*. Trans. F. Rosenthal. London: Routledge & Kegan Paul.

Ikeya, K. 2005. Livestock economy and camel pastoralism among the Raika in India. In *Pastoralists and their neighbors in Asia and Africa*, ed. K. Ikeya and E. Fratkin, 171–186. Senri Ethnological Studies 69. Osaka: National Museum of Ethnology Publications.

Iliffe, J. 1979. *A modern history of Tanganyika*. Cambridge: Cambridge University Press.

Ingold, T. 1980. *Hunters, pastoralists, and ranchers: Reindeer economies and their transformations*. Cambridge: Cambridge University Press.

Irons, W. 1979. Political stratification among pastoral nomads. In *Pastoral production and society: Production pastorale et société*, ed. L' Equipe Ecologie et Anthropologie des Sociétés Pastorales, 362–372. Cambridge: Cambridge University Press.

Ismagulov, O. 1998. Ethnogenesis of the Kazak people. In *History of Kazakhstan*, ed. A. K. Akhmetov and M. K. Kozybaev, 43–61. Almaty: Ministry of Science–Academy of Sciences of the Republic of Kazakstan, Gylym.

Israilova-Khar'ekhuzen, Ch. R. 1999. *Traditsionnoe obshchestvo kyrgyzov v period russkoi kolonizatsii vo vtoroi polovine XIX—nachale XX v. i sistema ikh rodstva*. Bishkek: Ilim.

Jackson, M. 1989. *Paths toward a clearing: Radical empiricism and ethnographical inquiry*. Bloomington: Indiana University Press.

Jackson, P. 2005. *The Mongols and the West, 1221–1410*. Harlow: Pearson Longman.

Jagchid, S. 1999. *The last Mongol prince: The life and times of Demchugdongrob, 1902–1966*. Bellingham, Wash.: Center for East Asian Studies, Western Washington University.

Jagchid, S., and P. Hyer. 1979. *Mongolia's culture and society*. Boulder, Colo.: Westview Press.

Jagchid, S., and V. Symons. 1989. *Peace, war, and trade along the Great Wall: Nomadic-Chinese interaction through two millennia*. Bloomington: Indiana University Press.

Jones, M., et al. Forthcoming. Dating millet cultivation on the Eurasian steppe.

Keesing, R. 1975. *Kin groups and social structure*. Orlando, Fla.: Harcourt Brace Jovanovich.

Kessler, A. 1993. *Empires beyond the Great Wall: The heritage of Genghis Khan*. Los Angeles: Natural History Museum of Los Angeles County.

Khaldûn, Ibn. 1967. *The Muqaddimah: An introduction to history*. Trans. F. Rosenthal. London: Routledge & Kegan Paul.

Khasanov, A. Kh. 1968. Iz istorii klassovoi bor'by v Kirgizii v kontse XIX veka. *Izvestiya akademii nauk kirgizskoi SSR* 2: 10–16.

Khazanov, A. M. 1983. *Nomads and the outside world*. Cambridge: Cambridge University Press, 1983.

Khorin nigetü tailburi toli [*The Dictionary of Twenty One Volumes*] 1979 [1977]. Huhhot: Inner Mongolian People's Press.

Khoury, P., and J. Kostiner, eds. 1990. *Tribes and state formation in the Middle East*. London: University of California Press.

Kirchhoff, P. 1955. The principles of clanship in human society. *Davidson Journal of Anthropology* 1: 1–10.

Koppers, W. 1954. Primitive man, state, and society. *Diogenes* 2, no. 5: 69–76.

Kozlov, V. 1974. On the concept of ethnic community. In *Soviet ethnology and anthropology today*, ed. Yu. Bromley. The Hague: Mouton.

Krader, L. 1963. *Social organisation of the Mongol-Turkic pastoral nomads*. The Hague: Mouton.

———. 1968. *Formation of the state*. London: Prentice-Hall.

Kuper, A. 1988. *The invention of primitive society: Transformations of an illusion*. London: Routledge.

———. 2004. Lineage theory: A critical retrospect. In *Kinship and family: An anthropological reader*, ed. R. Parkin and L. Stone, 79–96. Oxford: Blackwell. Reprinted from *Annual Review of Anthropology* 11 (1982): 71–95.

Kuranov, G. G. 1937. Predislovie. In *TsK VKP(b) i Soyuznoe Pravitel'stvo o Kirgizii (Cbornik dokumentov za 1919—1937 god)*, ed. G. G. Kuranov. Frunze: Kirgizosizdat.

Lancaster, W. 1981. *The Rwala Bedouine today*. Cambridge: Cambridge University Press.

Lapidus, I. 1990. Tribes and state formation in Islamic history. In *Tribes and state formation in the Middle East*, ed. P. Khoury and J. Kostiner, 25–47. Berkeley: University of California Press.

Lattimore, O. 1934. *The Mongols of Manchuria*. New York: John Day.

———. 1935. *The Mongols of Manchuria: Their tribal divisions, geographical distribution, historical relations with Manchus and Chinese, and present political problems*. London: George Allen & Unwin Ltd.

———. 1940. *Inner Asian frontiers of China*. American Geographical Society, Research Series No. 21. London: Oxford University Press.

———. 1962. *Studies in frontier history: Collected papers, 1928–1958*. Oxford: Oxford University Press.

———. 1976. From serf to sage: The life and work of Jamsrangiin Sambuu. *Journal of the Anglo-Mongolian Society* 3, no. 1.

———. 1980. Inner Mongolian nationalism and the pan-Mongolian idea: Recollections and reflections. *Journal of the Anglo-Mongolian Society* 6, no. 1.

Leach, E. 1961. *Pul Eliya: A village in Ceylon; A study of land tenure and kinship*. Cambridge: Cambridge University Press.

———. 1982. *Social anthropology*. London: Fontana Press.

Leacock, E., and R. Lee, eds. 1982. *Politics and history in band societies*. Cambridge: Cambridge University Press.

Lee, R., and I. DeVore, eds. 1968. *Man the hunter*. Chicago: Aldine.

Levchine, A. 1840. *Description des hordes et des steppes des Kirghiz-Kazaks ou Kirghiz-Kaissaks*. Paris: Imprimerie Royale.

Lévi-Strauss, C. 1969. *The elementary structures of kinship*. Boston: Beacon Press.

———. 1983. *The way of the masks*. Trans. S. Modelski. London: Jonathan Cape.

Lewis, G., trans. 1974. *The book of Dede Korkut*. Harmondsworth: Penguin.

Leys, N. 1976. *By Kenya possessed: The correspondence of Norman Leys and J. H. Oldham, 1918–1926*. Ed. J. Cell. Chicago: University of Chicago Press.

Lindholm, Charles. 1997. Charisma. In *The dictionary of anthropology*, ed. T. Barfield. Oxford: Blackwell.

Locke, J. 1978 [1690]. *Two treatises of government*. London: Dent.

Lowie, R. 1962 [1927]. *The origin of the state*. New York: Russell & Russell.

Mackenny, R. 1993. *Sixteenth-century Europe: Expansion and conflict*. London: MacMillan.

Mackerras, C. 1990. The Uighurs. In *The Cambridge history of early Inner Asia*, ed. D. Senor, 317–342. Cambridge: Cambridge University Press.

Maine, H. 1861. *Ancient law: Its connection with the early history of society and its relation to modern ideas*. London: John Murray.

Mair, L. 1972. *An introduction to social anthropology*, 2nd ed. Oxford: Oxford University Press.

———. 1977. *African kingdoms*. Oxford: Oxford University Press.

Malinowski, B. 1944. *A scientific theory of culture and other selected essays by Bronislaw Maninowski*. Chapel Hill: University of North Carolina Press.

Mann, M. 1986. *The sources of social power*. Vol. 1, *A history of power from the beginning to* A.D. *1760*. Cambridge: Cambridge University Press.

Marcus, G. 1980. *The nobility and the chiefly tradition in the modern kingdom of Tonga*. Memoir 42. Wellington: The Polynesian Society.

Markov, G. E. 1976. *Kochevniki Azii: Struktura khozyaistva i obshchestvennoi organizatsii* [*The Nomads of Asia: The Structure of the Economy and Social Organisation*]. Izdatel'stvo Moskovskogo universiteta.

Marshall, L. 1976. *The !Kung of Nyae Nyae*. Cambridge, Mass.: Harvard University Press.

Martin, V. 2001. *Law and custom in the steppe: The Kazakhs of the Middle Horde and Russian colonialism in the nineteenth century*. Richmond: Curzon.

Marx, K. 1964. *The German ideology*. Moscow: Progress Publishers.

———. 1974 [1845]. *The German ideology: Pt.1, with selections from pts. 2 and 3, together with Marx's introduction to a critique of political economy*. Ed. C. J. Arthur. London.

McKinnon, S. 2000. Domestic exceptions: Evans-Pritchard and the creation of Nuer patrilineality and equality. *Cultural Anthropology* 15, no. 1: 35–83.

Meeker, E. 2002. *A nation of empire: The Ottoman legacy of Turkish modernity*. Berkeley: University of California Press.

Middleton, J. 1965. *The Lugbara of Uganda*. New York: Holt, Rineheart and Winston.

Mills, C. W. 1956. *The power elite*. New York: Oxford University Press.

Minorsky, V. 1978. *The Turks, Iran, and the Caucasus in the Middle Ages*. London: Variorum.

Mitchell, T. 1991. The limits of the state: Beyond statist approaches and their critics. *American Political Science Review* 85, no. 1: 77–96.

Morgan, D. 1986. *The Mongols*. Oxford: Blackwell.

Morgan, L. H. 1964 [1877]. *Ancient society: Researches in the lines of human progress from savagery through barbarism to civilization*. New York: Holt.

Mosca, G. 1939. *The ruling class: Elementi di scienza politica*. New York: Mc-Graw-Hill.

Mostaert, A. 1957. Matériaux ethnographiques relatifs aux Mongols Ordos'. *Central Asiatic Journal* 2, no. 4: 241–294.

Mote, F. W. 1994. *Chinese society under Mongol rule, 1215–1368*. In *The Cambridge history of China*, vol. 6, *Alien regimes and border states, 907–1368*, ed. H. Franke and D. Twitchett. Cambridge: Cambridge University Press.

Munkh-Erdene Lhamsuren. 2006. The Mongolian nationality lexicon: From the Chinggisid lineage to Mongolian nationality (from the seventeenth to the early twentieth century). *Inner Asia* 8, no. 1: 51–98.

Nadel, S. F. 1942. *A black Byzantium*. London: Oxford University Press.

Namjilma, ed. 1988. *Khorin naimatu tailburi toli* [*Dictionary of twenty-eight volumes*]. Huhhot: Inner Mongolian People's Press.

Natsagdorj, S. H. 1967. The economic basis of feudalism in Mongolia. *Modern Asian Studies* 1, no. 3.

———. 1978. *Mongolyn feodalizmyn ündsen zamnal* [*The fundamental lines of Mongolian feudalism*]. Ulaanbaatar.

Nordholt, H. 1996. *The spell of power: A history of Balinese politics, 1650–1940*. Leiden: KITLV Press.

Ochir, T. A., and B. J. Serjee. 1998. *Mongolchuudyn obgiin lavlakh* [*Directory of Mongolians' obogs*]. Ulaanbaatar: Mongolian Academy of Sciences.

O'Donovan, E. 1882. *The Merv oasis*. London: Smith, Elder & Co.

Olcott, M. 1995. *The Kazakhs*. 2nd ed. Stanford, Calif.: Hoover Institution Press.

Onon, U. 1990. *The history and the life of Chinggis Khan: The secret history of the Mongols*. Leiden: Brill.

Otgonjargal, S. 2003. *XX Zuuny Mongolyn tuuükhiig shineer ergen kharakhui (1921–1990)* [*New perspectives on the history of twentieth-century Mongolia (1921–1990)*]. Ulaanbaatar: Admon.

Paksoy, H. 1992. Z. V. Togan: The origins of the Kazaks and the Özbeks. *Central Asian Survey* 11, no. 3.

Parsons, T. 1951. *The social system*. Glencoe, Ill: The Free Press.

Patterson, T. C. 1991. *The Inca empire: The formation and disintegration of a pre-capitalist state*. Oxford: Berg.

Pelliot, P. 1949. *Histoire secret des Mongols: Restitution du texte Mongol et traduction Francaise des chapitres I a VI*. Paris: Adrien Maisonneuve.

Petrov, K. 1961. *Ocherki feodalnykh otnoshenii u kirgizov v XV–XVIII vekakh* [*Studies of the feudal relations among the Kirghiz in the XV–XVIII centuries*]. Moscow-Leningrad: Nauka.

Phillips, E. 1965. *The royal hordes: Nomad peoples of the steppes*. London: Thames and Hudson.

Piot, C. 1999. *Remotely global: Village modernity in West Africa*. Chicago: University of Chicago Press.

Potapov, L. 1954. O sushchnost patriarkhalno-feodalnykh otnoshenii u kochevykh narodov Srednei Azii I Kazakhstana [On the nature of patriarchal-feudal relations among the nomadic peoples of Middle Asia and Kazakhstan]. *Voprosy Istorii* [*Questions of History*] 6, no. 6: 73–89.

Privratsky, B. 2001. *Muslim Turkistan: Kazakh religion and collective memory*. Richmond: Curzon.

Rabinow, P. 1989. *French modern: Norms and forms of the social environment*. Chicago: Chicago University Press.

Radloff, M. 1863. Observations sur les Kirghis. *Journal Asiatique* 6, no. 2: 309–328.

Ranger, T. 1983. The invention of tradition in colonial Africa. In *The invention of tradition*, ed. E. Hobsbawm and T. Ranger, 211–262. Cambridge: Cambridge University Press.

———. 1989. Missionaries, migrants, and the Manyika: The invention of ethnicity in Zimbabwe. In *The creation of tribalism in southern Africa*, ed. L. Vail, 118–150. London: James Currey.

Rasidondug, S., and V. Veit. 1975. *Petitions of grievances submitted by the people to the Bogd Khan*. Wiesbaden: O. Harrassowitz.

Ratchnevsky, P. 1991. *Genghis Khan: His life and his legacy*. Oxford: Blackwell.

Rattray, R. S. 1929. *Ashanti law and constitution*. London: Oxford University Press.

Renan, E. 1990 [1882]. What is a nation? In *Nation and Narration*, ed. H. Bhabha, 8–22. London: Routledge.

Riasanovsky, V. 1965 [1937]. *Fundamental principles of Mongol law*. The Hague: Mouton.

Richards, A. 1940. The political system of the Bemba tribe—North-eastern Rhodesia. In *African political systems*, ed. M. Fortes and E. Evans-Pritchard, 83–120. Oxford: Oxford University Press.

———. 1941. A problem of anthropological approach. *Bantu Studies* 15, no. 1: 45–52.

Rigby, S. 1995. *English society in the later Middle Ages: Class, status, and gender*. London: MacMillan.

Rinchin, Yi. 2001. *Monggol sodlol-un ügülel-ün tegübüri* [*Collected papers on Mongolian studies*]. Huhhot: Inner Mongolian People's Press.

Rives, J. 1999. *Tacitus: Germania*. Oxford: Clarendon Press.

Rockhill, W., ed. and trans. 1900. *The journey of William of Rubruck to the eastern parts of the world, 1253–55: As narrated by himself, with two accounts of the earlier journey of John of Pian de Carpine*. London: Hakluyt Society.

Rose, N. 1996. Governing "advanced" liberal democracies. In *Foucault and political reason: Liberalism, neo-liberalism, and rationalities of government*, ed. A. Barry, T. Osborne, and N. Rose. Chicago: University of Chicago Press.

Rossabi, M. 1988. *Khubilai Khan: His life and times*. Berkeley: University of California Press.

——. 2004. Introduction to *Governing China's Multiethnic Frontiers*, ed. M. Rossabi. Seattle: University of Washington Press.

Rowe, W. 2001. *Saving the world: Chen Hongmou and elite consciousness in eighteenth-century China*. Stanford, Calif.: Stanford University Press.

Rumyantsev, G. N. 1962. *Proiskhozhdeniye Khorinskikh Buryat* [*Origin of the Khori Buryat*]. Ulan-Ude: Nauka.

Rykin, P. 2004. The social group and its designation in middle Mongolian: The concepts *irgen* and *oboq*. In *Forum for Anthropology and Culture* 1, 183–210. St. Petersburg: Peter The Great Museum of Anthropology and Ethnology.

Sahlins, M. 1968. *Tribesmen*. Englewood Cliffs, N.J.: Prentice-Hall.

——. 1983. Other times, other customs: The anthropology of history. *American Anthropologist* 85: 517–543.

Salzman, P. 1979. Inequality and oppression in nomadic society. In *Pastoral production and society: Production pastorale et société*, ed. L' Equipe Ecologie at Anthropologie des Sociétés Pastorales, 429–446. Cambridge: Cambridge University Press.

——. 1999. Is inequality universal? *Current Anthropology* 40, no. 1: 31–61.

Sanders, A. J. 2003. *Historical dictionary of Mongolia*. 2nd ed. Lanham, Md.: Scarecrow Press.

Sanjdorj, M. 1980. *Manchu Chinese colonial rule in northern Mongolia*. London: Hurst.

Schneider, D. 1984. *A critique of the study of kinship*. Ann Arbor: University of Michigan Press.

——. 2004 [1972]. What is kinship all about? In *Kinship and family: An anthropological reader*, ed. L. Parkin and R. Stone. Oxford: Blackwell.

Schuyler, E. 1885. *Turkistan: Notes of a journey in Russian Turkistan, Khokand, Bukhara, and Kuldja*. 3rd American ed. New York: Charles Scribner's Sons.

Scott, J. 1998. *Seeing like a state: How certain schemes to improve the human condition have failed*. New Haven, Conn.: Yale University Press.

Semenov, P. 1998. *Travels in the Tian-Shan, 1856–1857*. Trans. L. Gilmour. London: Colin Thomas & Marcus Wheeler, The Hakluyt Society.

Service, E. 1975. *Origins of the state and civilization: The process of cultural evolution*. New York: Norton.

Shahrani, M. 1979. *The Kirghiz and Wakhi of Afghanistan: Adaptation to closed frontiers.* Seattle: University of Washington Press.

Shanin, T. 1989. Ethnicity in the Soviet Union: Analytical perceptions and political strategies. *Comparative Studies in Society and History* 31, no. 3: 409–424.

Shils, E. 1957. Primordial, personal, sacred, and civil ties. *British Journal of Sociology* 7: 113–145.

Shnirelman, V., and S. Panarin. 2001. Lev Gumilev: His pretensions as founder of ethnology and his Eurasian theories. *Inner Asia* 3, no. 1: 1–18.

Shorter, A. 1972. *Chiefship in western Tanzania: A political history of the Kimbu.* Oxford: Clarendon Press.

Silverblatt, I. 1987. *Moon, sun, and witches: Gender ideologies and class in Inca and colonial Peru.* Princeton, N.J.: Princeton University Press.

Sima Qian. 1982. *Shiji.* Beijing: Zhonghua Shuju.

———. 1993. *Records of the grand historian.* Vol. 3, *Han Dynasty II.* Trans. B. Watson. New York: Columbia University Press.

Simukov, A. D. 1933. Hotoni (Hotons). In *Sovrennaya Mongoliya* [*Contemporary Mongolia*] 3.

———. 1936. Materialy po kochevomu bytu naseleniya MNR [Materials concerning the nomadic life of the population of Mongolia]. *Sovremennaya Mongoliya* [*Contemporary Mongolia*] 2, no. 15: 49–57.

Sinor, D. 1990a. The Hun period. In *The Cambridge history of early Inner Asia,* ed. D. Sinor, 177–205. Cambridge: Cambridge University Press.

———. 1990b. The establishment and dissolution of the Türk empire. In *The Cambridge history of early Inner Asia,* ed. D. Senor, 285–316. Cambridge: Cambridge University Press.

Skrynnikova, T. 2006. Relations of domination and submission: Political practice in the Mongol empire of Chinggis Khan. In *Imperial statecraft: Political forms and techniques of governance in Inner Asia, 6th–20th centuries,* ed. D. Sneath. Bellingham, Wash.: Western Washington University, Center for East Asian Studies.

Smith, A. 2000. Theories of nationalism: Alternative models of nation formation. In *Asian nationalism,* ed. M. Leifer. London: Routledge.

Smith, W. R. 1885. *Kinship and marriage in early Arabia.* Cambridge: Cambridge University Press.

Sneath, D. 1999. Spatial mobility and Inner Asian pastoralism. In *The end of nomadism? Society, state, and the environment in Inner Asia,* ed. C. Humphrey and D. Sneath, 218–277. Durham, N.C.: Duke University Press.

———. 2000. *Changing Inner Mongolia: Pastoral Mongolian society and the Chinese state.* Oxford: Oxford University Press.

———. 2006. Introduction. Imperial statecraft: Arts of power on the steppe. In *Imperial statecraft: Political forms and techniques of governance in Inner Asia, 6th–20th centuries*, ed. D. Sneath. Bellingham, Wash.: Western Washington University, Center for East Asian Studies.

———. Forthcoming. Ritual idioms and spatial orders: Comparing the rites for Mongolian and Tibetan "local deities." In *Proceedings of the International Association of Tibetan Studies* (September 2003), Oxford University.

Soucek, S. 2000. *A history of Inner Asia*. Cambridge: Cambridge University Press.

Southall, A. 1956. *Alur society: A study in processes and types of domination*. Cambridge: Heffer.

———. 1988. The segmentary state in Africa and Asia. *Comparative Studies in Society and History* 30, no. 1: 52–82.

Spooner, B. 1971. Towards a generative model of nomadism. *Anthropological Quarterly* 44, no. 3: 198–210.

———. 1973. *The cultural ecology of pastoral nomads*. Reading, Mass.: Addison-Wesley.

Ssorin-Chaikov, N. 2003. *The social life of the state in subarctic Siberia*. Stanford, Calif.: Stanford University Press.

Starr, C. 1961. *The origins of Greek civilisation, 1100–650 B.C.* London: Jonathan Cape.

Stebnitzky, I. 1977 [1874]. Stebnitzky's journey in central and southern Turkomania. In *The country of the Turkomans: An anthology of exploration from the Royal Geographical Society*, 62–70. London: Royal Geographical Society & Oghuz Press.

Stewart, C. E. 1977 [1881]. The country of the Tekke Turkomans and the Tejend and Murghab rivers. In *The country of the Turkomans: An anthology of exploration from the Royal Geographical Society*, 124–172. London: Royal Geographical Society & Oghuz Press.

Stone, C. 1979. Ibn Fadlan and the midnight sun. *Saudi Aramco World* (March/April): 2–3.

Strathern, A. 1983. Tribe and state: Some concluding remarks. In *The conflict of tribe and state in Iran and Afghanistan*, ed. R. Tapper, 449–453. London: Croom Helm.

Sutton, D. 1990. Organisation and ontology: The origins of the northern Maori chiefdom, New Zealand. *Man* n.s. 25, no. 4: 667–692.

Szonyi, M. 2002. *Practicing kinship: Lineage and descent in late imperial China*. Stanford, Calif.: Stanford University Press.

Szynkiewicz, S. 1977. Kinship groups in modern Mongolia. *Ethnologia Polona* 3: 31–45.

Tambiah, S. 1985. *Culture, thought, and social action: An anthropological perspective*. Cambridge, Mass.: Harvard University Press.

Tapper, R., ed. 1983. *The conflict of tribe and state in Iran and Afghanistan*. London: Croom Helm.

———. 1990. Anthropologists, historians, and tribespeople on tribe and state formation in the Middle East. In *Tribes and state formation in the Middle East*, ed. P. Khoury and J. Kostiner, 48–73. Berkeley: University of California Press.

Thackston, W., trans. 1998. *Rashiduddin Fazlullah, Jami'u't-Tawarikh, compendium of chronicles*. Cambridge, Mass.: Harvard University, Department of Near Eastern Languages and Civilizations.

Thom, M. 1990. Tribes within nations: The ancient Germans and the history of modern France. In *Nation and narration*, ed. H. Bhabha, 23–43. London: Routledge.

Tishkov, V. 1994. Post-Soviet ethnography: Not a crisis but something more serious. *Anthropology and Archeology of Eurasia* 33, no. 3: 87–92.

Tolstov, S. P. 1934. Genezis feodalizma v kochevykh skotovodcheskikh obshchestvakh [The genesis of feudalism in pastoral nomadic societies]. In *Osnovnye problemy genezisa I razvitiia feodalnogo obshchestva*, 165–199. Moscow-Leningrad: Gosudarstvennoe sotsialno-ekonomicheskoe izdatelstvo.

Tolstov, S. P., T. A. Zhdanko, S. M. Abramzon, and N. A. Kislyakov. 1963. *Narody Srednei Azii i Kazakhstana [Peoples of Central Asia and Kazakhstan]*. Moscow: Izdatel'stvo Akademii Nauk SSR.

Tolybekov, S. 1971. *Kochevoe obshchestvo kazakhov v XVII–nachale XX veka. Politiko-ekonomicheskii analiz [The nomadic society of the Kazakhs in the seventeenth to the beginning of the twentieth century: A political-economic analysis]*. Alma-Ata: Nauka.

Toynbee, A. 1946. *A study of history*. Abridgement of volumes 1–4 by D. C. Somervell. Oxford: Oxford University Press.

Tseveendorj, D., ed. 2004. *Mongol ulsyn tüükh: Tergüün bot' [History of Mongolia, vol. 1]*. Ulaanbaatar: Admon.

Tubshinnima, G. 1985. *Barguchud-un teyken irelt [The historical arrival of the Bargas]*. Hailar: Inner Mongolian Cultural Press.

Tulibaeva, Zh. 2001. *Kazakhstan i Bukharskoe khanstvo v XVIII—pervoid polovine [Kazakhstan and the Bukhara khanate in the eighteenth and first half of the nineteenth centuries]*. Almaty: Daik-Press.

Uray, G., and H. Uebach. 1994. Clan versus thousand-district versus army in the Tibetan empire. In *Tibetan Studies*, ed. P. Kvaerne, 911–921. Oslo: The Institute for Comparative Research in Human Culture.

Urbanowicz, C. 1979. Changes in rank and status in the Polynesian kingdom of Tonga. In *Political anthropology: The state of the art*, ed. S. Seaton and H. Ciaessen, 224–242. The Hague: Mouton.

Vail, L., ed. 1989. *The creation of tribalism in southern Africa*. London: James Currey.

Vainshtein, S. 1980. *Nomads of south Siberia: The pastoral economies of Tuva*. Cambridge: Cambridge University Press.

Valikhanov, Ch. 1985. *Sobranie socinenii v pyati tomakh*. Alma-Ata: Glavnaya redaktsiya Kazakhskoi sovetskoi entsiklopedii.

Vambery, A. 1970 [1864]. *Travels in Central Asia: Being the account of a journey from Teheran across the Turkoman desert on the eastern shore of the Caspian to Khiva, Bokhara, and Samarcand performed in the year 1863*. New York: Praeger.

Van den Berghe, Pierre. 1995. Does race matter? *Nations and Nationalism* 1, no. 3: 357–368.

Verdon, M. 1983. *The Abutia Ewe of West Africa: A chiefdom that never was*. Berlin: Mouton.

Vernadsky, G. 1953. *A History of Russian*. Vol. 3, *The Mongols and Russia*. New Haven, Conn.: Yale University Press.

Viatkin, M. 1947. *Batyr Srym* [*Batyr Srym*]. Moscow-Leningrad: Izdatelstvo Akademii Nauk SSR.

Vinnikov, Ya. R. 1956. Rodo-plemennoi sostav i rasselenie kirgizov na territorii yuzhnoi kirgizii. In *Trudy kirgizskoi arkheologo-etnograficheskoi ekspeditsii*, ed. G. F. Debets. Moscow: Izdatel'stvo akademii nauk SSR.

Vitebsky, P. 2005. *Reindeer people: Living with animals and spirits in Siberia*. London: HarperCollins.

Vitkin, M. 1981. Marx and Weber on the primary state. In *The study of the state*, ed. H. Claessen and P. Skalnik, 443–454. The Hague: Mouton.

Vladimirtsov, B. 1934. *Obshchestvennyi stroi Mongolov. Mongolskii kochevoi feodalizm* [*Social order of the Mongols: Nomadic Mongol feudalism*]. Leningrad: Izdatelstvo Akademii Nauk.

Vreeland, H. H. 1962 [1954]. *Mongol community and kinship structure*. New Haven, Conn.: Human Relations Area Files.

Watson, B., trans. 1993. *Records of the grand historian*. Vol. 3, *Han Dynasty II*. New York: Columbia University Press.

Watson, J. 1982. Chinese kinship reconsidered: Anthropological perspectives on historical research. *The China Quarterly* 92: 589–622.

Weber, M. 1923. *General economic history*. London: Allen & Unwin.

———. 1947. *The theory of social and economic organization*. New York: Oxford University Press.

———. 1948. *From Max Weber: Essays in sociology*. Trans. and ed. by H. H. Girth and C. Wright Mills. London: Routledge & Kegan Paul.

———. 1949. *Max Weber: The theory of social and economic organization*. Ed. A. Henderson and T. Parsons. Glencoe, Ill.: The Free Press.

———. 1978. *Economy and society: An outline of interpretive sociology*. 2 vols. Ed. G. Roth and C. Wittich. Berkeley: University of California Press.

Wheeler, G. 1964. *The modern history of Soviet Central Asia*. London: Weidenfeld and Nicolson.

Whisenhunt, W. 2001. *In search of legality: Mikhail M. Speranskii and the codification of Russian law*. Boulder, Colo.: East European Monographs.

Wittfogel, K., and C. Feng. 1949. *History of Chinese Society: Liao 907–1125*. New York: MacMillan.

Wolfram, H. 1988. *History of the Goths*. Berkeley: University of California Press.

Woodburn, J. 1980. Hunters and gatherers today and reconstruction of the past. In *Soviet and Western anthropology*, ed. E. Gellner. London: Duckworth.

———. 1982. Egalitarian societies. *Man* 17, no. 3: 431–451.

Wright, D. 1998. The ambassadors' records: Eleventh-century reports of Sung embassies to the Liao. *Papers in Inner Asia* 29. Bloomington: Indiana University Research Institute for Inner Asian Studies.

Yorke, B. 1990. *Kings and kingdoms of early Anglo-Saxon England*. London: Routledge.

Yang, Haiching, and U. Bulag. 2003, *Janggiy-a qutughtu: A Mongolian missionary for Chinese national identification*. Mongolian Culture Studies 5. Cologne: International Society for the Study of the Culture and Economy of the Ordos Mongols.

Yapp, M. 1983. Tribes and states in the Khyber, 1838–42. In *The conflict of tribe and state in Iran and Afghanistan*, ed. R. Tapper. London: Croom Helm.

Yudakhin, K. 1990. *Kyrgyzcha-oruscha sözdük (Kyrgyzsko-russki slovar')*. Bishkek: Sham.

Zhou, Qingshu. 2001. *Yuan Meng shi zha [Collected papers on the Yuan and Mongols]*. Huhhot: Inner Mongolia University Press.

| *Acknowledgments* |

I would like to thank the many people who have helped me in the writing of this book, particularly my colleagues and friends at the Mongolia and Inner Asia Studies Unit, Cambridge University—Caroline Humphrey, Hurelbaatar, Uranchimeg, Hildegard Diemberger, Libby Peachey, David Gullette, and many others. But I owe a very special debt of gratitude to Christopher Atwood for the advice and many inspirational conversations that have contributed so much to this book.

| Index |